The Protestant Orphan Society and its social significance in Ireland, 1828–1940

MANCHESTER
1824

Manchester University Press

The Protestant Orphan Society and its social significance in Ireland, 1828–1940

JUNE COOPER

Manchester University Press

The right of June Cooper to be identified as the author of this work has been asserted by her in accordance with the Copyright, Designs and Patents Act 1988.

Published by Manchester University Press
Altrincham Street, Manchester M1 7JA, UK
www.manchesteruniversitypress.co.uk

British Library Cataloguing-in-Publication Data
A catalogue record for this book is available from the British Library

Library of Congress Cataloging-in-Publication Data applied for

ISBN   978 0 7190 8884 1   hardback

First published 2015

Typeset in Sabon and Gill by
Servis Filmsetting Ltd, Stockport, Cheshire
Printed in Great Britain by
by CPI Group (UK) Ltd, Croydon, CR0 4YY

Contents

Tables

Figures

Acknowledgements

To begin with, I would like to extend my thanks to Professor R. V. Comerford and Dr D. McLoughlin for their guidance and encouragement during the course of my studies at the National University of Ireland, Maynooth. I would also like to extend my appreciation to the director of the National Archives of Ireland, Aideen Ireland, who granted permission to use material from the Protestant Orphan Society collection in this book. In addition, I would like to mention Brian Donnelly and Zoë Reid, the National Archives of Ireland and Dr Raymond Refaussé, the Representative Church Body Library. Thanks also to the reading room staff who made my research possible at the National Archives, the National Library of Ireland, the Representative Church Body Library, the Royal Irish Academy, the National University of Ireland, Maynooth, the Early Printed Books Department, Trinity College Dublin, the Gwenydd Museum, Bangor and the National Archives, Kew. I also owe a debt of gratitude to the secretaries of the St Stephen's and Monaghan Protestant Orphan Societies, for their kind permission to examine private archival collections and to the secretary of the Meath Protestant Orphan Society who provided a short history of its work. I am most grateful to the team at Manchester University Press for the opportunity to publish my work and for their patience and guidance throughout the publishing process. In closing, I wish to offer special thanks to my family.

Abbreviations

ARDP	Association for the Relief of Destressed Protestants
CISSU	Church of Ireland Social Service Union
CPOS	Cork Protestant Orphan Society
CPOU	Charitable Protestant Orphan Union
DPOS	Dublin Protestant Orphan Society
ICM	Irish Church Missions
MPOS	Monaghan Protestant Orphan Society
NAI	National Archives of Ireland
NLI	National Library of Ireland
PORS	Protestant Orphan Refuge Society
RCBL	Representative Church Body Library
RCSI	Royal College of Surgeons Ireland
RIA	Royal Irish Academy
TCD	Trinity College Dublin
TPOS	Tipperary Protestant Orphan Society
WNHA	Women's National Health Association

Introduction

'The Protestant Orphan Society became a social bridge that linked together throughout the Church of Ireland the humble poor and the wealthy and the great'.[1] Founded in Dublin in 1828 by three Protestant artisans, and later managed by laymen and Church of Ireland clergymen, the Protestant Orphan Society in Dublin (DPOS) developed a carefully regulated large-scale boarding-out and apprenticeship scheme for the benefit of Protestant orphans. Its influence grew by degrees until the 1870s, by which time auxiliaries to the DPOS and separate county PO Societies had been set up throughout Ireland. Though not subject to the authority or direction of the parent body, local PO Societies were governed by the same guiding principles, particularly investment in children's education and, if necessary, long-term care. In 1868 the Antrim and Down POS stated, 'from the moment that the child is placed under the charge of the directors and guardians to the moment he sets out in the world, he is cared for by the Society'.[2] PO Societies endeavoured to 'stand in the place of a parent', to be a 'father to the fatherless', and to preserve the health, morals, respectability and religion of Protestant orphans, the rising Protestant generation.

This study examines the pioneering work and social service legacy of the DPOS, one of the most significant Protestant charities in nineteenth-century Ireland, against the background of over a century of political, religious and social upheaval from Catholic emancipation, the Great Famine, social reforms to Independence. While the Society's work pertains to the broader discourse on religious rivalry which merits attention, this study is intended primarily as an exploration of its immense social significance particularly given that, as Caroline Skehill suggests, 'statutory child welfare and protection social work' has its origins in boarding out.[3] There are two main aims: firstly, to uncover the true extent of the Society's social influence, reputation and contributions to the field of child and family welfare and the prominent figures who supported its work from Douglas Hyde to Ella Webb; secondly, to frame the experiences of the bereaved families, widows and orphans, whose lives it undoubtedly shaped, analysis which yields important insights into the social composition of the Church of Ireland, most significantly the Protestant poor, as well as aspects of childhood and family including the significance of siblings. The history of siblings and kinship is under-documented, particularly in the Irish context, despite the 'importance of sibling and cousin relationships, as well as the notion of friendship as a major component of both economic and domestic middle class life in the eighteenth and nineteenth centuries'.[4] Local PO Societies are discussed in relation to the charity's development and variations in management and rules, as well as applicant profiles and individual case histories. However, given that it was the parent body, the most respected and well-known PO Society and served all of Ireland prior to the formation of local PO Societies, the work of the DPOS warrants the most detailed analysis.

Evangelicalism was a key motivating factor for the founders and later supporters of PO Societies and central to the broader construction of the concept of childhood, particularly in the context of this study. The first PO Societies were founded at a time when few child welfare measures were in place. Regarded as specially connected to God and a sign of the fragility of life, orphans were viewed as distinct from other children and considered most deserving of charity. (Children were referred to as orphans or half orphans if only one parent was deceased.) In the years prior to the introduction of the Poor Law, 1838, orphans were found in gaols and Houses of Industry and after in workhouses, reformato-ries, industrial schools and orphanages. Lay Catholic orphan societies boarded out children from the late eighteenth century and continued to provide for orphans on a relatively small scale in the nineteenth. Margaret Aylward founded St Brigid's Outdoor Orphanage, or boarding-out insti-tution, in 1856.[5] Religious competition generated greater interest in the welfare of orphans – the children of the church – who in the case of the Church of Ireland became symbols of strength, vitality and the future.

Given the predominance of the institutionalisation of children, PO Societies' support of the 'family system' differentiated it from public poor relief provisions and many other charities aimed at orphans, a system which attracted the attention of social reformers in the 1860s. Anti-cruelty legislation was introduced in the second half of the nine-teenth century as reformist women such as Rosa Barrett, founder of the Dublin Aid Committee (later the NSPCC), advocated change. Children's health became an issue of national importance in the late nineteenth century amid high infant and child mortality rates which caused increas-ing concerns for the rising generation.[6] Throughout the nineteenth and early twentieth century, PO Societies expressed similar fears as the preservation of the Church of Ireland became 'inextricably linked' with the preservation of the rising Protestant generation.

The history of childhood, child welfare and the family in Ireland remain largely unexplored fields of research; however, there are several studies which serve as a foundation for scholars, such as Joseph Robins, *The Lost Children*,[7] Kenneth Milne, *The Irish Charter Schools*,[8] and Jane Barnes, *Irish Industrial Schools*.[9] In later studies such as Mary Raftery and Eoin O'Sullivan's *Suffer the Little Children*,[10] and Caitriona Clear's *Growing up Poor*,[11] greater attention is paid to children's experiences and perspectives. Maria Luddy devotes one chapter to child welfare in *Women and Philanthropy*, and observes that, 'the history of the child in Irish society has yet to be written'[12] – a view reiterated by Luddy in more recent years.[13]

So far, however, the main focus has been on the placement of children in institutions; there has been less discussion of boarding out. In her biography of Margaret Aylward,[14] Jacinta Prunty examines St Brigid's boarding-out institution. Moire Maguire's *Precarious Childhood*[15] investigates the lives of poor, illegitimate and abused children and the state's role in child welfare provision in post-independence Ireland. Maguire's study draws much needed attention to state foster care systems, and the history of the family. Nevertheless, the existing accounts do not present a comprehensive history of the origins and development of 'modern boarding out'.

The history of childhood has also been examined through the lens of illness and medical care. Alice Mauger and Anne MacLellan's *Growing Pains*[16] surveys the history of childhood illness and medical care over two centuries. These studies represent an important basis for an emergent body of scholarly work which delves further into children's experiences of growing up in nineteenth and twentieth-century Ireland.

To date, historians have overlooked the social significance of PO Societies. Luddy and Raftery both refer briefly to the POS system of boarding out; Robins offers slightly more detail on the Westmeath and Dublin PO Societies; Prunty considers the Society's work in terms of religious rivalry; and Oonagh Walsh, *Anglican Women*,[17] examines the work carried out by the Dublin POS in the early twentieth century in the broader context of women's philanthropy. Clergymen have written short histories of the Meath and the Armagh PO Societies, and the Cork, Limerick and Westmeath PO Societies have been the subject of three unpublished theses.

The greater part of the research material used for this study was sourced from the DPOS archival collection held in the National Archives of Ireland. DPOS annual reports include invaluable accounts of the charity's development, from the numerous auxiliaries which fundraised on its behalf to the foundation of separate local PO Societies. Minute books contain more in-depth discussion of the day-to-day management of the Society including orphan placement, inspections and transferrals, mothers' requests to reclaim their children, and the treatment of sick children. The Society also kept a number of registers to document bouts of serious illness, deaths of surviving parents and emigration. A small collection of letters from orphans, widows, clergymen and DPOS supporters offer rare personal testimonies of widows' reduced circumstances and children's transitions into adulthood.

The photographs that feature in this study offer the reader an extraordinary visual record of DPOS orphans at various stages of their lives, as young children, with their nurses, as adolescents and as adults. To a certain extent, these images also give some indication of the children's health at the time they were taken. They are mostly undated; however, the photographer, W. G. Moore, worked from a studio located at 11 Upper Sackville Street, Dublin from 1885 to 1900 which provides an approximate time line for the portraits; registers of case histories also act as a guide. Moore was the successor to Nelson and Marshall who advertised from 1860 to 1884. Additional portraits were taken by E. J. Lauder, Artists and Photographers, 22 Westmoreland Street, Dublin, in operation from 1880 to 1890.[18] Photographs of the *Clio* industrial training ship and *Clio* boys were sourced from the Gwynedd Museum, Bangor, Wales.

The private collections of Monaghan and Cork PO Societies, annual reports of the Kilkenny, Tyrone, Westmeath, Cavan PO Societies; minutes and annual reports of the Tipperary POS; short histories of the Meath and Armagh PO Societies; annual reports of the Limerick, Donegal, Antrim and Down, and Kerry PO Societies cast light on the variations of rules, management structures and the extent to which PO Societies worked autonomously. St Brigid's annual reports provide opposing views of PO Societies and highly significant insights into Catholic approaches to boarding out. Additional sources include the *Clio* Industrial Training Ship papers, which are held in the National Archives, Kew, Surrey, the *Journal of the Statistical and Social Inquiry Society of Ireland*, parliamentary papers, census returns, the *Church of Ireland Gazette*, Richmond District Lunatic Asylum registers and Church of Ireland parish registers and vestry minutes.

The overall structure of the study takes the form of eight chapters. Chapter 1 identifies the founders and supporters of the DPOS and their motivation for doing so. It also asks why the Church of Ireland invested in the children of the church at this time. Chapter 2 analyses the

Society's development, the grounds for support of private versus public poor relief for Protestant widows and children and stresses the crucial role that women played in the Societies' work. Chapter 3 examines the child welfare system implemented by the DPOS, and the extent to which its policies were forward thinking and child and family centred. Chapter 4 highlights the opposing views of the extensive social service carried out by PO Societies and the meaning of the charity for the Church of Ireland laity, particularly women. Chapter 5 examines applicant profiles, widows' reduced circumstances and health, attitudes to children's health, and bereavement and the attendant emotional effects. Chapter 6 questions whether in practice the POS apprenticeship system was one of effective child training or enforced child labour. Chapter 7 examines the marked shift in the Dublin POS approach to child welfare in the late 1890s and assesses the outcomes of these changes. Using individual case histories it also examines applicant case histories which include Sean O'Casey's sister. The final chapter uncovers the eminent public figures who supported PO Societies in the twentieth century, from Dr Ella Webb to Douglas Hyde, and the extent to which the decline in the Protestant population in the south had a corresponding effect on the status of PO Societies.

Notes

1 POS centenary, *Irish Times* (30 November 1928).
2 *Belfast News-letter* (7 March 1868).
3 C. Skehill, 'Child protection and welfare social work in the Republic of Ireland: continuities and discontinuities between the past and present', in N. Kearney and C. Skehill (eds), *Social Work in Ireland: Historical Perspectives* (Dublin: Institute of Public Administration, 2005), pp. 127–45, p. 135.
4 L. Davidoff, 'Kinship as a categorical concept: a case study of nineteenth century English siblings', *Journal of Social History*, 39:2 (Winter 2005), pp. 411–28, p. 412.
5 J. Prunty, *Dublin Slums, 1800–1925: A Study in Urban Geography* (Dublin: Irish Academic Press, 1998), p. 243.
6 A. MacLellan and A. Mauger (eds), *Growing Pains: Childhood Illness in Ireland, 1750–1950* (Dublin: Irish Academic Press, 2013), p. 2.
7 J. Robins, *The Lost Children: A Study of Charity Children in Ireland, 1700–1900* (Dublin: Institute of Public Administration, 1980).
8 K. Milne, *The Irish Charter Schools, 1730–1830* (Dublin: Four Courts Press, 1997).
9 J. Barnes, *Irish Industrial Schools, 1868–1908: Origins and Development* (Dublin: Irish Academic Press, 1989).

10 M. Raftery and E. O'Sullivan, *Suffer the Little Children: The Inside Story of Ireland's Industrial Schools* (Dublin: New Island, 1999).
11 C. Clear and M. Johnston, *Growing up Poor: The Homeless Young in 19th Century Ireland and Dublin Childhoods* (Galway: Galway Labour History Group. 1993).
12 M. Luddy, *Women and Philanthropy in Nineteenth Century Ireland* (Cambridge: Cambridge University Press, 1995), p. 70.
13 MacLellan and Mauger (eds), *Growing Pains*, p. 4.
14 J. Prunty, *Margaret Aylward 1810–1889: Lady of Charity, Sister of Faith* (Dublin: Four Courts Press, 1999).
15 M. Maguire, *Precarious Childhood in Post-Independence Ireland* (Manchester: Manchester University Press, 2009).
16 MacLellan and Mauger (eds), *Growing Pains*.
17 O. Walsh, *Anglican Women in Dublin: Philanthropy, Politics and Education in the Early Twentieth Century* (Dublin: UCD Press, 2005).
18 E. Chandler, *Photography in Ireland, the Nineteenth Century* (Dublin: Edmund Burke, 2001), p. 97.

I

Origins, 1828–30

It is to such Institutions as the present that we shall be indebted for the preservation of Protestantism.[1]

Introduction

Evangelicalism inspired renewed religious purpose, individualism, a missionary impulse and moral and social reform through philanthropy and education. It drew considerable support from all classes in Dublin,[2] a broad appeal which threatened the authority of the established church as well as Catholic and dissenting churches. The ensuing religious rivalry brought the issue of child welfare to the fore. While Protestant philanthropy was already extensive, real concerns were not expressed for the future of Protestant orphans, the rising Protestant generation, until 1828 amid growing Catholic middle-class confidence on the eve of emancipation and during a period of considerable economic distress among the Protestant artisan class in Dublin. The first chapter identifies the people behind the DPOS, both lay and religious, and examines the source of the founders' motivation given the broader social, religious and political milieu. It highlights the challenge to secure adequate funding and uncovers unanticipated divisions between committee members of the fledgling charity.

Religious revival

The essence of the evangelical message was individualism and the importance of the bible as a direct link to God, ideas which challenged the authority of mainstream churches.[3] The evangelist John Cennick preached in Dublin in 1746 until the arrival of John and Charles Wesley, key figures in the progress of the Methodist movement in Ireland.[4] John Wesley visited Ireland twenty-one times during the years between 1747 and 1789 and Methodist missionary stations were established and Irish speaking missionaries enlisted to spread the gospel.[5] Wesleyan Methodists seceded from the Church of Ireland in 1816 while Primitive Wesleyan Methodists remained within the margins of the established church. These two elements of Methodism did not unite until 1878 when the Methodist church was formally founded. Wesleyan Methodism had a particular appeal for artisans seeking advancement in society.[6]

Members of the Church of Ireland who wished to experience and embrace the vibrancy of revival preaching without seceding attended the Bethseda Chapel in Dorset Street, 'known as the Cathedral of Methodism'[7] and founded in 1784. Revd Benjamin Mathias was a central figure in its success while prominent laymen such as Arthur Guinness and Lord Roden were among its many enthusiastic supporters.[8] In the early nineteenth century, ministers of the evangelical wing of the Church of Ireland preached in ordinary Dublin parishes and in 'free churches' or proprietary chapels. Revd Thomas Kelly left the established church, formed a sect called the Separatists and founded chapels at Maryborough and Blackrock in Dublin.[9] Revd John Walker, a former minister at the Bethseda, set up the Walker's Society on Calvanist principles in 1804.[10]

There was also a high church revival in the Church of Ireland espoused by, among others, Archbishop Brodrick, John Jebb, Alexander Knox and Archbishop William Magee.[11] Evangelicals were criticised by the church establishment; however, Archbishop William Magee managed to overcome many of these differences by officiating at the Bethseda in 1825 and other proprietary chapels.[12] As J. R. Hill suggests, Magee 'did not so much give evangelicals a strategy, rather he sought to harness the rising evangelical impulse under the control and authority of the established church'.[13] The common thread which united the lay founders and clerical supporters of the DPOS was a commitment to evangelicalism.

The evangelical revival, the promotion of Christian morality following the 1798 rebellion, and intense criticism of the church from the 1780s, which included the charge of clerical neglect (in certain cases Protestants lapsed into Roman Catholicism as a matter of necessity),[14] brought about the 'age of graceful reform' of the Church of Ireland.[15] (Under the terms of the Act of Union, Ireland, 1800, the Church of Ireland and the Church of England were united.) The period was characterised by episcopal reform, church building and rebuilding funded by the Board of First Fruits,[16] and a growing evangelical spirit within the church as demonstrated by Revd Peter Roe, for example.[17] Moral reform agencies included the Association for Discountenancing Vice and Promoting the Practice of Christian Religion, known as the

Dublin Association, founded in 1792; the Hibernian Bible Society in 1806 and the Sunday School Society for Ireland in 1809. The Society for Promoting Education of the Poor in Ireland, or the Kildare Place Society, was formed in December 1811 with the firm aim of providing education without religious interference.[18] The Religious Tract and Book Society was founded in 1817; the Irish Society in 1818; the Scripture Society in 1822 and the Established Church Home Mission Society in 1828.[19]

Religious polarisation

Apart from restrictions on lease lengths and property rights, which were removed in 1778 and 1782 respectively, Catholics were free to engage in commercial industry which led to the rise of a Catholic middle class.[20] There was further relaxation of the penal laws in 1793, which among other concessions enabled Catholics to bear arms, parliamentary franchise equal to Protestants, and guild and corporation membership (though membership remained limited).[21] Caitriona Clear documents the rise of nuns in Ireland and identifies the upper middle-class profile of many of the women who founded religious orders and of those who funded the establishment of a growing network of convents during the Catholic revival amid growing religious rivalry.[22] Nano Nagle established the Sisters of the Charitable Instruction of the Sacred Heart of Jesus in 1776. Other orders included the Presentation nuns (1805), the Brigidines (1807), the Daughters of Charity (1810), the Irish Sisters of Charity (1815), and Catherine McAuley founded the religious congregation, the Sisters of Mercy, in 1831.[23] In 1800 there were 120 nuns in Ireland and by 1851 there were ninety-one convents and 1,500 nuns.[24]

James Warren Doyle, who served as Bishop of Kildare and Leighlin (JKL, James Kildare and Leighlin) from 1819 (at the age of thirty-three) until 1834, built churches, including the Carlow Cathedral, schools, formed confraternities and condemned the unjust treatment of Catholics. Bishop Doyle responded forcefully to the Church of Ireland Archbishop of Dublin, William Magee's charge delivered at St Patrick's Cathedral, Dublin, 22 October 1822, which was regarded 'as a declaration of religious war'[25] (alternative interpretations suggest that the issue of tithes and other criticisms of the church as well as mounting pressure from evangelical reformers were foremost in his mind).[26] Catholic bishops were urged to curb the progress of the Bible Society as controversial sermons[27] and the increased involvement of the established church in the bible movement were no longer tolerated.[28] Bishop Doyle and Bishop John MacHale (Mariona 1825–43 and Tuam 1834–81) challenged the popular bible movement and worked closely with Daniel O'Connell on the emancipation campaign.

Despite initial support for the Kildare Place Society (KPS), O'Connell, along with other Catholic patrons, withdrew his support over the issue of reading the bible without note or comment, and alleged, though unproven, proselytism, raised in letters written by Bishop MacHale over a period of three years from 1820 to 1823.[29] The Education Inquiry of 1825 concluded that, despite its many achievements, the KPS did not meet the needs of the majority of people.[30]

From 1822 the folk version of the Pastorini Prophecies, which predicted the extirpation of Protestants from Ireland in 1825, became increasingly well known and caused considerable alarm, remaining a 'constant anxiety' for Protestants.[31] The prophecies were circulated in tracts and through word of mouth by travellers and pedlars and dismissed by Catholic clergy and the middle-class laity who were eager to achieve emancipation.[32] The prophecies were particularly popular among the Catholic lower orders even after 1825.[33]

Despite assurances from O'Connell to the contrary, Conservative Protestants predicted that if Catholic emancipation were granted an outright Catholic revolution would ensue, that the union was therefore under potential threat, and that a Catholic ascendancy would follow.[34] The Duke of Richmond referred to the 'intimidation of Protestants', claiming that 'they bully and threaten the Protestants to sign their petitions, whilst many of the Protestants allow themselves to be bullied and none try to stop the current'.[35] However, there were liberal Protestant supporters of emancipation, Arthur Guinness, for example. The Roman Catholic Relief Act[36] was carried in April 1829, after which the inevitability of Protestant decline and Catholic ascendancy[37] was again noted by Archbishop Beresford.

Orphans in Dublin

The Incorporated Society for Promoting English Protestant Schools in Ireland was founded in February 1733.[38] The Charter Schools were intended for the education of poor Roman Catholics and 'the meanest Protestants' in 'useful skills and habits of industry' with the aim of both social and religious reformation.[39] However, the Commissioners of Education presented troubling accounts of the schools in their 1825 report which called an eventual halt to once large parliamentary grants.[40] Houses of Industry provided for the aged, the sick, lunatics and orphans[41] and in 1817 there were approximately 900 children in the Dublin House of Industry. Following a rise in admissions due to fever

epidemics, conditions deteriorated rapidly and it was no longer considered fit for children, who were subsequently apprenticed or sent to
Charter Schools.[42] The new admission restrictions inevitably meant that
more children were sent to its associated penitentiaries or left to wander
the streets.[43] The Mendicity Association, founded in 1818, gave employment to adult beggars in order to keep them off the streets during the
day. It also provided orphans with day time care in the institution and
paid women beggars employed by the institution, who had their own
homes, a small allowance to keep the children at night.[44]

By the 1820s a number of Protestant charities had been founded specifically for orphans. The Bethseda Orphan School was founded shortly
after the Bethseda Chapel in 1786;[45] Margaret Este and Mrs Edward
Tighe established the Female Orphan House in 1790, which was funded
by voluntary subscriptions, donations and a parliamentary grant and
in 1807 there were 140 children under its care; the Masonic Female
Orphan School, Jervis Street, a boarding school for the daughters of
deceased freemasons was established in 1792; the Methodist Female
Orphan School, White-friar Street, was founded in association with the
Church of Ireland in 1804; and Pleasants' Asylum, 75 Camden Street,
was founded in 1818. Many of these orphanages catered for relatively
small numbers, operated age restriction policies, admitted only full
orphans and in the case of the Methodist Female Orphan School and the
Female Orphan House admitted only girls.

In the mid-eighteenth century, the Patrician Orphan Society was
founded in Dublin to serve the Catholic poor as a substitute for the
foundling hospitals.[46] Catholic tradesmen founded the St Joseph's
female orphanage in 1770. In addition, laymen founded Catholic
orphan societies in Dublin as well as Cork and Waterford.[47] Nine
Catholic orphan societies were established in Dublin from 1822 to
1829 and due to restrictions on Catholic charity[48] were not organised
on a large scale. A number were aimed at young children with age
limits of four and five.[49] Three of the societies admitted a total of 480
children from 1817 to 1840.[50] By 1834 twenty-four Catholic orphan
societies existed in Dublin providing for 800 orphans.[51] Children were
sent to farmers near Dublin and in counties Wicklow and Carlow.[52]
(Fosterage was an ancient Irish custom.[53]) In 1834 Thomas Osler,
Assistant Commissioner, reported that the Catholic orphan societies
were 'strictly Lay Associations' and that the Roman Catholic clergy
were relatively unfamiliar with them and 'did not interfere, unless
their advice was specifically requested'.[54] St Bonaventure's Charitable
Institution and Orphanage was founded in 1820, and like many of the
other Catholic orphan societies 'sought to prevent Protestant agencies

receiving Catholic children'.[55] Nuns carried out widespread work among the poor and managed orphanages from convents by the early nineteenth century.[56]

Founding fathers

At the beginning of the long eighteenth century, Protestants were a majority in Dublin; however, following rapid urban population growth, by the early nineteenth century they had become a distinct minority.[57] In 1836 the Protestant population of inner city parishes comprised, for example, '2,700 (St. Michan's), 2,380 (St. Paul's), 2,808 (St. George's) and 6,946 (St. Thomas's)'.[58] The three founding fathers of the Protestant Orphan Society were Protestant tradesmen named James Kelly, a hosier, Cathedral lane, St Peter's parish; Joseph Williams, a tape weaver, Meeting-house Yard, Mullinahack, St Catherine's parish, and John Stanton, a glover from Ellis Quay, which extended from Queen Street to Silver Street in the parish of St Paul.[59]

Weaving in the Liberties had once been a flourishing trade, employing high numbers because of the labour intensiveness of the work. (The Meath Hospital was founded in 1753 to provide medical care for Protestant weavers among other deserving cases. Labourers, tradesmen and servants were among the most frequently treated for fever according to the records of Dr Steeven's Hospital from 1816 to 1817.[60]) In 1792, there were 60 master clothiers, 400 broad cloth looms, and 100 looms in the Liberties with employment for approximately five thousand people.[61] Given that import tariffs protected their share of the home market, Dublin manufacturers were not in favour of the Union which would expose them to unwanted English competition.[62] Nevertheless, under the terms of the Act of Union, 1800, these tariffs were retained until 1808 and then gradually reduced. On 28 June 1822 a petition was sent to the Lord Lieutenant on behalf of the unemployed weavers of the city and Liberties of Dublin, who had endured hardship due to the 'decaying trade'.[63] The petition was also sent to the Dublin Society, Linen Board and Mendicity Association, and was signed by 'upwards of 2,000 members of the trade'.[64] John Brady, Secretary to the Linen Memorial, reported that there were 5,000 of both sexes who 'are at present idle and starving'.[65]

From the eighteenth century, there were downturns in the silk trade,[66] established by Huguenots in the Liberties, Dublin, and Spittlefields in London.[67] The silk trade declined further after 1824 and the act to repeal the aforementioned import tariffs which had once protected silk, wool and cotton manufacturers from English competition; production and employment decreased by more than fifty per cent.[68] In 1824 a number of silk weavers sought employment in Spittlefields, London, while other tradesmen emigrated to North America.[69]

In 1826 James Forrest, British, Irish, and Foreign Silk Mercery and Lace Warehouse, 28 Grafton Street, advertised 'All Irish goods he will dispose of at First Cost Price for ready money. He trusts a liberal and patriotic public will appreciate his motives in making sales without any profit, whatsoever, during this time of public distress'.[70] In the same year the Committee for the Relief of Distressed Manufacturers was formed. Severe unemployment pushed weavers on to the streets to protest in July 1826. Shortly after, fever epidemics hit cities, Dublin, Cork and Belfast.[71] The broad silk weavers of Dublin submitted a petition in 1828 to the House of Commons as they were 'reduced to the most deplorable state of destitution and misery, through want of sufficient employment'.[72] The Dublin linen hall was no longer used as a market after 1828.[73] Related trades such as hosiery were also in a perilous state. As a result of the decline in employment and wages, which had been reduced from £1 5s in 1800 to 10s per week in 1836, a number of hosiers sought work in Nottingham; by 1836 there were no more than 200 hosiers in employment. It was observed that 'the long credit which the English capitalists can afford to give, causes excessive importation, and the manufacturers here therefore cannot compete with them'.[74]

In 1810 the glovers' guild had supported proposals for repeal of the union in light of the non-materialisation of expected benefits and the saturation of the Irish market with English goods.[75] At the same time, an Irish parliament was considered imperative to Irish interests. Anti-union sentiment was expressed by Protestants and also by Catholics, who had not yet been granted emancipation.[76] According to Select Reports on the Irish poor, two operatives reported in 1816 that there had been 1,500 men, women and children employed in the thriving glove trade.

> Some years back, gloves were made for the regiments stationed here; *all now are sent from England*. There are about 200 hands employed, 30 men, *with no regular employment*, the rest women and children. Some occasionally get a day's work, and are in a trifling degree supported *by their wives*; the generality of them are in a most deplorable state.[77]

William Stanley provided an account of trades in Dublin in the 1830s; referring to the inadequate supply of skilled tradesmen and the importation of gloves, he claimed, 'few can be found who know how to sew and finish gloves, and still fewer who can cut them out'.[78] Stanley believed that the deficiency of training schools for young women and the rules regarding apprentices lay at the root of the problem. He commented further on the 'poverty of the mass of the people' in Meath, Kildare and Wicklow and the effects on other trades including shoemaking, tailoring, and brass and tin working.

Due to a combination of mechanisation, the reduction of tariffs on imports which opened up the home market to cheaper English products, the 'de-gentrification' of Dublin,[79] the 'major bank crisis in England',[80] and the organisation of trade societies particularly of journeymen and silk weavers, once comfortable tradesmen and their families found themselves in sharply reduced circumstances.[81] In 1827 the Mendicity Association reported that, 'The shops are idle, the trades people unemployed and the mass of the population suffering from privation'.[82] It also stated that the 'unprecedented' number of '736 trades people (and their families)' had sought relief.[83]

Initial years

According to the DPOS's first annual report, the founders had learned at a funeral of a mutual acquaintance that his widow felt compelled from the effects of poverty to give up her children to a Roman Catholic orphan society, as she had been unable to secure relief from a Protestant source. The 'Protestant Orphan Society' was founded on 30 November 1828 and each founding member 'put down a penny in the churchyard of St. Catherine's'.[84] (Arthur Guinness was a parishioner of St Catherine's and in this parish gathered support for Catholic emancipation.[85]) The objective was 'to support a society formed for the laudable purpose of keeping from Poverty, Misery and Vice the orphans of our poorer fellow Protestants'.[86] The founders viewed the establishment of the DPOS as a solution to the destitution they had witnessed in their own community.

> That in communion with our fellow Protestants of the city of Dublin and called upon at a period when poverty and distress surround the dwellings of widows and finding it necessary as far as in our power to promote their comfort, deeply impressed with their exigencies; we in conformity with the true spirit of our religion deem it expedient to come forward to use every effort to effect a measure (hitherto unheeded and unthought of) and to render every exertion and assistance to alleviate their sufferings.[87]

The founders were described in subsequent years as 'three poor men, themselves alive to the blessings of a scriptural discipline'.[88] They aimed to offer relief to the most destitute of Protestant orphans under the age of eight years, and to offer them 'blessings of a moral and religious education and afford them such pecuniary means of relief as the funds of the society might with safety permit'.[89] The orphans were boarded out to Protestant families and later apprenticed to Protestant masters.

On 4 January 1829 the original committee members assembled at the Tailors Hall, Back Lane, to set the rules of the newly formed society. (Tailor's Hall dates back to 1706 and was one of the largest guild halls in Dublin also used by hosiers, saddlers and tanners and as a meeting place for Methodists and the Grand Lodge of the Freemasons.) Members of the first DPOS committee, which included Joshua Tate, Thomas Elward, Samuel Rea, Abel Mcintosh, John Stanton and John Britain, met again at Tailor's Hall on 24 May 1829. It was decided at this meeting that a further twenty-four members would be appointed to collect on behalf of the committee.[90] Other committee members included William Wilson, a boot and shoemaker, William Gore, a skinner, Edward Drew, a foreign fruit merchant, and Samuel Stead, a tailor.[91]

The DPOS committee members met every Tuesday evening at eight o'clock. Initially, they collected penny-a-week subscriptions in the 'atmosphere of small sums collected in the West end of the City of Dublin' but soon moved into 'the guinea atmosphere of the East end of the city round about the Rotunda'.[92] The founders hoped that holding its first annual meeting at the Rotunda would attract the attention of influential Protestants. The meeting was a success in this respect as Protestant clergymen and 'highly respectable laymen attached themselves to the society and in the most efficient manner have zealously exercised their influence on its behalf'.[93] Among the prominent lay committee members were George Boileau Esq. of Huguenot descent[94] and Robert Lanigan Esq., a magistrate, committee member of the Mendicity Society,[95] and a trustee of the Society for Bettering the Condition of the Poor in Ireland.[96] The meeting was also attended by a 'great number of the lower classes, men with frize coats, and women with decent but very humble dress; I see also not a few who are orphans themselves, reared in Protestant Charter Schools'.[97] Other former Charter School boys were identified at the meeting as 'devoted members of the Protestant Orphan Society'.[98] In the months that followed, sufficient funds were raised by voluntary subscription to admit nine orphans. The DPOS elected children from all over Ireland until separate local PO Societies were founded. A further nineteen children were admitted in the initial year. The first annual report and a public appeal were printed and circulated in early 1830.[99]

The DPOS was a specific type of child welfare, one that served the respectable poor, artisan and middle-class widows in reduced circumstances. Almost a century after its foundation, the Archbishop of Dublin noted that the DPOS had always represented a 'kind of insurance for the poor'.[100] The Guardian Assurance Company, 'for assurance on lives and survivorships Endowments for children', was established in 1821. It had offices in London and Moore Street, Dublin. The Clerical, Medical and General Life Assurance Society, which claimed that it was the first to extend 'the benefit of life assurance to persons not in a sound state of health', was situated at No. 1 Eden Quay, Sackville Street, Dublin.[101] It too granted annuities and endowments for children; however, these safeguards were out of reach for most. A Society such as the DPOS afforded the artisans the opportunity to contribute to a fund which would pay out after their deaths. It was all the more significant because artisans had founded the Society. It was essentially a family strategy designed to maintain the respectability of Protestant widows and orphans.

It was also envisaged that the Society would act as a shield to preserve children's Protestantism. The urban Protestant poor were generally neglected apart from in specific areas such as the Liberties.[102] In 1828 Henry Richard Dawson, then aged thirty-six, was installed Dean of St Patricks, after which he had a census made of the Protestants of the Dean's liberties which brought to light their 'great ignorance and misery' and that they were 'much more numerous than had been anticipated'.[103] The Dean founded schools for adults, children and infants in the area and became involved with other 'benevolent institutions'.[104] Such work was thought to have prevented Protestants from lapsing into Roman Catholicism as a result of clerical neglect.[105]

Fears that Protestants would be subsumed into Roman Catholicism through such clerical neglect were also expressed in the first DPOS annual report, 1830, which referred to the number of Catholic orphan societies in Dublin (seven Catholic orphan societies were founded in Dublin between 1825 and 1828)[106] and reported that poor Protestant families subscribed to them.[107] DPOS minutes of committee meetings also provide similar evidence: 'the above child was recommended by a lady to a Roman Catholic school but his sister would not agree to it, none of the family on either side having been Roman Catholics'.[108] In later years, the Limerick POS reflected on the foundation of the DPOS: 'their hearts sank within them when they outdid one another in recounting the numerous cases in which poor Protestant orphans had been entrapped by nuns into the nineteen Romish Orphan Asylums of Dublin'.[109] Although suspicions of Catholic orphan societies appear overstated in certain instances, there was a firm basis for concerns that Protestant orphans were being neglected by their own church.

An article written about the self-supporting institutions in Dublin referred to reports made by Thomas Osler, Assistant Commissioner, which stated that 'the orphan societies are mostly Roman Catholic, as in Dublin the poorest classes are almost universally of that religion; but they are not necessarily confined to any particular sect, and one case occurred of an orphan of Protestant parents being put under the care of a Protestant family by a Roman Catholic Society'.[110] While this cannot be judged as proselytism, it does explain the founders' 'reproachful indignation at the non existence amongst the Protestant community of an asylum for the relief of destitute Protestant orphanage'.[111] J. R. Hill suggests that Fr Cornelius Nary had considered ways to bring about the conversion of Protestants in the early eighteenth century in the context of dwindling Protestants numbers in the rest of Europe.[112]

In 1831 the *Christian Examiner and Church of Ireland Magazine* referred to the foundation of the DPOS.[113]

> The Protestant Orphan Society is a most interesting one. It was founded by a few Protestant tradesmen, who were induced to do it, by perceiving, that as Government, in accordance with the views of the Romish party, had closed the doors to the Foundling Hospital, the Charter Schools, and all similar establishments, and that the activity of the monks, Jesuits, Scapularians, Confraternities, Sisters of Charity, and the whole swarm of Romans that are now in Dublin was in proportion to their numbers, resolved, as far as in them lay, to preserve Protestant orphans from being carried away to swell the numbers and the triumph of the Romanists.[114]

Florence Davenport Hill noted in the 1860s that the DPOS had been founded to assist Protestant orphans who 'until that period ... had frequently found refuge in the numerous institutions established by benevolent Roman Catholics; but in these, not unnaturally, conversion to the creed of their benefactors became, if not absolutely a condition, generally a consequence of the children's admittance'.[115] Protestants viewed the closure of the Charter Schools, the foundation of Catholic orphan societies, and convents funded by a confident and united Catholic middle class as unsettling signs of encroachment.

The established church and the DPOS

Although evangelicalism was not fully embraced by the Church of Ireland until after disestablishment, it had by then influenced the church in a number of profound ways: observance of the Sabbath, domestic discipline, respectability, individualism, piety and philanthropy.[116] St Catherine's vestry minutes contain references to the enlistment of the laity as overseers to maintain observance of the Sabbath: 'the laity overseers hitherto appointed to prevent the breach of the Sabbath day, the same continues to be shamefully profaned in this parish by the publicans, obstinately continuing to sell spirituous and other liquors to the lower classes of society at hours prohibited by which means poor families are deprived of their earnings'.[117] This suggests that the foundation of the DPOS was but an extension of the church-related work being carried out by laymen.

Twenty-seven laymen, mainly Protestant artisans, formed a collectors' committee of the DPOS, one of whom acted as assistant secretary. Clergymen and prominent laymen formed a second committee which comprised fifteen clergymen and six gentlemen, a secretary and treasurer. In 1830, vice presidents of the DPOS included the provost of Trinity College and the Dean of St Patrick's. Clergymen and laymen met every Friday at three o'clock at Mr Watson's, No. 7, Capel Street. The collectors' committee met at the Tailor's Hall, Back Lane, every Tuesday evening at eight o'clock and collected subscriptions of one penny per week or upwards. Committee members stressed the point that the DPOS's management structure contrasted with that of other leading charities: 'it differs from every other charitable association in this country, as the government of the society is not as in other societies confined to the wealthier classes of subscribers. All classes poor as well as rich are eligible and by existing laws a certain number of both must annually be elected'.[118] The system was intended to bridge the social gap of 'class extremes' within the Church of Ireland. Evangelicals valued the individual regardless of rank,[119] an idea which gradually permeated the Church of Ireland and was clearly reflected in the management structure and general ethos of the DPOS.

Both committees shared the same powers and one committee could not make a final decision on any matter without the other's consent:

> The general committee is divided into two branches; or rather the business of the society is conducted by two committees one composed of clergy and the other composed exclusively of operative mechanics and other respectable individuals of inferior station. These two committees have equal powers, have exactly the same duties to perform and no act of one is valid until sanctioned by the other.[120]

In subsequent years, the above system became unworkable mainly because of differing opinions and miscommunication which led to delays in the decision making process.[121] The collectors did not retain their own committee. However, for example, James Shaw, who was listed as a member of the original collectors' committee was named as a member of the managing committee in the 1840s. From the late 1830s, a committee of clergymen and laymen managed the Society. The DPOS office was located at 16 Upper Sackville Street.

The Archbishop of Dublin, William Magee, lent his name as first patron (initially, the Society had approached the Primate of Armagh): 'Your committee have further to state that a manuscript copy of the rules having been laid before his grace the Archbishop of Dublin he kindly consented to become our patron and liberally contributed towards our funds'.[122] Magee most probably viewed the Society as a worthy cause – however, one that should continue to operate within the boundaries of the church. He referred to the DPOS as a mechanism to counteract the perceived Catholic threat: 'we are not kidnappers; our object is but to hinder our people from being kidnapped'.[123] Much of the language used in the first annual report was characteristically evangelical, particularly its references to being part of Christ's army – warriors and soldiers of Christ were other terms used by evangelicals.[124]

In its early annual reports, a number of prominent evangelical clergymen were listed as DPOS committee members. Caesar Otway founded the *Christian Examiner* with Revd Joseph Henderson Singer in 1825. He was also literary editor of the *Dublin Penny Journal* which was in circulation from 1832 to 1836 and wrote under the pseudonym 'Terence O'Toole'. Otway was a trustee of the Society for Bettering the Condition of the Poor in Ireland and assistant chaplain at the Magdalen Chapel, Leeson Street, Dublin.[125] One of the original DPOS committee members, he was subsequently appointed Honorary Secretary of the Charitable Protestant Orphan Union and referred to as an 'invaluable friend and supporter'.[126]

Born in County Dublin in 1786, Joseph Henderson Singer co-founded the Established Church Home Mission[127] and was a leading voice of the evangelical party in the Church of Ireland.[128] An entry in a register of incoming letters to the DPOS, dated 10 May 1833, referred to Singer's association with the charity and recorded that, 'he expressed a desire that his name might be removed from the list of the committee'.[129] There is no reason given for his request. Singer was chaplain of the Magdalen Asylum and appointed Bishop of Meath in September 1852. He died on 16 July 1866.

The aforementioned Dean of St Patrick's was assisted in his work in the Liberties by several clergymen. Among them were Hastings from St James's, Kingston from St Catherine's, Halahan from St Nicholas's, Burroughs, rector from St Luke's.[130] The Very Revd the Dean of St Patrick's became the first Vice President of the DPOS, and Revds Halahan, Burroughs and Kingston became DPOS committee members.

Revd Arthur Thomas Burroughs was curate of St James's parish in the 1820s and a committee member of the Hibernian Church Missionary Society.[131] He also sought support for the parochial school of Saint Nicholas Without, a charitable school for the poor:, 'the benevolent attendance or generous benefaction of the public is earnestly entreated to preserve from decay and debt the charitable school of a parish equally populous and poor, which is unable to support its own establishment without the aid of the benevolent inhabitants of other parishes'.[132] Prior to his death, aged thirty-seven, he served as rector of St Luke's parish.[133]

Born in 1791, George Blacker, a Trinity graduate, served for several years as curate of St Andrew's; he was also chaplain of the city corporation.[134] Revd Blacker became vicar of Maynooth in 1840 where he continued to live until his death in 1871. He wrote local histories such as the *Castle of Maynooth* in 1853. Revd Blacker served on the DPOS committee from its earliest years.[135]

John Richard Darley was born in 1799 and later served as Bishop of Kilmore, Elphin and Ardagh. Darley had been a schoolmaster for many years in Dundalk. He married William Conyngham Plunket's sister in 1851 and 'sought to reunite the Primitive Methodists in Ireland with the Church of Ireland'.[136] He died in Cavan in 1884.

Additional committee members included Revd Robert Stevelly, DPOS treasurer, and a Hibernian Temperance Society committee member; Revd J. A. Bermingham, the secretary for the DPOS from its earliest years, and later the chairman of the Mendicity Institution;[137] Revd George Kelly curate of St Mary's parish; Revd James Gregory, later Dean of St Bridget's Cathedral, Kildare; Revd Michael Boote who co-founded the North Strand Sunday and Daily Schools in 1837.

While many of the clergymen and laymen mentioned in the first annual report played relatively insignificant roles in the Society's actual management, Revd Thomas Robert Shore was a notably active supporter. Shore served as curate of St Michan's parish and chaplain to the Smithfield Penitentiary;[138] he was appointed Honorary Secretary of the Society for the Relief of Indigent Roomkeepers in the 1830s and later chaplain to the Newgate Prison and the House of Industry. Through his many public roles, he gained extensive and invaluable experience of poverty and destitution which proved particularly useful in his work with the DPOS.

The Charitable Protestant Orphan Union

The governing rules of the DPOS were officially introduced on 12 January 1830 and stated that only children of Protestant parentage were admissible; however, not all committee members agreed with this policy.[139] Following the receipt of several urgent applications from mixed marriage families in February 1830, certain committee members suggested a review of the terms of eligibility.[140] Others dismissed the idea, contending that to do so would violate the Society's original principles. In the first year only four mixed marriage cases were elected; the others were 'invariably rejected because one parent was Roman Catholic'.[141] On this basis, on 16 March 1830, the committee reconfirmed its ruling to receive only children whose parents were both Protestant. 'In order therefore that this question might be set at rest forever a motion was submitted to this effect that the orphans of Roman Catholics either on the father's or mother's side be and are inadmissible'.[142] There were twenty-nine votes for and nine against.[143] Two of the original found-ers voted in favour and one voted against. With only limited funds at their disposal, the DPOS was forced to refuse several applications from Protestant families. Moreover, the charity was founded for the specific purpose of assisting respectable Protestant families. The committee remained divided on the issue, and after a resolution was passed which stated that 'none but the orphans of Protestant parents be admissible', it was reported that 'several of the committee have taken offence at the same and have resigned up their collection books and places on the com-mittee'.[144] A subsequent resolution requested the formal resignation of those who objected to the rule with immediate effect.

The committee members who left the DPOS founded a separate orphan society which they named the Charitable Protestant Orphan Union. Soon after, the DPOS committee noted that they had heard 'with upset that more seceding members have endeavoured to estab-lish a society in opposition to this exclusively Protestant institution by the illegitimate and degrading means of impugning the principles and maligning the character of its friends'.[145] Representatives of the charities remained on acrimonious terms for seven months until the DPOS com-mittee members recommended on 9 November 1830 that all Protestants should maintain a degree of unity.[146] Nevertheless, the two charities continued to work separately until 1898.

Conclusion

During economically turbulent times and inspired by the spirit of evan-gelicalism, three artisans came together to affect change in their own community. The inevitability of Catholic emancipation, the increased number of convents and religious orders, and looming fears of the unknown brought home Protestant artisans' weakened position and prepared the ground for the foundation of the DPOS. A number of the committee members were or had been members of other poor relief and moral reform agencies which gave them first-hand experience of poverty. Divisions within the charity in its initial years prompted the foundation of the CPOU amid soured relations between once unified committee members; it was made clear at this juncture that only children of Protestant parentage were eligible to the DPOS. The Society was a lay parish charity aimed at respectable bereaved Protestant families who had fallen on hard times; however, it did not remain so for long. The next chapter examines the foundation of auxiliaries and local PO Societies throughout Ireland against the backdrop of cholera epidemics and the Great Famine.

Notes

1 DPOS annual report, 1830, NAI, POS papers, 1045/1/1/1–7, p. 22.
2 See I. Whelan, *The Bible War in Ireland: The 'Second Reformation' and the Polarization of Protestant-Catholic Relations, 1800–1840* (Dublin: Lilliput Press, 2005), p. 60.
3 J. R. Hill, *From Patriots to Unionists: Dublin Civic Politics and Irish Protestant Patriotism, 1660–1840* (Oxford: Clarendon Press, 1997).
4 D. W. Bebbington, *Evangelicalism in Modern Britain: A History from the 1730s to the 1980s* (London: Routledge, 1989), p. 1.
5 Whelan, *Bible War*, p. 87.
6 *Ibid.*, p. 11
7 D. Bowen, *The Protestant Crusade in Ireland, 1800–70: A Study of Protestant-Catholic Relations between the Act of Union and Disestablishment* (Dublin: Gill and Macmillan, 1978), p. 68.
8 P. Comerford, 'An innovative people: the Church of Ireland laity, 1780–1830', in R. Gillespie and W. G. Neely (eds), *The Laity and the Church of Ireland, 1000–2000: All Sorts and Conditions* (Dublin: Four Courts Press, 2002), pp. 170–96, p. 175.
9 W. Curry, *The Picture of Dublin: or, Stranger's Guide to the Irish Metropolis* (Dublin: W. Curry jun. and Co., 1835), p. 193.
10 *Ibid.*
11 A. Acheson, *History of the Church of Ireland, 1691–1996* (Dublin: Columba Press, APCK, 1997), pp. 153–7.
12 *Ibid.*, p. 157.
13 Hill, *Patriots to Unionists*, p. 335.
14 Acheson, *History of the Church of Ireland*, p. 109; see also Bowen, *Protestant Crusade*, p. 61.
15 Acheson, *History of the Church of Ireland*, p. 121; see also, Whelan, *Bible War*, pp. 52–5, p. 55.
16 W. G. Neely, 'The Clergy, 1780–1850', in T. Bernard and W. G. Neely (eds), *The Clergy of the Church of Ireland 1000–2000: Messengers, Watchmen and Stewards* (Dublin: Four Courts Press, 2006), pp. 142–56, p. 147.
17 Acheson, *History of the Church of Ireland*, p. 133.

18 Whelan, *Bible War*, p. 84.

19 *Ibid.*, p. 236.

20 M. Wall, 'The rise of a Catholic middle class in eighteenth-century Ireland', *Irish Historical Studies*, 11:42 (1958), pp. 91–115.

21 See J. R. Hill, 'Protestant ascendancy challenged: the Church of Ireland laity and the public sphere', in Gillespie and Neely (eds), *The Laity and the Church of Ireland*, pp. 150–69, pp. 158–65.

22 C. Clear, 'The limits of female autonomy: nuns in nineteenth century Ireland', in M. Luddy and C. Murphy (eds), *Women Surviving: Studies in Irish Women's History in the 19th and 20th Centuries* (Dublin: Poolbeg Press, 1990), pp. 15–50, p. 29.

23 *Ibid.*; see also C. Enright, '"Take this child": a study of Limerick Protestant Orphan Society, 1833–1900' (MA dissertation, University of Limerick, 2003).

24 Clear, 'The limits of female autonomy', p. 21.

25 Bowen, *Protestant Crusade*, p. 91.

26 Whelan, *Bible War*, pp. 156–7; see also, Hill, *Patriots to Unionists*, p. 336.

27 Acheson, *History of the Church of Ireland*, p. 162.

28 *Ibid.*

29 See Whelan, *Bible War*, pp. 134–7; See Acheson, *History of the Church of Ireland*, p. 123.

30 S. M. Parkes, *Kildare Place: The History of the Church of Ireland Training College and College of Education 1811–2010* (Dublin: CICE, 1984), pp. 18–20.

31 Whelan, *Bible War*, p. 143; Bowen, *Protestant Crusade*, p. 63.

32 Whelan, *Bible War*, p. 145.

33 *Ibid.*

34 B. Jenkins, *Era of Emancipation: British Government of Ireland, 1812–1830* (Quebec: McGill-Queen's Press, 1988), p. 65.

35 *Ibid.*, p. 64.

36 10 Geo. IV, c. 7 (13 Apr. 1829).

37 Comerford, 'An innovative people', p. 182.

38 Milne, *Charter Schools*, p. 23.

39 *Ibid.*, pp. 8–12; S. J. Connolly, *Religion, Law and Power: The Making of Protestant Ireland, 1660–1760* (Oxford: Oxford University Press, 1992), p. 304; Robins, *Lost Children*, pp. 68–9.

40 N. Yates, *The Religious Condition of Ireland, 1750–1850* (Oxford: Oxford University Press, 2006), p. 54; see Milne, *Charter Schools*.

41 P. Gray, *The Making of the Irish Poor Law, 1815–43* (Manchester: Manchester University Press, 2009), p. 12.

42 Robins, *Lost Children*, p. 119.

43 *Ibid.*, p. 115.

44 *Ibid.*, p. 129.

45 *The Dublin Almanac and Register of Ireland for 1847* (Dublin: Pettigrew and Oulton, 1847), p. 939.

46 N. Acheson, B. Harvey, J. Kearney and A. Williamson, *Two Paths, One Purpose: Voluntary Action in Ireland, North and South: A Report to the Royal Irish Academy's Third Sector Research Programme* (Dublin: Institute of Public Administration, 2004), p. 12.

47 Robins, *Lost Children*, p. 119.

48 Prunty, *Dublin Slums*, p. 236.

49 *First Report of the Commissioners for Inquiring into the Condition of the Poorer Classes in Ireland 1834*, p. 22, HC 1835 (369), vol. xxxii.

50 D. J. Keenan, *The Catholic Church in Nineteenth-Century Ireland: A Sociological Study* (Dublin: Gill and Macmillan, 1983), p. 127.

51 Robins, *Lost Children*, p. 119.

52 *The Penny Magazine of the Society for the Diffusion of Useful Knowledge*, 3:113 (Winter 1834), pp. 171–2.

53 Robins, *Lost Children*, p. 3.

54 *The Penny Magazine*, pp. 171–2.

55 Luddy, *Women and Philanthropy*, p. 77.

56 Clear, 'The limits of female autonomy', p. 28.

57 Comerford, 'An innovative people', p. 173.

58 K. Milne, *Protestant Aid, 1836–1936: A History of the Association for the Relief of Distressed Protestants* (Dublin: APCK, 1986), p. 3.

59 DPOS annual report, 1830, NAI, POS papers, 1045/1/1/1–7; see also 'Centenary of the Protestant Orphan Society', *Irish Times* (30 November 1928), www.irishtimes/archive.com, 10 Jan. 2012.

60 E. M. Crawford, 'Typhus in nineteenth-century Ireland', in G. Jones and E. Malcolm (eds), *Medicine, Disease and the State in Ireland, 1650–1940* (Cork: Cork University Press, 1999), pp. 121–37, p. 129.

61 S. Lewis, *Irish Topographical Dictionary* (London: S. Lewis and Co., 1837), p. 534.

62 D. Dickson, 'Death of a capital? Dublin and the consequences of union', in P. Clark and R. Gillespie (eds), *Two Capitals: London and Dublin, 1500–1840* (Oxford: Oxford University Press, 2001), pp. 111–32, p. 114.

63 *Freeman's Journal* (1 July 1822).

64 *Ibid.*

65 *Ibid.*

66 Hill, *Patriots to Unionists* p. 201.

67 *The Penny Cyclopaedia of the Society of Useful Knowledge* (London: Charles Knight and Co., 1841), p. 490.

68 O. MacDonagh, 'The age of O'Connell, 1830–45', in W. E. Vaughan (ed.), *A New History of Ireland, V: Ireland Under the Union, 1801–1870, I* (Oxford: Oxford University Press, 1989), pp. 158–68.

69 *The Penny Cyclopaedia*, p. 490; K. A. Miller, *Emigrants and Exiles: Ireland and the Irish Exodus to North America* (Oxford: Oxford University Press, 1985), p. 176.

70 *Freeman's Journal* (13 May 1826).

71 A. Cosgrove and W. E. Vaughan (eds), *A New History of Ireland: A Chronology of Irish History to 1976* (Oxford: Clarendon Press, 2005), p. 307.

72 *Journal of the House of Commons,* 83 (1828), p. 221.

73 Hill, *Patriots to Unionists,* p. 285.

74 *Third Report of the Commissioners for Inquiring into the Condition of the Poorer Classes in Ireland, 1836,* p. 27, HC 1836 (43), vol. xxx.

75 Hill, *Patriots to Unionists,* p. 266.

76 *Ibid.,* p. 279.

77 *Appendix to First Report of the Commissioners for Inquiring into the Condition of the Poorer Classes in Ireland, Appendix (C) – Parts I and II – Part I: Reports on the State of the Poor, and on the Charitable Institutions in some of the Principal Towns, with supplement containing answers to queries,* p. 24c, HC 1836 (35), vol. xxx; *Part II: Report on the City of Dublin, and supplement, containing answers to queries,* p. 25c, HC 1836 (35), vol. xxx.

78 W. Stanley, *Facts on Ireland* (Dublin: R. Milliken and Son, 1832), p. 25.

79 Dickson, 'Death of a capital?', p. 127.

80 S. Magee, *Weavers and Related Trades, Dublin, 1826* (Dublin: Dun Laoghaire Genealogical Society, 1995), p. 1.

81 Dickson, 'Death of a capital?', p. 127.

82 *Freeman's Journal* (7 May 1827).

83 *Freeman's Journal* (14 May 1827).

84 DPOS annual report, 1830, NAI, POS papers, 1045/1/1/1–7, p. 2.

85 Comerford, 'An innovative people', p. 181.

86 'Constitution and rules of a proposed Protestant Orphan Society submitted by committee to general meeting; with amendments as passed in 1828', NAI, POS papers, 1045/6/2/1.

87 *Ibid.*

88 J. B. M'Crea, Minister Independent Church, *The Cause of Irish Protestant Orphans: The Cause of Godliness and Loyalty* (Dublin: Richard Moore Tims, 1833), p. 21.

89 DPOS annual report, 1830, NAI, POS papers, 1045/1/1/1–7, p. 8.

90 'Constitution and rules of a proposed Protestant Orphan Society submitted by committee to general meeting; with amendments as passed in 1828', NAI, POS papers, 1045/6/2/1.

91 *The Treble Almanack: Containing: I. John Watson Stewart's Almanack II. The English Court Register III. Wilson's Dublin Directory with a New Correct Plan of the City* (Dublin: sold by all booksellers, 1830), pp. 65–127.

92 'Centenary of the Protestant Orphan Society', *Irish Times* (30 November 1928).

93 DPOS annual report, 1831, NAI, POS papers, 1045/1/1/1–7, p. 7.

94 G. Lawless Lee, *The Huguenot Settlements in Ireland* (London: Longmans, 1936), p. 216.

95   *Freeman's Journal* (14 May 1827).
96   *The Treble Almanack* (1832), p. 180.
97   DPOS annual report, 1830, NAI, POS papers, 1045/1/1/1–7, p. 39.
98   *Ibid.*
99   See retrospective look at the POS management in minutes general commit-
     tee, 1856–61, NAI, POS papers, 1045/2/1/6, pp. 286–8.
100 'Protestant Orphan Society', *Irish Times* (9 April 1921).
101 *The Treble Almanack* (1830), pp. 206–7.
102 Comerford, 'An innovative people'.
103 'Diocesan intelligence England and Ireland, Dublin', *Church of England
     Magazine*, 11:321 (Winter 1841), p. 435.
104 *Ibid.*
105 Comerford, 'An innovative people', p. 174.
106 Keenan, *The Catholic Church*, p. 127.
107 DPOS annual report, 1830, NAI, POS papers, 1045/1/1/1–7, p. 2.
108 Minutes, 6 Sept. 1829, NAI, POS papers, 1045/2/1/1.
109 D. Massy, *Footprints of a Faithful Shepherd: a Memoir of the Rev.
     Godfrey Massy, B.A., vicar of Bruff, and hon. sec. of the Limerick
     Protestant Orphan Society; with a sketch of his times* (London, Dublin:
     Selley, Jackson & Haliday, 1855), p. 319.
110 From a Correspondent, 'Self-supporting institutions for orphans among
     the Irish Poor', *The Penny Magazine of the Society for the Diffusion of
     Useful Knowledge*, 8:455 (Summer 1839), pp. 171–2, p. 171.
111 DPOS annual report, 1830, NAI, POS papers, 1045/1/1/1–7, p. 2.
112 J. Liechty, 'The problem of sectarianism and the Church of Ireland', in
     A. Ford, J. McGuire and K. Milne (eds), *As by Law Established: The
     Church of Ireland since the Reformation* (Dublin: Lilliput Press, 1995),
     pp. 204–22, p. 221.
113 Letter to the editor, 'Protestantism placed on the defensive in Ireland',
     Christian Examiner and the Church of Ireland Magazine, 11:86 (1831),
     pp. 725–32, p. 732.
114 *Ibid.*
115 F. Davenport Hill, *Children of the State: The Training of Juvenile Paupers*
     (1st edn, London: Macmillan and Co., 1868), pp. 118–19.
116 P. Jalland, *Death in the Victorian Family* (Oxford: Oxford University
     Press, 1996), p. 19.
117 St Catherine's vestry minutes, 27 Sept. 1830, RCBL, p. 312.
118 DPOS annual report, 1830, NAI, POS papers, 1045/1/1/1–7, p. 11.
119 Whelan, *Bible War*, p. 68.
120 DPOS annual report, 1830, NAI, POS papers, 1045/1/1/1–7, p. 11.
121 *Ibid.*, 1834, p. 13.
122 *Ibid.*, p. 9.
123 DPOS annual report, 1830, NAI, POS papers, 1045/1/1/1–7, p. 40.
124 Whelan, *Bible War*, p. 61.
125 *The Treble Almanack* (1832), p. 180.

126 CPOU annual report, 1842, p. 15, RIA

127 Bowen, *Protestant Crusade*, p. 67.

128 L. Lunney, 'Singer, Joseph Henderson', *Dictionary of Irish Biography*, www.dib.cambridge.org, 12 Sept. 2012.

129 Register incoming letters, 10 May 1833, NAI, POS papers, 1045/3/1/1.

130 R. S. Brooke, *Recollections of the Irish Church* (London: Macmillan and Co., 1877), pp. 24–5.

131 *The Treble Almanack* (1832), p. 172.

132 *Freeman's Journal* (20 May 1826).

133 *Freeman's Journal* (12 October 1854).

134 Anon., Revd D. Huddleston, 'Blacker, George Dacre (1791–1871), Church of Ireland clergyman', *Oxford Dictionary of National Biography*, www.oxforddnb.com, 9 Oct. 2012.

135 DPOS annual report, 1830, NAI, POS papers, 1045/1/1/1–7.

136 B. H. Blacker and Revd M. C. Curthoys, 'Darley, John Richard (1799–1884), schoolmaster and bishop of Kilmore, Elphin, and Ardagh', *Oxford Dictionary of National Biography*.

137 DPOS annual report, 7 July 1842, NAI, POS papers, 1045/1/1/11–17.

138 *Ibid.*, p. 204.

139 'Constitution and rules of a proposed Protestant Orphan Society submitted by committee to general meeting; with amendments as passed in 1828', NAI, POS papers, 1045/6/2/1; see also a retrospective view of the foundation of the CPOU found in the minutes of the DPOS committee, 16 Sept. 1859, NAI, POS papers, 1045/2/1/6, pp. 286–8, p. 287.

140 Minutes, 9 Feb. 1830, NAI, POS papers, 1045/2/1/1.

141 A retrospective view of the foundation of the CPOU found in the minutes of the DPOS committee, 16 Sept. 1859, NAI, POS papers, 1045/2/1/6, pp. 286–8.

142 Minutes, 30 Mar. 1830, NAI, POS papers, 1045/2/1/1, p. 35.

143 Retrospective view of earlier meetings discussed 16 Sept. 1859, NAI, POS papers, 1045/2/1/6, pp. 286–8.

144 Minutes, 30 Mar. 1830, NAI, POS papers, 1045/2/1/1, p. 35.

145 *Ibid.*

146 *Ibid.*, 9 Nov. 1830, p. 40.

2

PO Societies and the Poor Law, 1830–50

Favourably as the committee would regard the Poor Law for the aged and infirm; they cannot consent that the orphan children of their fellow Protestants should be thrown into a position calculated to undermine their faith, and deteriorate their morals, and which experience has proved to be one attended with an awful mortality in the case of children.[1]

Introduction

At a time when only rudimentary elements of a 'poor law' were in place, the DPOS embarked on a period of expansion through the foundation of parish auxiliaries. Local PO Societies, which were not subject to the direction of the parent body in Dublin, were also formed. Thus, by 1838 when the Poor Law was extended to Ireland, the charity had become an established source of private poor relief for respectable Protestants in reduced circumstances. Though an extensive public poor relief measure, the Poor Law was intended to stigmatise pauperism. Workhouses were regarded as dens of proselytism and immorality, and as a 'badge of shame'. Given the Protestant minority status which was magnified in the workhouse environment, respectable Protestant widows with dependents sought and were encouraged to seek private rather than public assistance. This chapter explores the Protestant mindset post-emancipation and argues that religious rivalry accounted for the growing support of PO Societies pre-Poor Law and that the charity was self-promoted as a superior alternative to workhouses post-Poor Law on the basis that its system had succeeded where the Poor Law failed: it maintained widows and children's health, well-being, respectability and future prospects.

Preserving a Protestant presence in Ireland

Catholic emancipation did not solve the Irish question as liberals had predicted leading to widespread agrarian unrest. Conflict over the tithe, a tax charged on agricultural produce for the support of the Church of Ireland and its clergy, eventually proved irrepressible for a number of reasons: the poor harvest of 1829, unresolved Catholic grievances post-emancipation and encouragement from Bishop James Doyle to refuse payment.[2] In 1831 there were serious outbreaks of violence, for example, in Newtown Barry, Wexford, and the Carrickshock incident in Kilkenny, during which seventeen people died, the majority of whom were policemen.[3] Protestants in Kilkenny also resisted payment of tithe.[4] Moreover, there was opposition to priests' dues which led to the foundation of the Threshers, a secret society, in the west of Ireland.[5] From 1832 to 1834 accounts of intimidation and murder abounded.[6] Church of Ireland clergy experienced grave difficulties during the 1830s due to the withholding of tithe until they were provided with relief in 1832.[7] The Tithe Composition Act was carried in 1832 and the 1833 Church Temporalities (Ireland) Act[8] resulted in the internal reform of the Church of Ireland.

Protestant emigration in the pre-famine years was attributable, in part, to fear of attacks during the tithe war and to concerns that they no longer had a viable future in a country where their status was fast diminishing.[9] As Desmond Bowen contends, 'At all times the culturally besieged Protestants feared assimilation through intermarriage and sometimes feared annihilation through some kind of jacquerie'.[10] J. B. M'Crea, Independent minister, Ebenezer Chapel, Dublin, referred to Protestant emigration and the 'security which many of the reformed are seeking on foreign shores'.[11] Protestant converts emigrated steadily in the late eighteenth and nineteenth century,[12] for example, a convert, an ex-policeman and blacksmith from County Mayo, was boycotted by the local priest for a decade before he eventually emigrated to Canada.[13] Protestant tenant farmers refused to pay the exorbitant rents set by landlords, leaving Catholics to take up the land.[14] There were reports that a number of Protestants had planned to leave as soon as their leases had expired 'as they had no chance of a renewal on fair terms. The landlords now care no more for a Protestant than for a Roman Catholic'.[15]

As O'Connell appeared to have bypassed Protestant opinion on the issue of the repeal of union,[16] former liberal Protestant supporters and the general Protestant population became increasingly defensive and alarmist.[17] The National School System, to be managed by the National Commission and by the majority church in each locality was rejected by the Church of Ireland and subsequently by Presbyterians.[18] The decision to do so led to further Protestant alienation and the foundation of the Church Education Society in 1839.[19] (Church of Ireland schools remained independent until 1860.[20])

Protestant societies and associations were founded in the 1830s during a period of continued economic depression to preserve a Protestant presence in Ireland. The Protestant Conservative Association was founded in 1832.[21] The Protestant Association of Ireland registered voters and aimed to protect persecuted Protestants in the south.[22]

The *Dublin University Magazine* called attention to Protestant emigration in 1833:

> We have no desire to magnify this evil beyond its just dimensions, but we ask, of what use will be the Protestant press – the Conservative Clubs – our Tory Principles – even the Established Church herself, when the Protestant population has emigrated? – of what use will be the protecting measure, when there are no Protestants to protect? It will, then, be mere idiotcy, or, at least, a waste of time and talent to devise plans for the support of the Protestant interest, when those who are the bone and sinew of that body shall have abandoned the country forever. The magnitude of this evil will stand revealed still more plainly when we reflect on the value of the character and principles of that class.[23]

The report on the condition of the poorer classes (1836) brought to light that 'the Protestants see their numbers daily diminishing, and they think if they remain at home they will be exposed to violence'.[24] The report identified the sharply reduced circumstances of once respectable families.

> I often meet with cases of great distress where the parties have been respectable; widows of clergymen, doctors, attorneys, and merchants, and of gentlemen who had been officers. We have lost some of our members (speaking of the Room-keepers' Society), who have been reduced by distress to discontinue their subscriptions. I have known many persons who had been members of the institution who have been subsequently obliged to seek relief from the institution.[25]

The Association for the Relief of Distressed Protestants (ARDP) was founded on 1 October 1836 after the Poor Relief Commission's report.[26] In the 1840s Revds H. R. Halahan, Eugene O'Meara, and R. J. McGhee, Alexander Leeper and Dr John Ringland were members of both the ARDP and DPOS committees. Church of Ireland Christian fellowships were founded in the 1830s to assist Protestants in times of hardship and to encourage religious practice.[27]

The development of county PO Societies pre-Poor Law

From 1832 onwards, Roman Catholics could openly give land for the purpose of building churches and schools.[28] The rising Catholic middle class contributed to the foundation of ninety-one convents by the 1840s[29] while ninety-seven churches were established under Daniel Murray's episcopate from 1809 to 1852.[30] Further concessions were granted under the Charitable Donations and Bequests (Ireland) Act, 1844 and the Maynooth grant was increased in 1845. Protestant evangelicalism also grew steadily and by the mid-1830s a colony for converts had been established in Dingle, and Revd Edward Nangle had founded the Achill mission.

In the pre-Poor Law years, Houses of Industry and Mendicity Associations remained essential sources of poor relief. In 1834 Henry Inglis recalled a visit to the Dublin Mendicity Society where 2,145 people were reliant on charity and of these '200 were Protestant'.[31] Moreover, he stated that the bulk of its subscriptions came from the Protestant rather than the Roman Catholic middle class.[32] J. B. M'Crea, Independent minister of the Ebenezer Chapel, Dublin, D'Olier Street (opened 5 November 1820), delivered a speech on the subject of Irish Protestant orphans in 1833.[33]

> I had previously no idea, though quite aware of the spirit and feeling of the respective communities, that so large a capital was supplied by Protestant benevolence for the almost exclusive service of the Roman Catholic population. I could not imagine, that with the reiterated boastings of the increasing wealth of the Popish body, so little was done by it toward the support of our public hospitals; whilst the mass of mendicants, paupers, and invalids, relieved by those institutions, are members of that communion by which Protestants are stigmatised, persecuted, and proscribed.[34]

M'Crea reported that from a total of 8,000 Protestants in a 'southern town of great importance', there were ninety-one Protestant orphans 'of whom fifty five live entirely by semi-mendicancy and the rest are maintained by individual charity or the precarious returns of casual employment'.[35] M'Crea also heavily criticised the 'heartless proprietary', for their neglect. Two years later, he submitted a petition to the House of Commons requesting an investigation into Roman Catholic societies.

> A petition of John Benjamin McCrea; praying the House to appoint a Select Committee to inquire into the number, nature, operations and tendency of Monastic, Conventional, and other houses of seclusion in Ireland, their comparative finances, numbers of inmates, and the rules of their internal government and economy since the year 1825; and to obtain particularly all possible information respecting the several houses of the Society of Jesus, the Institute of the Blessed Virgin Mary, the Confraternity of Carmelites, and the Monks of La Trappe, with their constitutions, tests, declarations and resources.[36]

According to its annual reports, the ARDP was founded as, 'all the charitable institutions of this city being founded on general principles and consequently chiefly occupied by Roman Catholics who are the great majority of the poorest part of the population so that consequently our poor Protestant brethren are neglected in their daily ministrations'.[37] Given the absence of legal provisions for the support of orphans at this time,[38] increasing Roman Catholic influence, claims that the 'Church of Rome' reported a rise in intermarriages[39] and increasing Protestant emigration,[40] the DPOS sought to expand.[41] Initially, auxiliaries were set up in many Dublin parishes to collect subscriptions. The outbreak of cholera, which first appeared in Belfast in March 1832 followed by Dublin, Cork, Waterford, Limerick and Galway,[42] placed fresh demands on private charity. Many orphans were taken in by relatives while other destitute children and widows resorted to begging.[43] St Vincent's Hospital (by the Sisters of Mercy)[44] and the Cholera Orphan Society were founded in the wake of the epidemic.

The Cork POS was founded in 1832. In the 1830s approximately one-third of the population in the city parishes of Cork were Protestant.[45] Owing to the growing number of orphans on its roll, thirty-nine in its first year, the Cork POS employed an Assistant Secretary and Travelling Agent, 'to conduct the complicated machinery of the Society's exertions, and to form Auxiliary Associations in the country'.[46] The 'common cause' promoted by the Society in Cork, as in Dublin, was the preservation of bereaved Protestant families:

> The pressing dangers to which the destitute children of our brethren are exposed, call imperatively upon every Protestant of honest and conscientious feeling, from the peer to the mechanic, to come forward and support this Society, so closely connected with the happiness and stability of our country – it calls on the benevolent to cast in of that which God hath given them, to aid in raising up the orphan's head from the father's tomb – to dry the falling tear of helpless misery – to staunch the bleeding heart of widowed grief.[47]

The annual report was enthusiastic and urgent in its pleas to the public: 'increased support must be sought – warmly attached patronage must be acquired – and the luke-warm and the timid roused to decision'.[48] The orphans of mixed marriages as well as Protestant parentage were admissible. Almost half of the orphans who were admitted to the Society had lost either one or both parents to cholera.[49]

In 1832 applications for the admission of ninety-three cholera orphans from Limerick were sent to Dublin; however, as the DPOS was still in its infancy, many of the children had 'perished' before help was forthcoming.[50] The Limerick POS (LPOS) was subsequently founded by Revd William Maunsell on 25 February 1833 to assist families in distress.[51] Revd Maunsell died of fever in 1836; the Vicar of Bruff, Revd Godfrey Massy, who 'scarcely received any clerical income'[52] during the tithe war, was subsequently appointed co-secretary. In his history of Limerick, Fr John Begley refers to Massy in the following terms: 'full of the idea of converting the papists, a very common idea at the time, he made a survey of the parish to find out his prospects in the new field that was opening out before him, and did not overlook his formidable adversary, the priest'.[53] According to Massy, the priest was indeed a force to be reckoned with. Well-connected with the resident gentry, Dean MacNamara was thought responsible when a respectable Protestant family 'lapsed into popery'. Massy said of MacNamara, 'his smooth, oily manners and insinuating address, his electioneering power and ready wit secured his welcome at the table of the rich. While his singular skill in ruling and pleasing the mob made him a perfect dictator among the poor'.[54] During Massy's appeal for funds, the indifference of absentee landlords was mentioned as well as the cold responses of the resident landlords who it was stated were overburdened with requests for assistance.[55]

The LPOS was regarded as 'proof to the drooping Protestant, that he is still cared for'.[56] The Society was said to bring together 'all sorts and conditions' of Protestants to ensure their 'mutual welfare'.[57] The orphans of mixed marriages were admitted.[58] Also referred to as the Protestant Orphan Friends' Society, in 1840 there were 215 orphans under its care.[59] It is important to restate that many of the PO Societies which formed after the DPOS were not connected to it or subject to its direction. In its 1834 annual report, the DPOS clarified its position:

> The Carlow Association, Kingstown and Limerick have been formed, having the same object, and on the same principles as your own, though not in connexion with it. In Cork, also, a society has been instituted for the relief of Protestant orphans; differing, however, from yours in extending its benefits to children, of whom only one parent has been Protestant.[60]

Local PO Societies were typically founded if the DPOS could not admit orphans due to lack of funds.

Newly formed PO Societies corresponded with the parent body primarily in the initial months of establishment to seek advice on general management. The Vicar of Clogheen formed the County Tipperary POS (TPOS) on Tuesday 8 December 1835. The Earl of Glengall presided. The TPOS resolved at its inaugural meeting held at the Courthouse, Clonmel, on 16 December 1835, that 'requests be made to the Protestant Orphan

Society in Dublin for information respecting the duties of the assistant secretary, the annual expense of each orphan and the salary allowed to nurses'.[61] Prior to the foundation of a separate local society, the Dublin POS was likely to have admitted children from that county. As a rule children were returned to that parish and thereafter became the responsibility of the local PO Society. The TPOS accepted applications from Protestant and mixed marriage families. Meetings were held throughout the county which resulted in 'some auxiliaries'[62] being formed.

> Preparatory to this meeting circulars were addressed to the noblemen and influential Protestant gentry of this great county, and, with very few exceptions, favourable answers were returned, and liberal donations and subscriptions promised. The list of noblemen and gentlemen, who on the instant, became guardians of the charity is sufficient evidence of the respectable and influential patronage which it received ... They sent deputations throughout the county, in order to make known the objects of the Society, and to create a general interest in its favour.[63]

In the early decades of the nineteenth century, Protestant landlords, such as the Tandys, encouraged growth in areas such as Mountshannon, where a Protestant church was built and Protestant labourers and tradesmen were introduced to the area.[64] By the early 1830s over five hundred Protestants resided there along with a population of 1,682 Catholics.

Protestants also migrated to other parts of Tipperary such as Templemore where by the early 1840s there was a population of 3,685.[65] Cloghjordan was mentioned in the 1838 TPOS annual report as having a 'considerable Protestant population'.[66] The Society had received several applications from that area. Infantry regiments were consistently stationed in Tipperary town throughout the nineteenth century which is reflected in the names that featured in the annual reports and with the applications made to the Society, which are discussed in the next chapter. Military barracks were built in the town in 1879.[67] The Kilkenny POS was founded in January 1836[68] and provided for orphans 'either or both of whose parents may have been Protestants, a preference however to be given in all cases where both parents shall have been Protestants'.[69] The Society admitted a small number of orphans.

PO Societies and the Poor Law

Opponents of the Irish Poor Law included the Church of Ireland Archbishop of Dublin, Richard Whately, who believed the measure did not fit the Irish context.[70] The Earl of Roden and the Earl of Glengall, previously mentioned in relation to the Dublin POS and the Tipperary

Table 2.1 POS development, 1832–44

County POS	Year founded
Cork	1832
Limerick	1833
Clare	1835
Tipperary	1835
Kilkenny	1836
Drogheda	1838
King's County	1839
Leitrim	1839
Sligo	1839
Kerry	1840
Roscommon	1840
Westmeath	1840
Longford	1841
Queen's County	1841
Tyrone	1843
Carlow	1844
Meath	1844
Cavan	1844

Source: DPOS annual report, 1845.

POS, were also vocal opponents. When the Poor Law bill was read before the House of Lords, Roden objected to it because 'it would ruin the best gentry'[71] which was described as an exaggerated plea. He also presented a petition from the corporation of tailors at the third reading and stated that the bill 'has spread the greatest alarm and dismay among all classes of the community in Ireland'.[72] Daniel O'Connell also opposed the bill while William Smith O'Brien pointed out that it did not take into account the unsuitability of workhouses for pauper children.[73] Workhouse relief under the Poor Law (Ireland) Act, 1838, divided the country into 130 poor law unions.

Founded in 1840, the Westmeath POS aimed to prevent Protestant widows and orphans becoming dependent on workhouse relief.[74] The Tipperary POS (TPOS) annual report, 1840, described the Protestant population as a 'small defenceless flock' which 'must be carefully watched'.[75] After the extension of the Poor Law, the TPOS insisted 'that no political arrangement to alleviate, "according to law", the destitution of the poor of this land, can or ought to supersede, in the south of Ireland at least, the necessity of these institutions'.[76] The DPOS resolved

in 1840 that 'while we feel grateful to the Government of the Country
for making a legal provision for our destitute Poor, we are fully per-
suaded that the Work-house is not a suitable asylum for our Protestant
Orphans'.[77] The grounds for opposition to the placement of Protestant
orphans in workhouses were threefold: deterioration of physical health
and moral health, religious interference, and poor education with no
future prospects. Greater concerns were raised for children who had to
remain in workhouses over long periods and were therefore more likely
to be corrupted than those temporarily dependent on indoor relief.[78]

PO Societies were among many private charities to point out the inad-
equacies of the Poor Law. In England Captain E. P. Brenton founded the
Society for the Suppression of Juvenile Vagrancy in 1830. The Society,
which became known as the Children's Friend Society in 1834, organised the emigration of destitute and orphan children to the Cape of
Good Hope and Canada.[79] Vice-patronesses of the Society included the
Countesses of Cork, Carysfort and Wicklow. Captain Brenton stated in
1837 that 'we ask for a comparison between the relative merits of our
school, and the workhouses, the prison, the penitentiaries, the hulks,
the madhouses, and the penal colonies; for all these owe their being
to the neglect of the education of this mighty empire'.[80] PO Societies
also objected to the placement of children in workhouses because the
Poor Law failed to provide them with apprenticeships, and education
in workhouse schools was inadequate.[81] In 1841 TPOS committee
members remarked, 'the Poor Law could hold out to these children no
prospect of future independence or comfort'.[82] The DPOS annual report
of the same year contains similar comments:

> Under the provisions of the Poor-Law Act, very little is contemplated
> beyond the mere support of paupers; no arrangement whatever is made
> with the view of bettering the condition of the children under their care in
> after life. Your committee would then ask, are the Children of Protestant
> Parents, with such serious disadvantages as these, to be encouraged to
> enter and remain in a Poor-house, there to live and die paupers?[83]

Joseph Robins observes that destitute Protestant orphans sent to workhouses were 'placed at the mercy of Catholics in those areas where the
guardians, and consequently the workhouse officers, were mainly of
the Catholic faith; Protestants could not look on with equanimity'.[84] By
1845 there were 123 workhouses in Ireland.[85]

The DPOS compared its methods with the 'Poor-house system' in
1842 based on information supplied by Dublin Poor Law Guardians.
The DPOS deemed its system superior 'with regard to both moral effects
and economy',[86] and predicted that as soon as such findings became

known, 'there will be no more necessity for handing over to the Poor-house, the orphans of our brethren'.[87] At this time, the DPOS confirmed its commitment to 'the defence, preservation, and support of poor Protestant children'.[88]

> The fact cannot be denied that when the Orphan Children of Protestants, both of whose Parents are dead, have been admitted into the Dublin Poor-houses, they have in some instances been registered as members of the Church of Rome. Children of seven and eight years of age have also been permitted to change their religion, and to such an extent was this system carried, that the Government Commissioners were compelled to interpose their authority, in order to check the growing evil. The reports of cases, brought the notice of the Poor-Law Guardians, in addition to other sources of information, which not un-frequently occupy a prominent place in the columns of the public press, and which bear upon them the stamp of truth, are, your committee conceive, a sufficient warrant for expressing more than a doubt as to the propriety of allowing Orphans of Protestant parents to enter a Poor-house.[89]

Although regulations were in place to deter interference with children's religion, such as a requirement of parental consent for under fifteens to change their religion in the workhouse register and only in cases where the Poor Law Guardians were certain that the original entry was incorrect, the measures did not appear to have included orphans and foundlings.[90] In Dundalk Union Workhouse in 1842 such a case arose. Two orphans, aged nine and eleven, were admitted to Dundalk Union Workhouse when it was opened on 14 March 1842 and on that day were registered Protestants. The family had moved to Dundalk from Newry; the children's mother had died of cholera. After their father's (a carpenter) subsequent death in 1837, 'the children became orphans in a district in which they had neither friends nor relations'.[91] The Vicar of Dundalk, Elias Thackery, who had for a time contributed from private means to their care, presented evidence that the parents and the children had always been Protestant. The union-house register said otherwise, 'admitted on the 14th March, and entered as Protestants. But in the margin of the book is this remark, opposite to the name of these children:- "R. Catholic, by order of the Board of Guardians, dated April 4th, 1842 – T. O'Reilly, master'.[92] The case became a precedent and the Poor Law Commissioners concluded that the Board of Guardians had violated the 49th section of the Irish Poor Relief Act, 1838.[93] Several local PO Societies were founded in the following years. (The Louth POS was founded in 1850.[94]) The DPOS persisted in its claims that workhouses were unsuitable shelters for Protestant children, and that the implementation of the Poor Law rather than reducing the relevance of PO Societies had, in fact, called for their 'more hearty assistance'.[95]

During the 1840s, efforts were made to maintain existing DPOS auxiliaries and to promote the foundation of additional auxiliaries. The Belfast auxiliary reported in November 1844, 'the attendance was large and respectable, especially of ladies'.[96] Revd Thomas Gregg, who was on a deputation from Dublin, spoke at the meeting reminding the audience of its Christian duty to care for destitute orphans; 'he also showed the misery in which various orphans had been found at the time when the Society's protection was afforded them'.[97] Revd O'Meara, the Visiting Secretary, who was responsible for raising the DPOS profile, credited Revd Thomas Drew with the foundation and support of the Belfast POS auxiliary and the 'progress of the orphans cause in Belfast and the neighbourhood'.[98] Born on 26 October 1800 in Limerick city, Thomas Drew became a prominent evangelical and member of the Orange Order. A curate in County Antrim before his appointment to Christ Church, Belfast, in 1833, he founded the Church Accommodation Society in 1838 and though regarded as a formidable leader – the driving force behind church building, and numerous and highly beneficial social reforms, such as medical care for the poor – he was viewed as a controversial figure in other respects, who lost favour with the more moderate Bishop Richard Mant.[99] Drew was also a secretary of the Belfast General Relief Fund during the famine which raised funds in Belfast for the relief of the poor throughout Ireland.[100] He garnered support from Methodists and Presbyterians in Belfast who were also admissible to the DPOS. It is likely the auxiliary was founded due to a fall off in employment for weavers in the predominately Protestant area of Ballymacarrett.[101] Subsequently, Protestant orphans from Belfast and the surrounding areas were admitted to the DPOS.[102] The Belfast auxiliary continued to collect the funds necessary for the children's upkeep.

Despite the outward appearance of support, the gentry gave only a tepid response to requests for funds. In 1843 Revd C. H. Minchin, the DPOS, vowed to 'try by every means in his power to prevail on our rich gentry to remove the stigma by multiplying their subscriptions, and thus giving practical proof that they have the prosperity of the institution really at heart'.[103] The Society continued to appeal to the better off members of the church for donations to assist the Protestant poor: 'the law of opinion is against him, the coldness, the distrust, and not unfrequently undisguised hostility, and harassing persecution ... they not merely profess the same religion as yourselves; but on account of that religion they suffer hardships and trials to which you are strangers'.[104] As mentioned earlier, the Society was viewed as a 'social bridge' for the 'class extremes' within the church.

From the early 1830s, attempts were made to establish DPOS auxiliaries outside Ireland. In May 1832, the committee advertised an appeal to the Protestants of England in the *Record* newspaper, London: 'A door has been opened, though to a trifling extent and as yet with little success, to introduce through the medium of the public press – this society to the notice of the Protestants of England'.[105] After a number of deputations, auxiliaries were eventually founded in Manchester, Liverpool, Newcastle upon Tyne, Eccles, Hull, North Repps, Norwich, Nottingham and Southport, though donations were not substantial. The Society's highly significant influence on Scottish boarding-out schemes is considered in chapter 4.

Women's role

It was common for women to participate in charitable work primarily as fundraisers while men took on a more public role.[106] Women – clergymen's wives, daughters and other committed women of the church – became involved in the DPOS collection process from 11 July 1832 onwards: 'Mr. D. gives notice that he will on next Wednesday evening move to solicit religious females to collect for this society'.[107] In 1833, 143 women subscribed to the DPOS. In this year alone, women stood out as leading donors, making up 56.81 per cent of the total collected.[108] By 1834, twenty-nine women collected subscriptions on behalf of the DPOS. Twenty-seven men collected in the same year.[109] 'Your funds have been largely increased through collections which have been made among the upper classes of life by many benevolent ladies in the city and in the country'.[110] Women were acutely aware that they too were susceptible to widowhood and possible destitution.

The anonymous author of *The Orphans of Glenbirkie*, published in 1841 to raise funds for the DPOS, was thought to have been a woman connected with the Deaf and Dumb Society, which was founded by Revd Edward Herbert Orpen. 'The profits arising from the sale are to be devoted to the rescue of the numerous orphans of our destitute brethren from the miseries attendant on poverty'.[111] Copies were sold by booksellers and at the office of the DPOS, 16 Upper Sackville Street, Dublin and ran into a second edition. The author was initially told that 'the tale is too romantic; but the romance of the story owes nothing to her fancy or invention, for the entire incidents were derived from the story of James and Jannette Forrest, contained in the Protestant Orphan report for 1837'.[112] The family on whom the story was based lived in Hamilton, Scotland.

> Jannette Forrest was the daughter of a most respectable farmer in the neighbourhood of Hamilton who left her a free house, well furnished, and upwards of one hundred pounds. She married Forrest, and in a little more than four years his extravagance and dissipation left her houseless and penniless. He locked her up at night in their empty house, and returned the keys to the landlord. Her feelings when she discovered herself to be thus forsaken may be imagined – but there was none to witness them; and when the door was opened some days afterwards, she was found lying upon a bed in a state of decided lunacy. For years this continued, unconscious of her bereavement, with the exception of occasional ravings about her children until last April.[113]

Mr Forrest had taken the children, a boy and a girl, and following his death, which was caused by a fall from a horse, they were 'received under the protection' of the DPOS. Jannette was unaware of their whereabouts and remained so until the DPOS committee was informed of her story and arranged their return.

The author of the book also wrote *Norman Lyndesay, the Orphan Mute: A Narrative of Facts*, in aid of the Juvenile Deaf and Dumb Society, among others, such as *The Little Chimney Sweep*, which included true stories of the deprivation of child slaves and child mortality among chimney sweeps. *The Orphans of Glenbirkie*, and other works by the same author, informed the wider public of the challenges faced by the deaf, by Protestant widows and orphans, and of the exploitation and endangerment of child workers. On 10 October 1846, Miss Jane Phelps, Wilton, Salisbury, England, wrote to the DPOS committee stating that 'the cash sent for the copies of *Orphans of Glenbirkie* may be applied to Society's use'.[114] These books as well as the printed annual reports enhanced the Society's reputation and elevated its status promoting an air of respectability which in turn improved the orphans' future prospects: the DPOS aimed, where possible, to maintain children in the same class as their fathers.

These books were unquestionably important social commentaries which had no doubt been inspired by Charles Dickens's classic portrayal of Oliver Twist. Dickens used fiction to express his criticism of social ills, particularly the treatment of children, and his astute observations shaped future social reform measures. Workhouses were depicted as entirely unsuitable for children; juvenile delinquency and street trading were also themes. Dickens also helped to redefine Victorian childhood by challenging contemporary attitudes with sentimentalised notions of children and childhood.[115] Charlotte Brontë, the daughter of an Irish clergyman, Patrick Brontë (Brunty) published Jane Eyre in 1847. Brontë's poignant portrayal of a young orphan offers important insights into the treatment of charity children in the nineteenth century.[116] Significantly, Arthur Bell Nicholls, Patrick Brontë's curate, who married Charlotte Brontë in 1854, raised money for the Protestant Orphan Society in 1870, which, following the disestablishment of the Church of Ireland, lost part of its income (applicable to Percy Place training home) and appealed for funds.[117]

Protestant famine relief work

Charges of 'souperism' have largely overshadowed the good work of many Church of Ireland ministers and their families, some of whom died through concerted efforts to alleviate the suffering of others.[118] Even mild typhoid fever struck all classes causing more deaths among those with less immunity – the better off.[119] All relief workers ran the risk of contracting fevers. The Dublin Parochial Association was founded in the Chapter House of Christ Church in 1847 to 'assist the parochial clergy by equalising the distribution of charity throughout the city'.[120] In early 1847, 'one in ten' people admitted to the North Dublin Union Workhouse were Protestant.[121]

Some two hundred doctors and medical students died in 1847,[122] and in Mayo, Cork and Armagh medical relief was severely lacking.[123] Dr Neason Adams ran the dispensary at Dingle from 1834 to his death in 1859.[124] Born in 1824, Joseph Kidd, a Quaker, and Limerick native, a homœopath, and future physician to Benjamin Disraeli, arrived in Bantry in 1847. Medical relief in the area at the time was wholly inadequate due to the illness of one of the local physicians. Not long after his arrival, he recorded the death of Revd Dr Trail who had 'died of exhaustion'.[125] Kidd treated fever and dysentery with considerable success.[126] The Archbishop of Dublin, Richard Whately, who too was a faithful supporter of homœopathy, donated much needed funds to provide convalescing fever patients with rice (it was more palatable than Indian meal), milk, bread and fuel.[127]

Kidd remained in Bantry for two months and in a resolution passed by the Bantry Relief Committee, the Vicar of Bantry, Revd Mr Murphy, proposed and Revd Mr Begley, acting parish priest, seconded, 'that thanks of this committee are due to Joseph Kidd, Esq. M.R.C.S. for his assiduous and kind attention to the sick poor of Bantry'.[128] Arthur Guinness was another advocate of homœopathy. He and a number of other Church of Ireland clergymen and laymen founded the Irish Homœopathic Society in Dublin in 1845. Guinness reported in 1846 that a whole convent in Dublin had been converted to homœopathy by Charles Luther, a homœopath who had been practising in Dublin from the 1830s.[129] Revd William Smyth Guinness, rector of Rathdrum, and local superintendent of DPOS orphans, was also a member of the Irish Homœopathic Society.[130]

PO Societies and the Great Famine

Revd Thomas Gregg, Dublin POS (DPOS) committee member, died after thirteen days of severe illness on 22 April 1846:

> Mr Gregg with a generosity that made him heedless of his own temporal welfare, bestowed his money and his time (too truly it may be added) and his health in the service of this society. (Rescuing the orphan ready to perish or in procuring funds.) In him the church has lost one of the noblest examples of living faith. While we mourn his loss may it be given to us to emulate his example.[131]

Revd John Nash Griffin was appointed secretary in Revd Gregg's stead.[132]

The Poor Law Amendment Act, 1847, provided outdoor relief and also placed the burden of poor relief on local ratepayers.[133] In the same year, the DPOS assisted a number of families though it regretted it could not do more without jeopardising the future well-being of all newly admitted orphans as well as those already in its care. At a meeting dated 2 July 1847, the committee discussed current applications and approved twelve urgent cases.[134] The Meath POS was equally cautious regarding the release of funds during the famine years.[135]

In Cork during the 'female industrial movement' poor women made clothes from the gingham material produced by Cork weavers which was then bought by the Ladies' Clothing Association to provide the poor with clothing.[136] Cork gingham was sold by the Board of Manufacture[137] and the Ladies' Auxiliaries Association promoted the revival in Dublin.[138] As mentioned in the next chapter, the DPOS girls wore gingham dresses. Lady Dunraven, a Limerick POS subscriber,[139] supported Limerick weavers.[140] Among other initiatives, embroidery schools, the Ladies' Industrial Society of Ireland, and convent industrial schools were set up to meet the demands of the famine. Protestant and Catholic clergy and Poor Law Guardians throughout the country also supported the movement.[141]

At the close of 'black 47', the Cork POS committee reflected on the devastation of that year:

> So eventful a year as the present over the orphan society nor perhaps has ever been recorded in the annals of our country. Famine has scattered its

blight over our now depopulated county sowing thickly the seeds of pestilence and fever almost amounting to plague, cuts off thousands upon thousands of our fellow creatures. Amongst these are to be found the parents of many respectable and comfortable families whose orphan children are now thrown upon charity of the benevolent … The names of 50 applicants are already upon our books and when our clergy are relieved from the pressure of labour which at present occupies them how numerous may we expect will be the claimants upon the society's funds.[142]

In March 1849, the DPOS noted the 'unprecedented monetary difficulties' and the 'afflicted land'. It indicated that it had 'help from England during the famine' because of the 'greatly diminished resources of our fellow Protestants'.[143] A letter was received from Arklow, County Wicklow, offering a sum of money towards the upkeep of cholera orphans from the town. The chairman stated, 'let him know that there will be others who have lost both parents from the "ravages of cholera" and that we will proceed as normal'.[144] The manner in which the committee dealt with the request proved its impartiality. For example, during a four month period, the Society received sixty-four applications but admitted only five orphans. The DPOS noted at length the far-reaching impact of the cholera epidemic of 1849:

The extent of the ravages of Cholera, in Dublin and many other parts of Ireland, is very imperfectly known to those who did not feel its consequences, owing to the want of any official accounts to record the magnitude of the calamity: but soon this Society felt those consequences, in the appeals of multitudes of Orphans. In every year there have been many applications before your Committee, in behalf of children whose parents belonged rather to the middle than the lower ranks of society: the number of applicants of that class was augmented to a lamentable extent towards the close of the past year. On the list of candidates were Orphans of professional men, of those who held respectable situations, of some comfortable farmers, and of tradesmen, whose children never knew the want of comfort until they were suddenly deprived of a parent's care: to these add, the Orphans of one who was for many years a Member of your Committee, and who had long sincerely and cordially devoted his time and exertions to the work of this Society, and then some idea may be formed of the weight of misery that has pressed and is still pressing upon this institution.[145]

Reluctant to overburden its funds, the DPOS did not approve all applications for the year 1849.

The Kilkenny POS (KPOS) also revealed the perilous state of its funds in 1849, 'that it is a subject of painful regret that the circumstances in which the Society is now placed not only renders it unable to receive several urgent applications for the admission of Orphans, but that the

Table 2.2 Countrywide applications to the DPOS, 1849

Election date	Applications	Admissions	%
January	48	6	12.5
March	56	20	35.7
May	58	12	20.7
July	59	12	20.3
September	58	6	10.4
November	64	5	7.8

Source: DPOS annual report, 1849.

most strenuous exertions will be necessary for the maintenance of the children at present under its care'.[146] Despite having already admitted ten children for that year, the committee had been 'compelled to reject every further application for admittance'.[147] There was even discussion that it might be necessary to 'remove' some of the orphans already under its charge. Although circulars had been sent to the 'landed proprietors, resident and non-resident' in the hope of gathering funds, apart from a 'few exceptions', their pleas went unheard.[148] The KPOS reminded its subscribers that it was

> essentially a poor man's Society – to encourage the Protestant of the humble class amidst the many difficulties and discouragements to which, in such a country as this, they are peculiarly exposed, by convincing them that they are not forgotten by their richer brethren, and by relieving them from what perhaps is the sorest of the many trials incident to their low estate – the agonising reflection that, when they shall be no more, their children will be left to choose between destitution on the one hand and apostasy on the other.[149]

Revd James Graves was a member of the KPOS committee. Graves was one of the founding members of the Royal Society of Antiquaries of Ireland and contributed hugely to the field of archaeology in the second half of the nineteenth century. Both Thomas Shaw Esq., Kilree, Kells, County Kilkenny, another KPOS committee member, and Revd Graves were members of the Kilkenny Archaeological Society.[150]

Missions

Redemptorists and other religious orders such as the Passionists, the Oratorians and Rosminians set up missions in England and Wales in the 1840s and 1850s 'in the hopes of winning a harvest of conversions'.[151] The Vincentians preached in Athy in 1842 and in Dingle in

1846 to challenge the reported successes of Protestant missionaries.[152] In Scotland the Edinburgh Irish Mission was established in 1842 to counteract Catholic attempts to convert Protestants and to advance Protestantism through the conversion of Catholics.[153] The *Belfast News-Letter* reported in 1846 that the Sisters of Mercy and Catholic missionaries were in Western Australia and, while their main focus was the conversion of 'the aboriginal tribes', they had 'attracted many Protestant observers'.[154]

Fr Gentili and Fr Furlong carried out a 'spiritual harvest' over a sixteen month period from January 1847 to April 1848 during which time they had preached at fifteen missions in England and visited Ireland on three occasions. While the missions were aimed mainly at the 'spiritual advancement of Catholics', there were numerous accounts of Protestant conversions. At one mission the 'fishers of men caught in their apostolical net fifty-three Protestants'.[155] There were reports that in total 'at least four hundred Protestants' had been converted.[156] Among them were converts returning to the Roman Catholic church. In London, an Anglican minister and his family converted.[157] Back in Dublin, during the third mission and a typhus fever outbreak, Fr Gentili died on 26 September 1848.

Alexander Dallas officially formed the Society for Irish Church Missions to Ireland (ICM) on 29 March 1849 (however, he had been laying the foundations for its establishment from before 1845),[158] which received the majority of its funding from English sources.[159] While there was a degree of Irish Protestant support there was also intense criticism of its controversial methods.[160] Its main bases were in Connemara and Dublin.[161] Dallas firmly believed that the famine had been a sign of the 'second coming'; the millenarian prediction gave urgency to his mission. The ICM's goal was to 'to communicate the gospel to the Roman Catholics and converts of Ireland by any and every means which may be in accordance with the United Churches of Ireland and England'.[162] Protestants asserted that moral reform and social order depended on access to the bible and Ulster was held up as an example of the pacifying effects of Protestantism. The Oxford Movement, which began after the Church Temporalities Act, 1833, anti-ritualism, John Henry Newman's conversion in 1845 and European revolutionary spirit, fuelled support for the ICM.[163]

In 1849 Dr Paul Cullen, whose family 'represented the Catholic gentry class' was appointed Archbishop of Armagh.[164] Daniel O'Connell had assured Cullen in 1842 that, 'If the union were repealed and the exclusive system abolished, the great mass of the Protestant community would with little delay melt into the overwhelming majority of the nation. Protestantism would not survive the Repeal ten years'.[165] By 1850 there were 1,250 nuns and 2,500 priests in Ireland.[166] Irene Whelan contends that 'Catholic religious practices in Ireland were shaped by the Protestant challenge'.[167] The character of the Church of Ireland was equally shaped by Catholic revival; PO Societies represented one of its most crucial defence strategies and by 1850 sixty DPOS auxiliaries had been founded in parishes throughout Dublin, in Derry, Belfast, Enniskillen, Newry, Monaghan and Wicklow.

Conclusion

The confident eighteenth-century Protestant identity was replaced with a defensive, conservative, self-reliant and insular character as power gradually transferred from Protestant to Roman Catholic hands. The foundation of an alternative to national schools in the form of the Church Education Society signalled the increasing polarisation of 'the two peoples'.

An additional element of this shift was the promotion and development of a private poor relief system in the form of PO Societies, aimed at respectable bereaved Protestant families, and, in the case of certain local PO Societies, mixed marriage families. The reasons for the promotion of private relief were threefold: first, Protestant children were the religious minority in workhouses; second, children's physical health was compromised; and, thirdly, widows and children were thought to be in danger of 'moral contamination' and, thus, likely to lose their respectability. The inability of PO Societies to approve all applications, the admission of Protestants to workhouses during the famine, and Roman Catholic missionary activity abroad suggest that there was a legitimate demand for PO Societies which prompted further development. The next chapter examines in detail the boarding-out system developed by the DPOS and local PO Societies in the first half of the nineteenth century.

Notes

1 DPOS annual report, 1843, NAI, POS papers, 1045/1/1/11–17, p. 15.
2 Acheson, *History of the Church of Ireland*, p. 142.
3 See R. Tobin, *The Minority Voice: Hubert Butler and Southern Irish Protestantism, 1900–1991* (Oxford: Oxford University Press, 2012), p. 15.
4 *Ibid.*, p. 15.
5 D. Bowen, *Souperism: Myth or Reality* (Cork: Mercier Press, 1970), p. 54.

6 K. Madden, *Forkhill Protestants and Forkhill Catholics, 1787–1858* (Quebec: McGill-Queen's Press, 2005), p. 91.

7 *Ibid.*

8 3 & 4 Will. IV, c. 37 (14 Aug. 1833).

9 Miller, *Emigrants and Exiles*, p. 295.

10 Bowen, *Protestant Crusade*, p. 132.

11 M'Crea, *The Cause of Irish Protestant Orphans*, p. 12.

12 See M. Moffitt, *The Society for the Irish Church Missions to the Roman Catholics, 1849–1950* (Manchester: Manchester University Press, 2010).

13 Miller, *Emigrants and Exiles*, p. 234.

14 *Ibid.*, p. 235.

15 *Third Report of the Commissioners for Inquiring into the Condition of the Poorer Classes*, p. 10.

16 Hill, 'Protestant ascendancy challenged', p. 165.

17 Hill, *Patriots to Unionists*, p. 283.

18 See Acheson, *History of the Church of Ireland*, p. 143.

19 *Ibid.*

20 Moffitt, *Irish Church Missions*, p. 35.

21 J. R. Hill, 'The Protestant response to repeal: the case of the Dublin working class', in F. S. L. Lyons and R. A. J. Hawkins (eds), *Ireland Under the Union: Varieties of Tensions. Essays in Honours of T. W. Moody* (Oxford: Clarendon Press, 1980), pp. 35–68, p. 40.

22 'On the emigration of Protestants', *Dublin University Magazine*, 1:5 (1833), pp. 411–82, p. 471.

23 *Ibid.*

24 *Third Report of the Commissioners for Inquiring into the Condition of the Poorer Classes*, p. 10.

25 *Ibid.*, p. 103.

26 Milne, *Protestant Aid*.

27 J. Crawford, *The Church of Ireland in Victorian Dublin* (Dublin: Four Courts Press, 2005), p. 53.

28 Prunty, *Dublin Slums*, p. 236.

29 Clear, 'The limits of female autonomy'.

30 Prunty, *Dublin Slums*, p. 237.

31 H. D. Inglis, *Ireland in 1834: A Journey throughout Ireland, during the Spring, Vol. 1* (London: Whittaker and Co., 1835), p. 16.

32 *Ibid.*, p. 17.

33 M'Crea, *The Cause of Irish Protestant Orphans*, p. 12.

34 *Ibid.*

35 *Ibid.*, p. 11.

36 *Journal of the House of Commons*, 90 (1835), p. 249.

37 Milne, *Protestant Aid*, p. 5.

38 Robins, *Lost Children*, p. 156.

39 Minutes, 1831, NAI, POS papers, 1045/2/1/1.

40 DPOS annual report, 1832, NAI, POS papers, 1045/1/1/1–7.

41 *Ibid.*
42 G. O'Brien, 'State intervention and the medical relief of the Irish poor, 1787–1850', in G. Jones and E. Malcolm (eds), *Medicine, Disease and the State in Ireland, 1650–1940* (Cork: Cork University Press, 1999), pp. 195–207, p. 201.
43 See figures in Robins, *Lost Children*, pp. 156–7.
44 Acheson, Harvey, Kearney and Williamson, *Two Paths, One Purpose*, p. 12.
45 Hill, Patriots to Unionists, p. 26.
46 Cork POS annual report, 1832, p. 6, RIA.
47 *Ibid.*, p. 7.
48 *Ibid.*
49 *Ibid.*
50 Massy, *Footprints of a Faithful Shepherd*, p. 320.
51 *Ibid.*
52 *Ibid.*, p. 315.
53 See J. Begley, *The Diocese of Limerick from 1691 to the Present Time, Vol. 3* (Dublin: Browne and Noble, 1938), p. 482.
54 *Ibid.*
55 Massy, *Footprints of a Faithful Shepherd*, p. 324.
56 *Ibid.*, p. 345.
57 *Ibid.*
58 *Ibid.*, p. 327.
59 Mr and Mrs S. C. Hall, *Ireland: Its Scenery, Character, Vol. 1* (London: How and Parsons, 1841), p. 343.
60 DPOS annual report, 1834, NAI, POS papers, 1045/1/1/1–7, p. 12.
61 Minutes, 16 Dec. 1835, Ireland, County Tipperary POS papers, MS 32,521 (with the Permission of the Board of the National Library of Ireland).
62 TPOS annual report, 1837, NLI, County Tipperary POS papers, MS 32,530/A(2), p. 5.
63 *Ibid.*
64 B. S. Elliott, *Irish Migrants in the Canadas: A New Approach* (Quebec: McGill-Queen's Press, 2004), pp. 29–31, p. 30.
65 *Ibid.*
66 TPOS annual report, 1837, NLI, County Tipperary POS papers, MS 32,530/A(2), p. 5.
67 W. O'Shea, *A Short History of Tipperary Military Barracks (Infantry), 1874–1912* (Tipperary: Walter O'Shea, 1998).
68 Kilkenny POS annual report, 1849, p. 5, RIA.
69 *Ibid.*
70 Gray, *The Making of the Irish Poor Law*, p. 210.
71 *Ibid.*
72 *Mirror of Parliament*, 5:2 (Spring 1838), p. 4,193.
73 Robins, *Lost Children*, pp. 159–60.
74 *Ibid.*

75 TPOS annual report, 1840, NLI, County Tipperary POS papers, MS 32,530/A(5), p. 14.
76 *Ibid.*
77 DPOS annual report, 1841, NAI, POS papers, 1045/1/1/11–17, p. 11.
78 Robins, *Lost Children*, p. 257.
79 C. Neff, 'The Children's Friend Society in Upper Canada, 1833–37', *Journal of Family History*, 32:3 (Summer 2007), pp. 235–59, pp. 236–7.
80 E. P. Brenton, *The Bible and Spade: or, Captain Brenton's account of the Children's Friend Society* (London: James Nisbet and Co., 1837), p. 37.
81 Robins, *Lost Children*, pp. 159–60, pp. 223–5.
82 TPOS annual report, 1841, NLI, County Tipperary POS papers, MS 32,530/A(6), p. 17.
83 DPOS annual report, 1841, NAI, POS papers, 1045/1/1/11–17, p. 10.
84 Robins, *Lost Children*, p. 252.
85 D. Webster Hollis, *The History of Ireland* (Wesport, CT: Greenwood Publishing Group. 2001), p. 92.
86 DPOS annual report, 1841, NAI, POS papers, 1045/1/1/11–17, p. 10.
87 *Ibid.*, p. 11.
88 *Ibid.*, p. 10.
89 *Ibid.*, p. 11.
90 Robins, *Lost Children*, p. 245.
91 *Minutes of Proceedings of Dundalk Union, relative to two pauper children*, HC 1842 (545), xxxvi.
92 *Ibid.*
93 *Ibid.*
94 DPOS annual report, 1850, NAI, POS papers, 1045/1/1/18–23.
95 DPOS annual report, 1843, NAI, POS papers, 1045/1/1/11–17, p. 15.
96 *Belfast News-letter* (19 November 1844).
97 *Ibid.*
98 Minutes, 29 Oct. 1847, NAI, POS papers, 1045/2/1/4, p. 169.
99 P. Long and C. J. Woods, 'Thomas Drew', *Dictionary of Irish Biography*; see M. Hill and D. Hempton, Evangelical Protestantism in Ulster Society, 1740–1890 (London: Routledge, 1992); C. Kinealy and G. MacAtasney, *The Hidden Famine: Hunger, Poverty and Sectarianism in Belfast, 1840–50* (London: Pluto Press, 2000).
100 C. Kinealy, *Charity and the Great Hunger in Ireland: The Kindness of Strangers* (A&C Black, 2013), p. 57.
101 Kinealy and MacAtasney, *The Hidden Famine*, p. 32.
102 Register of applications, 1837–50, NAI, POS papers, 1045/5/2.
103 DPOS annual report, 1843, NAI, POS papers, 1045/1/1/11–17, p. 21.
104 *Ibid.*, 1845, p. 14.
105 DPOS annual report, 1832, NAI, POS papers, 1045/1/1/1–7, p. 10.
106 E. Malcolm, 'Hospitals in Ireland', in A. Bourke (ed.), *Field Day Anthology of Irish Writing: Irish Women's Writing and Traditions* (New York: New York University Press, 2002), pp. 705–21, p. 706.

107 Minutes, 11 July 1832, NAI, POS papers, 1045/2/1/2.
108 DPOS annual report, 1833, NAI, POS papers, 1045/1/1–7.
109 *Ibid.*, 1834.
110 *Ibid.*, 1831, p. 13.
111 By the author of *Norman Lyndesay*, *The Orphans of Glenbirkie: A Story Founded on Facts* (Dublin: Protestant Orphan Society, 1841), p. 6.
112 *Ibid.*, p. 8.
113 *Ibid.*
114 Register incoming letters, 1846, NAI, POS papers, 1045/3/1/3.
115 S. Mitchell (ed.), *Victorian Britain: An Encyclopaedia* (London: Routledge, 1988), p. 141.
116 G. Williams, *Barnardo: The Extraordinary Doctor* (London: Macmillan Press, 1966), p. 11.
117 A. H. Adamson, *Mr Charlotte Brontë: The Life of Arthur Bell Nicholls* (Quebec: McGill-Queen's Press, 2008), p. 22.
118 Acheson, History of the Church of Ireland, pp. 187–91.
119 T. Dyson and C. Ó Gráda (eds), *Famine Demography: Perspectives from the Past and Present* (Oxford: Oxford University Press, 2002), p. 35.
120 R. McCarthy, 'The role of the clergy in the Great Famine', in *The Great Famine: A Church of Ireland Perspective* (Dublin: APCK, 1996), pp. 9–13, p. 10.
121 C. Ó Gráda, 'Church of Ireland mortality during the famine', in *The Great Famine*, pp. 13–16, p. 14.
122 Dyson and Ó Gráda (eds), *Famine Demography*, p. 35.
123 W. Kidd, R. H. McCall (ed.), *Joseph Kidd 1824–1918, Limerick-London-Blackheath: A Memoir* (Privately published, 1983), p. 210.
124 P. Comerford, 'A bitter legacy?', in *The Great Famine*, pp. 5–9, p. 6.
125 Kidd, *Joseph Kidd*, p. 209.
126 *Ibid.*
127 *Ibid.*
128 *Ibid.*, p. 251.
129 Correspondence, 'Dr Guinness to Dr Drysdale', *British Journal of Homœopathy*, 5:19–20 (1847), p. 124. See also R. U. Chonaire, 'The Luther legacy: homeopathy in Ireland in the nineteenth century', *Journal of the Irish Society of Homeopaths* (2010), pp. 17–24.
130 C. Luther, *A Concise View of the System of Homœopathy* (Dublin: J. Fannin and Co., 1845), p. vi.
131 Ibid.
132 *Ibid.*, p. 71.
133 Kinealy and MacAtasney, *The Hidden Famine*, p. 100.
134 Minutes, 2 July 1847, NAI, POS papers, 1045/2/1/4.
135 Revd R. Athey, 'A short history of the Meath Protestant Orphan Society compiled on the occasion of its centenary' (Privately printed, 1944), p. 5.
136 M. Cronin, 'The female industrial movement, 1845–52', in B. Whelan

(ed.), *Women and Paid Work in Ireland, 1500–1930* (Dublin: Four Courts, 2000), pp. 69–85.

137 *Freeman's Journal* (9 September 1850).
138 Cronin, 'The female industrial movement', p. 74.
139 Massy, *Footprints of a Faithful Shepherd*, p. 412.
140 See full account in Cronin, 'The female industrial movement', p. 74.
141 *Ibid.*, p. 75.
142 Minutes, 1847, RCBL, CPOS papers, PRIV MS 519.1.
143 Minutes, 23 Mar. 1849, NAI, POS papers, 1045/2/1/4, p. 268.
144 *Ibid.*, 9 Nov. 1849, p. 308.
145 DPOS annual report, 1849, NAI, POS papers, 1045/1/1/18–23, p. 13.
146 Kilkenny POS annual report, 1849, p. 7, RIA.
147 *Ibid.*
148 *Ibid.*
149 *Ibid.*
150 Kilkenny Archaeological Society, *Transactions of the Kilkenny Archaeological Society*, 1:3 (1852), p. 286.
151 D. G. Paz, *Popular Anti-Catholicism in Mid-Victorian England* (Stanford, CA: Stanford University Press, 1992), p. 85.
152 I. Whelan, 'Political controversy in Ireland, 1800–50', in K. A. Francis, W. Gibson, R. Ellison, J. Morgan-Guy and B. Tennant (eds), *The Oxford Handbook of the British Sermon 1689–1901* (Oxford: Oxford University Press, 2012), pp. 169–83, p. 180.
153 Moffitt, *Irish Church Missions*, p. 15.
154 *Belfast News-letter* (18 May 1846).
155 G. B. Pagani (ed.), *Life of the Rev. Aloysius Gentili L.L.D. Father of Charity, and Missionary Apostolic in England* (London, Dublin: Richardson and Son, 1851), p. 262.
156 *Ibid.*, p. 263.
157 *Ibid.*
158 See account of the build up to the foundation of the society in Moffitt, *Irish Church Missions*, pp. 46–51.
159 *Ibid.*, p. 134.
160 *Ibid.*, pp. 134–54.
161 *Ibid.*, p. 36.
162 Prunty, *Margaret Aylward*, p. 42.
163 T. Robinson, *Connemara: The Last Pool of Darkness* (Dublin: Penguin Ireland, 2008), p. 233.
164 Bowen, *Protestant Crusade*, p. 260.
165 *Ibid.*, p. 263.
166 E. J. Larkin, *The Historical Dimensions of Irish Catholicism* (New York: Arno Press, 1984), p. 58.
167 Whelan, 'Political controversy in Ireland', p. 180.

3

The 'family system', 1830–50

Leave thy fatherless children, I will preserve them alive;
and let thy widows trust in me.[1]
Jeremiah xlix. ii.

The large number of children frequently taken by friends shows how extensive is the benefit often conferred by affording even a temporary shelter to
the orphans; by this means, the widow, or the elder member of the family,
is often given the opportunity to make successful efforts for obtaining a
livelihood and may be enabled to take back with gratitude a charge. If left
with them at first, it must have paralysed these efforts and kept the whole
family in abject pauperism.[2]

Introduction

The Dublin POS (DPOS) was the 'parent body' and thus directly
responsible for the design and implementation of the boarding-out
and apprenticeship schemes which became a blueprint for later PO
Societies. Boarding out was by no means a widely accepted child
welfare model in the first half of the nineteenth century; for the most
part, orphans were placed in institutions such as orphanages, Houses
of Industry, Charter Schools, goals and workhouses. Few, if any, contemporary charities aimed to assist the family as a whole. Moreover,
orphanages tended to be gender specific which meant siblings were
separated. A flexible approach to the provision of short and long-term
care was also not characteristic of early nineteenth-century charities.
This chapter examines the development of the DPOS ethos, governing rules and policies with respect to eligibility, benefits for widows,
boarding out, children's health, and apprenticeship to determine the
extent to which the system could be deemed child and family oriented.
References are also made to the policies of early local PO Societies such
as Limerick and Tipperary.

Access to PO Societies

The DPOS served respectable Protestant families and imposed rigid application procedures to deter 'undeserving' applicants. The admission criteria were clear: legitimacy of birth; one or both parents deceased; father alive but incapacitated, due to mental or physical ill health, and unable to support his family. Children of widows who remarried were inadmissible and if widows remarried while their children were already in the Society's care, they were considered no longer in need of assistance;[3] only children of Protestant parentage, which included Methodist and Presbyterians and other 'dissenting churches' were admitted to the DPOS up until 1898 when the DPOS and CPOU amalgamated and children of intermarriages were admissible (county PO Societies accepted children from mixed marriage families).

Originally, only children under eight were accepted; the limit was raised to nine in the 1830s (the limit was raised again in later years). Children of subscribers bereft of both parents were prioritised. During the period under review here, 95 per cent of the applications received by the DPOS were from widows. Before admitting any child every effort was made to identify any 'suitable' Protestant relatives in comfortable circumstances prepared to care for the children. The 'lower orders', tradesmen on the committee, were enlisted to verify applicants' circumstances, for 'they are by their circumstances in life most likely to be made acquainted with cases of distress, and best fitted to detect and guard against imposition'.[4] In Limerick applications were investigated for two months to prove the validity of the claims.[5] Marriage, baptismal and burial certificates were required, without which applications were postponed or refused.[6]

The DPOS committee did not officially admit children until the quarterly meetings. However, it was resolved in 1831 that to effectively deal with urgent cases between quarterly meetings, 'a small sum may be drawn from the treasurer until such time as the helpless and perishing child shall be brought before quarterly meetings',[7] which was a form of out-relief. Children were 'elected' to the Society roll; that is a list of names was presented to the committee and they were required to 'elect' the candidates deemed most 'deserving'.

Applicants

Applicants to PO Societies were from a range of backgrounds. For example, the Tipperary POS (TPOS) reported that 20 per cent of the children admitted in 1836 were police orphans and 10 per cent soldiers' children. In 1836 the TPOS sent a circular with a copy of its rules to the commanding officer of each regiment in Clonmel and Caher.[8] In reply Captain Griffiths of the Royal Artillery, 'enclosed £1 from the officers and £1 from the non commissioners, Gunners and Drivers of that corps as donations'.[9] In 1839 just under 30 per cent of admissions to the TPOS were police orphans; by 1840, two years after the Tithe War had ended, the number had fallen to 18 per cent. (The Peace Preservation Police was formed in 1814, a 'national police' in 1822, and the Irish Constabulary and the Dublin Metropolitan Police in 1836.[10] Catholics entered the constabulary from 1836 onwards.[11])

Labourers' children represented on average 30 per cent of the total annual applications to the TPOS during this period.[12] Tradesmen's children – tailors, saddlers, butchers, weavers, and shoemakers – were also admitted, albeit in fewer numbers. Jewellers, accountants, shopkeepers, farmers and teachers were also nominally represented. Labourer and police orphans were the most well-represented among those admitted to the Kilkenny POS. The Kilkenny POS reported in 1849 that 78 per cent of its applicants were widows and 10 per cent widowers; in 12

Table 3.1 Kilkenny POS applicants, 1837–48

Occupation	No.
Bailiff	1
Blacksmith	1
Carrier	1
Cutler	1
Farmer	1
Gatekeeper	2
Labourer	12
Nailor	1
Organist	1
Parish clerk	1
Police constable	6
Servant	4
Shoemaker	1
Soldier	4
Tailor	1
Tallow chandler	1
Unable to labour	1
Weaver	1
Writing clerk	1
Total	**42**

Source: Kilkenny POS annual report, 1849.

per cent of cases, both parents had died.[13] In Limerick the orphans of doctors, soldiers, the police, clergymen and tradesmen, among others, were received.[14]

DPOS registers contain occupational data relating to deceased fathers which is illustrated in figure 3.1. The following occupations are listed in order of decreasing frequency: servants, shoemakers, clerks, labourers, police, carpenters, farmers, tailors and weavers. The Association for the Relief of Distressed Protestants (ARDP) reported in 1841 that over a three year period 1,260 Protestant servants, 'the most valuable members of the social system', sought assistance.[15]

After the foundation of auxiliaries in the north of the country, Protestant children from Belfast, Fermanagh and Armagh were admitted to the DPOS and boarded out in Wicklow. In all but a few cases, the fathers had been tradesmen.[16] Children of a police sergeant, a surgeon and a foreman were also admitted. The Society for the Relief of Sick and Indigent Roomkeepers also contains references to the destitution experienced by tradesmen. Prior to his work with the DPOS, which is examined in more detail later in the chapter, Revd Thomas R. Shore, curate of St Michan's parish, was honorary secretary of the Roomkeeper's Society. In 1834 he reported:

> The third class, who are in occasional distress, these are principally poor tradesmen, who would not get an employment in a shop, and are below the rank of journeyman (they might be about 16,000 or 18,000 in Dublin, reduced to distress by sickness). Of the classes above mentioned, I think that the second and third are most rapidly increasing in number. Vast numbers of persons – women – have been reduced from the third class to the second.[17]

The annual reports of the ARDP also referred to the 'many cases of great distress where the parties had been respectable: widows of clergymen, doctors, attorneys and merchants, and of gentlemen who had been officers'.[18] There is evidence that the better off succumbed to fever in relatively large numbers.[19] Reports from the Parochial Visitors' Society, which was founded in 1840, also refer to the Protestant poor. William Clementson, divinity student, visitor of St Anne's parish, reported on 3 January 1844 that he had 'called upon 110 families and have paid upwards of 500 visits, confining myself almost exclusively to poor Protestant room keepers'.[20] Henry Hutchings, visitor of St Mary's, stated that 'nothing can be more encouraging than the reception which the poor Protestants have given their parochial visitor, they are very happy at being sought after, and if in distress, pour out all their woes in one long message to their minister'.[21]

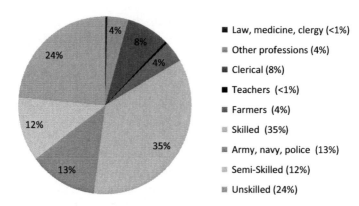

Figure 3.1 DPOS applicants' occupational profile, 1829–50.
Source: register of applications, 1829–50, NAI, POS papers, 1045/5/2/1–2.

Evidence drawn from DPOS registers and case files suggests that men who had once worked as skilled tradesmen resorted to labouring because of declines in their trades and unemployment.[22] In certain cases, applicants recorded their husbands' occupations as 'labourer' and their husbands' former trade, for example, as 'weaver'.[23]

Widowhood

Joseph Williams, co-founder of the DPOS, could not have known in 1828 that only six short years later his own family would come to depend on the charity for assistance. Before his untimely death, Joseph had been appointed assistant secretary to the DPOS. The Williams family lived in Mullinahack, St Catherine's parish, Dublin. In her application to the DPOS Mrs Williams recorded her occupation as a hat trimmer and sought the admission of her three sons Charles (two), John (four) and Joseph junior (nine). All three boys were elected to the Society roll in April 1834 and sent to a nurse in Carnew, County Wicklow. Mrs Williams was heavily pregnant with her fifth child at the time and her daughter was born less than one month after her sons' admissions to the Society.[24]

A number of women experienced a gradual deterioration in their circumstances due to their husbands' ill health, unemployment and underemployment. A young man, a smith, 'had not long been doing business for himself when paralysis of the right side and limbs consequently obliged him to give up his forge ... from that time gradually he grew worse'.[25] His wife was 'with child' during his illness. She died during childbirth three days after her husband's death. Until her admission to the DPOS, their little girl was cared for by her grandmother who was described as 'very old and poor'.[26]

Mental illness and 'immorality' also led once comfortable families to live in reduced circumstances. Two girls were admitted to the DPOS after their father died. He had 'very excellent means' until shortly before his death, 'when mental disability came out' and 'would have left a very handsome property in benefices to his children'.[27] His fortune was reduced considerably and his daughters were left without any means of support. In another case an aunt admitted her nephew to the DPOS because his mother was dead and his father was 'unsound in body and mind'.[28]

A widow was left destitute with a four and a half year old child when her husband, who had been a 'gentleman and held a commission in the Royal Service' was 'reduced to the greatest distress through drunkenness'.[29] His wife was 'lying in the Adelaide Hospital at the time of the election in a very bad state and not expected to recover'.[30] In a number of cases, widows died shortly after their children's admission.

The Dublin POS: services for widows

The DPOS provided children with long or short-term care as required by widows who could reclaim their children when they so wished, as long as the committee was satisfied that it was in the children's best interests. Widows themselves, the clergymen dealing with their applications and the subscribers who supported the applications, repeatedly requested the admission of the youngest dependents so that widows could seek employment. A widow returned to Ireland from New York in 1838. The local clergyman reported that she had three children, her last born only months before her husband's death. The widow attempted to 'carry on in small jobs to pay for the children's support but expended the greater part of her wages on paying a nurse to care for her youngest child while she attended work'.[31] She requested that the DPOS care for her infant child, 'for as it takes all her wages to pay for the nursing of two she has no means to pay for the third or to clothe herself or them, consequently the children are almost naked'.[32] The placement of children with private unregulated nurses was precarious, as brought to light in later baby farming scandals, particularly given that these women were not subject to any form of vetting or inspections, or accountable to any higher authority. As discussed later in the chapter, PO Societies provided widows with the assurance that their children's placement would be regulated, and though not always effective it accounted for widespread support of its system.

In April 1841 a widow stated, 'I have no trade or way of earning support for my three children, were they settled I would look out for a situation as it is now my whole dependence'.[33] The clergyman who recommended the case stated, 'she is obliged to watch a child of two and a half, too young to be left in the care of its sister'.[34] He suggested that if the DPOS elected the younger child, the widow could work and her daughter could attend school, which had dual benefits for the family. It was common for widows to depend on elder siblings, extended kin, friends and neighbours for child care; however, while an invaluable source of temporary support, it was not a long-term solution.

In 1849 Josiah Smyly, an eminent doctor with links to the DPOS as discussed later in the chapter, was requested by the committee to enquire into the circumstances of a widow whose husband had died after a 'lingering disease', leaving her three children 'in great destitution'. Smyly reported that 'when in health her husband was able to keep her in comfortable circumstances, she is now so reduced as to be happy to get into humble service'.[35] He also informed the committee that the widow had placed her children with a nurse in the country (unregulated) while she worked which had cost more than her wages. Finally, he stated that without the assistance of the DPOS, the widow would be forced to give up her employment. Smyly recommended the children's admission as they would otherwise become dependent on what he described as, 'the repulsive aid of the poor house'.[36] Analysis of applicant case histories suggests that despite their straitened circumstances, many widows struggled on independently for long periods before they sought assistance from PO Societies in order to keep their children 'out of the workhouse',[37] which is considered in more detail in chapter 5.

Boarding out

The DPOS developed a boarding-out system, the rules of which county PO Societies adapted to meet local needs. Given that the old method of boarding out[38] involved little or no supervision or focus on the orphans' educational progress, the DPOS was innovative in a number of respects not least its implementation of effective safeguards to ensure the children's continued well-being. The first safeguard was the careful selection of respectable nurses. Parish clergymen were required to recommend nurses and verify their claims. Moreover, as an additional precaution the DPOS resolved in 1830 that, 'inspectors will be occasionally sent down by the Society to see if the nurses are in comfortable circumstances according to the statements contained in certificates'.[39] Generally, children were placed with respectable Protestant farming families, 'That in the house of a decent farmer recommended and constantly visited by the local clergyman, a child is not in a more favourable position for health, morals and religion'.[40] Once approved, nurses were presented with certificates which confirmed their religion; acreage of farm; and the number of cows in their possession. The ages of the applicants' youngest children were also documented as, generally, women with infants were not selected as wet nurses. The nursing certificates also detailed the nurses' personal appearance – her hair, eyes, demeanour and height. These certificates were a means of identification to prevent abuses of the system and were also used in foundlings hospitals. The nurses were paid annually to cover the children's food, lodging, washing and education and were made accountable to the authority of the clergymen in their own parish and to the DPOS committee.

In order to help children settle in to their new homes, they were generally boarded out with their siblings, a child-oriented measure which recognised and met the specific needs of young children. Children were sent to houses of strangers and had to adjust to their new surroundings which was likely to have been an overwhelming change. The presence of siblings when first placed at nurse gave children, particularly younger children, a sense of security and comfort during the difficult transition. Elder children were encouraged to care for their younger siblings and often took the place of a parent after parental death, with girls becoming 'little mothers', a responsibility that few took lightly and in many cases extended throughout their lives. In large families elder siblings 'acted as an intermediate generation between parents and younger children'.[41] The DPOS endeavoured to place siblings together. On 4 December 1835, the committee resolved, 'that a letter be written to Reverend J. Webber stating that the two children allocated to Nurse –, one brother and sister, … it is most desirable not to separate'.[42] In the case of the Limerick POS, the children referred to the nurses as their 'aunts' which helped the children to settle and indicated the often temporary nature of their stay.[43]

Inspections

Regular inspection was the second and most important safeguard. Children were placed with families who lived in close vicinity of the glebe or parsonage house. Local clergymen, who were also referred to as 'Local Superintendents', worked for the DPOS on a voluntary basis, and were expected to monitor the children's attendance at day and Sunday school and to report any problems to the Dublin committee. (Prior to the establishment of PO Societies, clergymen, their wives and daughters had always contributed to the care of the 'children of the church' – 'orphans who became reliant on its bounty)'.[44] Most local superintendents took their role as the children's guardians very seriously. They corresponded regularly wtih the committee regarding the children's placements and, if necessary, admonished nurses on its behalf.

In addition, while the committee was thankful for the 'watchful eye of the parochial clergymen', in order to ensure the children's continued well-being, it was resolved in 1835 that 'all of the orphans be in future inspected twice in each year once in winter and once in summer'.[45] The appointed committee members carried out unannounced inspections and reported on the children's educational progress and physical and moral health, and the nurses' homes. Moreover, nurses were obligated to attend annual meetings and church with the children which broadened the Society's supervisory scope in the best interests of the orphans.

The Tipperary POS (TPOS) also made unannounced visits to its nurses and it is likely that all subsequent PO Societies followed suit. Children were inspected 'two or three times within the year' and 'the uncertainty of the period at which the inspector may present himself, and the conviction that no symptoms of neglect will be lightly passed over, have proved wholesome stimulants to the due discharge of the duties which the Society has imposed, and which the Nurses have voluntarily undertaken'.[46] TPOS committee members carried out the duties which were described as 'by no means pleasant and attended with much trouble and inconvenience'.[47] The TPOS appointed two inspectors from the parish to undertake the supervision of children while boarded out and while apprenticed.[48] (St Brigid's Orphanage, a Catholic boarding-out institution, founded in the 1850s, also carried out unannounced inspections.[49])

Minutes of DPOS committee meetings and annual reports reveal that it was the resident laity as well as clergymen and 'official inspectors' – committee members – who watched over the children; the whole parish, from clergymen and their wives, to neighbours and other parishioners, became overseers who were encouraged to report changes in the children's appearance or absences from church or school. The DPOS reported in 1843 that 'the parental care taken of them [the orphans] by the Reverend and his lady who live close to them'[50] had greatly improved the children's 'wretched health'.[51] However, the DPOS did not formally introduce 'ladies' committees' at this time. (The founders of the DPOS clearly outlined their intention to appoint laywomen to undertake these duties in 1829.) The Limerick POS (LPOS) appears to have been the first PO Society to arrange local 'ladies' committees' from 1837, if not earlier.[52] The children's good health was attributed to the care taken

Figure 3.2 Group of DPOS orphans in uniform, date unknown.

by the 'Visiting Ladies' who were mainly the wives of the LPOS committee members.[53]

To distinguish the orphans from other children and therefore make them more visible to parish overseers, children were dressed in distinctive clothing. Members of auxiliaries, members of the church, and neighbours were therefore able to detect marked changes in the children's appearance more easily. It was also important that the children were respectably dressed in order to present a positive public image of the charity. The Charitable Repository in Bandon dressed its female pupils in uniforms 'to make them more amenable to discipline'.[54] The TPOS girls were described as 'the little girls in blue'.[55] In Dublin the girls were dressed in gingham uniforms.

Uniforms were also a way of telling apart DPOS orphans from foundlings:

A letter be written to the managers of St Peter's Repository expressing the mortification we feel at finding that the same peculiar pattern of frock worn by the female orphans has been furnished to some of the foundling girls belonging to St Peter's parish who are at nurse in the County of Wicklow whereby the distinctive character of the dress is rendered useless, and we incur the liability of having these children mistaken for Protestant orphans which may, in many ways, lead to a very great inconvenience.[56]

Children were not placed in any home in which nurses also cared for foundlings – abandoned children, generally, though not always of illegitimate birth. The DPOS was a respectable charity which aimed to maintain the respectability of widows and orphans. If its subscribers had discovered that DPOS orphans were associated with 'immorality', it would have tarnished the Society's good reputation.

Unsuitable homes

For many nurses, caring for the orphans was an act of benevolence, a favour or good turn which they hoped would be reciprocated. There is evidence that former DPOS nurses applied to the Society for assistance in widowhood.[57] At the first DPOS annual meeting parents were implored to consider their own children's futures: 'fathers and mothers then, you may leave your children orphans, I address you in behalf of those orphans yonder; the mercy you bestow upon them, may cause mercy to be bestowed upon your children'.[58] The DPOS supplemented nurses' wages with bonuses during hard times, gratuities for the care of sick children, who required extra attention and nourishment, and annual supplies of clothing. Influential doctors', gentlemen's and clergymen's names featured in the DPOS reports as committee members, patrons and vice-patrons; it was a highly reputable charity, one which elevated the nurses' status. The same families carried out the work over generations.

However, despite the best efforts of many of the DPOS local superintendents to select good homes and the generally high standard of nursing, some of the placements, particularly in the early years, were entirely unsuitable. The committee sent two inspectors to investigate the case of a young orphan boy who had left his nurse's home and was reportedly missing. The nurse had not informed the committee and had received four months' allowance despite the child's disappearance. In response the committee resolved on 4 December 1835, 'That we conceive the clergymen into whose charge the orphan was entrusted to have been neglectful of the interest of the Protestant Orphan Society in not reporting the absence of the child from the nurse that to be forthwith written to on this subject to ascertain how long the child has been absent from the parish'.[59] These cases shaped future DPOS policies and improved the lot of other children. It is interesting to reflect on the founders' original rules dated 1828, 'every proper investigation shall then take place and such remedy be adopted for the prevention of any further neglect of duty'.[60] For every case of neglect there was a corresponding reform measure.

In 1836 the DPOS committee introduced stricter nurse selection guidelines: 'Five members with secretaries shall be appointed to a standing sub-committee to whom shall be confided the selection of nurses'.[61] Dublin, and later county PO Societies such as Tipperary, supplied nurses with a set of rules for the care of the orphans. 'N.B. It is requested that a copy of these rules be kept in the Dwellings of the nurses in some conspicuous place, so as to be seen by all who may visit them'.[62] Nurses became conduits for moral reform and 'good nurses' became models for expected standards of parental care.

Revd Thomas Shore was thirty-four when he began his work with the DPOS and became a key figure in the DPOS committee:

> In every Society the member most willing to work has found that a very large proportion of the work will be left for him to do; and, accordingly, I soon experienced the truth of this – as the books of the Society will show, as, from about the year 1836, the entire management of the department of "Nurses and Orphans" devolved on myself alone. Gaining additional experience every year, and ardently and anxiously devoted to the orphans, and the Society which sheltered them, I willingly gave myself to the work.[63]

During his tenure as 'General Superintendent of Orphans', Shore detected a number of cases of neglect; for example, in 1836, he discovered that a nurse had sent a twelve-year-old boy in her care to work as a servant for her son. Shore reported that he had ascertained by personal investigation that the orphan 'had been in Dublin at intervals since the last annual meeting for several weeks together acting as servant to his nurse's son, who keeps a dairy in Wood Street'.[64] The nurse was dismissed and the orphan transferred to another location. In 1841 the committee reiterated its commitment to the children's welfare: 'the utmost care is taken (founded on the personal inspection of a member of the committee), to have the several localities where orphans are placed, suited to the age and sex of the children'.[65] Revd Shore appears to have been the driving force behind such progress.

While most nurses adhered to the rules set by the DPOS, others proved less cooperative:

> The subcommittee having carefully considered the peculiar circumstances in which they are placed respecting the management of orphans located in the parishes of Tullow and Ardoyne, circumstances which are so peculiar that they cannot carry out their operations respecting orphans in either of those parishes in the same manner and on the same terms as they do

in all other parishes in which orphans are located without running the risk of giving offence when they have not the least intention of doing so. Circumstances so peculiar as to have prevented the managing committee from carrying into execution the order after which they felt it their duty to issue, respecting some nurses in those parishes in August last ... This subcommittee will not henceforward undertake or be responsible for the inspection, superintendence or care of any orphans located in the parishes of Ardoyne or Tullow, neither will we locate any orphans in either of those parishes or transfer or remove to the apprentice class or otherwise any orphan there from without having previously received the directions in each case from the managing committee.[66]

The minutes of earlier meetings suggest that there had been difficulties with two specific nurses who had been warned on two separate occasions that if the children's standard of hygiene did not improve, the children would be removed. The labour intensiveness of cleaning for women who also had their own children to care for and their own duties on the farm meant that the committee's expectations were often unachievable. The children were eventually transferred to other nurses.[67]

Shore, whose work with the Society was unpaid until the late 1840s, remained a central figure in the DPOS until the early 1850s. The committee trusted him emphatically and praised his tireless efforts on behalf of the orphans:

One of its members, who had devoted himself to the regulations of the internal affairs of the Society; and who for several years, had relieved the Committee from all anxiety as to the care of the Orphans while at nurse, by voluntarily and gratuitously undertaking the entire charge of the regulation, inspection, and superintendence of the nurses.[68]

In August 1851, the committee again referred to Shore's 'zeal and efficiency'.[69] Entries in the subcommittee minute book detail the hours he spent 'in the office', preparing for 'the dispatch of new orphans', 'the transferral of orphans' and 'foregoing inspections', which took weeks to complete.[70]

Medical care

Medical care in Ireland comprised voluntary hospitals, county infirmaries and dispensaries, originally supported entirely by charity and subsequently organised under the Dispensary Act, 1805. After 1840 the number of dispensaries gradually increased in number. By 1846, there were 204 dispensaries in Leinster, each one serving an average population of 9,675.[71] Legislation introduced during the famine to improve public health included the Nuisances Removal Act, 1848, and the Disease Prevention Act, 1849. In County Wicklow, where DPOS orphans were boarded out, there were sixteen dispensaries, each of which served an average population of 7,887, six fever hospitals and two infirmaries, which suggests that the children had relatively sufficient access to medical care.[72] Conversely, in Leitrim there were eight dispensaries to serve an average population of 19,412, one fever hospital and only one infirmary.[73]

DPOS medical officers

Dr Samuel Litton became one of the first doctors on the DPOS committee. He was a governor and consulting physician of the Hospital for Incurables, Donnybrook Road.[74] (Robert J. Graves was among the other renowned names associated with the hospital.) Dr James Pope was a member of the first DPOS committee and also a member of the Hibernian Temperance Society of which Philip Cecil Crampton Esq. was president.[75]

Another committee member, Dr Maurice Collis, was an attending surgeon at the Meath Hospital and lived at 113 Merrion Square, Dublin.[76] His nephew and namesake was appointed as surgeon to the Meath Hospital in 1851 following his uncle's resignation, later appointed Examiner in Surgery in the Queen's University, and an Examiner in the Royal College of Surgeons. His work on cancer has been described as a 'medical classic'.[77] Howard Cooke, MD and surgeon with an address at 73 Blessington Street, Dublin, was also listed as a medical adviser for the DPOS.

Dr John Ringland had spent time on the DPOS committee before his departure in 1846. The committee 'wished for his success and assured him of the sense they entertain of the ability and attention with which he has devoted his talents and his time to care of those among our orphans who required medical treatment as well as the kindness and sympathy he has always evinced towards those suffering little ones'.[78] Ringland had studied at Sir Patrick Dun's, and the Meath and the Rotunda hospitals; he delivered George Bernard Shaw in 1856.[79] He was also listed as a committee member of the ARDP in 1847.

Dr Josiah Smyly was appointed surgeon to the Meath Hospital in 1832. He was an esteemed and highly respected surgeon.[80] He was described in later years as 'the unobtrusive Christian man, the genial philanthropist, ever ready to assist the poor with his professional advice and his purse'.[81] Smyly was Vice-President of the RCSI.

Dr Alfred Henry McClintock was elected a member of the DPOS committee in October 1847 in place of the late Doctor Litton.[82] As part of his duties, he inspected applicants' claims on the north side of the city. Another esteemed doctor, McClintock introduced hugely beneficial sanitary reforms to the Rotunda Lying in Hospital, of which he was master in the 1850s, among many other achievements. Described as a 'quiet, deeply religious man', he was also a member of the Benevolent Fund Society of Dublin.[83]

Children's health

The DPOS recommended that infants remain with their mothers, where possible, until they had finished teething as convulsions during dentition was a common cause of infant mortality.[84] For example, in 1843 the DPOS committee ordered that 'orphan – be not taken from his mother until after the next election as his health is at present delicate owing to his getting his teeth'.[85] Revd Shore drew attention to the dangers associated with the early removal of infants from their mothers again in 1850 when he reported that while young dependents were the 'greatest impediment to the mothers' exertions', if removed too early they would 'suffer exceedingly by the change' and 'some have died during the progress of dentition'.[86] Despite already following a general policy of leaving infants with their mothers until after dentition, it resolved formally that all newly elected orphans under eighteen months (though in numerous cases children remained with their mothers for far longer) were to remain with their mother or relatives with a paid allowance from the Society until they were physically strong enough to be transferred to their nurses.[87]

The DPOS sent children to healthy country districts because fresh air, a change of air, was medically recommended for the maintenance of good health and for recuperating after bouts of illness.[88] Sea bathing and sea air were also recommended. (Sea bathing became a popular leisure pursuit in the eighteenth century.[89] Sir John Floyer, Dr Richard Russell and Dr William Buchan were all well-known advocates and in Scotland, the benefits for delicate children were stressed.[90]) Children were placed in homes which were 'convenient to a dispensary and sea-bathing'.[91] The availability of pure milk was another extremely significant reason for children's placement in the country. Children were only sent to homes where there was a plentiful supply of 'good milk'. In urban areas milk was often watered down thereby reducing its nutritional value. The city dairy yards were unsanitary and contaminated water was used to adulterate the milk.[92]

The DPOS application form required information as to whether or not the orphan in question had received the small pox vaccination. In some cases DPOS medical officers recorded that they had inoculated the children when they were admitted.[93] The Cow Pock Institution was founded in 1804 to collect and administer small pox vaccinations mainly in the city. The Vaccination Extension Act, 1853[94] gave powers to boards of guardians to vaccinate.[95]

There is evidence that the aforementioned medical men were instrumental in greatly improving DPOS orphans' health. The minutes of committee meetings state that Mr Jepps, the DPOS secretary, 'had waited upon Doctors Smyly and Collis relative to the proposed consultations respecting the health of the orphans – both gentlemen most readily agreed to these wishes and arranged to meet at Mr Smyly's house at two o'clock. Accordingly, notices have been sent to the other medical gentlemen and the sub-committee requesting their attendance'.[96] Following the discovery of health problems among the children, the subcommittee of medical officers compiled a report and forwarded 'special instructions' to the nurses 'embodying the recommendations contained in the report'.[97] In February 1846, against the background of the famine, the committee again convened to discuss the children's health.

> A letter be written to the several superintendents of our orphans requesting that they would have the kindness to give directions to the respective nurses to apply in every case of sickness for a ticket of recommendation to the Dispensary so that our children may have, without delay, the benefit of the local medical assistance, as we conceive that orphans wholly dependent on the bounty of others, and actually resident in the district, are fairly to be classed among the numbers of those whose relief and assistance dispensaries are established.[98]

Local doctors were also directly involved in the maintenance of the children's health. They regularly wrote to the Dublin committee with recommendations for the treatment of sick orphans whom they had recently attended.[99] Local superintendents (clergymen and their wives), school teachers and nurses also informed the committee when children were ill.[100] Carefully chosen nurses gave children with persistent illnesses specialist care. 'Invalid children to be located with Mrs – and Mrs – residing at Balbriggan as occasion offers at the rate of ten pounds per annum'.[101] These women played an integral role in the low mortality rates among DPOS orphans. In 1846 a gratuity was given to a nurse in Dunganstown 'in consideration of the great trouble she was subjected to by ill health of newly elected orphans, one of whom was inoculated with small pox secretly by her mother just previous to their being sent to nurse'.[102] Ringworm was detected among some of the children and 'Beatson's Lotion' was the recommended cure.[103] Three boys were sent to a nurse in Delgany, County Wicklow, 'who were placed in her care for the cure of ringworm'.[104] The doctor certified their recovery but the committee advised that the boys remain there for an additional month. In October 1846, a teacher at the Cronroe School, Glanely, County Wicklow, reported a young girl 'has a sore head – a woman is curing it for 5/c'.[105] In a separate case, in 1847 a doctor prescribed sea bathing for a girl with 'sore eyes'.[106]

In the same year there were a minor number of cases in which nurses gave children up because of the 'dearness of provisions' and in one case because of a death in the nurse's family.[107] The committee provided each nurse with an additional grant because of the 'increased price of provisions this season, in consequence of the failure of the potato crop'.[108] Masters, too, reported their inability to keep their apprentices: 'in consequence of the loss of the potato crop, he fears he will not be able to support his apprentice, begs advice'.[109] Throughout Black '47 reports of sick children continued to rise. In some cases children were in extremely poor health and admitted to hospital.[110] Four children could not attend the 1847 annual meeting because their nurses were ill with fever.[111] It was thought advisable that they did not attend to prevent its spread. Five other children had whooping cough and for the same reason were directed not to attend. Those who did attend were inspected and noted as being free from coetaneous disease.[112] Despite a number of disease outbreaks, the DPOS recorded consistently low mortality rates which are illustrated in figure 3.3

Burial societies were commonplace during the first half of the nineteenth century because the 'lower orders' were unable to pay funeral

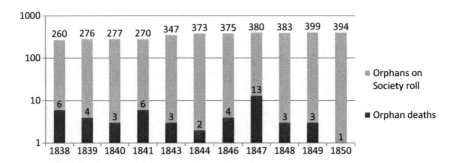

Figure 3.3 DPOS child mortality rates, 1838–50.
Source: DPOS annual reports, 1838–50, NAI, POS papers, 1045/1/1/1–23.

expenses. Charitable lay people set up burial societies to raise funds to assist bereaved families. The Protestant Benevolent Burial Society was founded in 1834, 'some benevolent persons having witnessed the hardships endured by many of their Protestant brethren for want of suitable means of internment for their friends'.[113] It was customary for nurses, DPOS committee members and the other boarded-out children to attend the funerals of any orphans who died while under the Society's care. Forty-two children and fourteen nurses and their families attended the funeral of – who died in June 1847. He was considered a 'very delicate child when first received from Belfast in April last'.[114] The boy was interred in Kiltegan churchyard.

Local superintendents were frequently praised for their dedication to the orphans' care[115] and objected to practices that appeared to compromise the children's health. Revd William Smyth Guinness, rector of Rathdrum, and as discussed in chapter 2 a member of the Irish Homœopathic Society, among other superintendents in County Wicklow, disapproved of sending orphans to Dublin to attend the Society's annual meetings. Smyth Guinness informed the DPOS committee in 1850 that 'the younger children have suffered severely in many instances from being obliged to take so long a journey and recommended that some change should be made'.[116] Women, most probably the nurses or clergymen's wives, were also likely to have raised the issue. Despite the justified concerns of the superintendents, the committee chose to retain the practice, 'of the past eighteen years'.[117] The committee reminded the superintendants that the children's presence induced people to donate to the Society and recommended that in future all children attend, 'except in cases of delicacy of health'.[118] Moreover, the annual meetings provided an additional opportunity for committee members, lay subscribers and the children's mothers, who were known to attend, to inspect the children. Attendance at the meetings also encouraged nurses to maintain the children's clothing and general health.

Families reunited

If widows' circumstances improved through remarriage, emigration, or other means, they generally applied to the DPOS for 'repossession' of their children. (In the broader context, it was common for pauper families to leave their children in workhouses before they went abroad to seek employment. These children were essentially 'temporary orphans' who were later reclaimed by their parents.[119]) The DPOS thoroughly investigated applications from widows, siblings and other members of the family who wished to reclaim their children. 'The committee always make the strictest inquiries for their relatives and never give them but where they are convinced it is for the benefit of the orphan'.[120] Inspectors visited the applicants' residences and judged the suitability of the surroundings. Another important consideration was whether the children were being reclaimed purely as a source of labour.

For the most part, the DPOS appear to have cooperated as much as possible with widows. In 1841, the committee reported that 'the child was taken away by the mother who has become rich having married well in London'.[121] The boy had been boarded out for six and a half years. In September 1845 a widow requested the return of her daughter, after which the committee made enquiries and 'having ascertained that it would be for the advantage of the child'[122] approved the application. In the same week the committee received another letter from a mother wishing to 'thank the Society for the kindness shown to her child, stating that she wishes to withdraw her'.[123] Children sometimes had to make extensive journeys abroad to reunite with their mothers. In 1846 a widow, who had remarried in Quebec, approached the Society for her son who had been under its care for a number of years. The committee agreed to send the boy, 'provided we are satisfied with the character of Mr – the boy's stepfather'.[124] It was routine practice in these cases for the committee to seek verification of claims and to confirm the widows' circumstances and step-parents' character from contacts (clergymen) in the destination country. The Society typically approved these cases and contributed to the children's travelling expenses.[125] There is also evidence, particularly during the famine, that in rare cases widows were in position to take back children after their other children had died, leaving them in 'improved circumstances'.[126]

'Make the children independent'[127]

The Kildare Place Society (KPS), which used the Lancasterian system, supported the theories of Pestalozzi, who emphasised the necessity for kindness and encouragement of pupils and recommended manual activities in the classroom.[128] The Society was the first in Ireland to do so.[129] In the eighteenth century Pestalozzi had warned against the neglect of destitute children.[130] After 1831, the KPS was no longer state funded and struggled under the weight of financial strain. The Church Education Society (CES), founded in 1839, took over the KPS college in 1855.[131] Alexander Leeper, rector of St Audeon's parish, principal of the CES College for twenty years, was also secretary to St Mary's POS auxiliary, a member of the main DPOS committee, and an influential figure in its management. The DPOS and other PO Societies ensured that children attended schools 'conducted on such principles as we would approve, which are those of the Church Education Society'.[132] Revds Thomas Kingston and John Nash Griffin were members of both the DPOS and the CES committees.

In the early nineteenth century, many child workers, particularly chimney sweeps in Dublin and Cork, were cruelly treated by their masters and placed in grave danger on a daily basis. In Dublin initially a Protestant Sunday School Society and later a Roman Catholic school offered them assistance after such 'systematic cruelty', which included child murder, was publicly condemned.[133] While conditions improved after the use of the 'sweeping machine', the ARDP, founded in 1836, reported that a ten-year-old chimney sweep had been forced to scavenge for food and was sold to his master for £1.[134]

Prior to the reduction in parliamentary grants, Charter Schools had once been the principal source of juvenile training. Agriculturally based reformatories were founded in Germany from the 1820s,[135] houses of refuge were established in New York in the 1820s which provided juvenile delinquents with education and apprenticeships, and, in 1839, in France, voluntary run farming colonies were established to help reform young offenders.[136] In the 1830s a Church of Ireland clergyman in Wexford, Revd William Hickey, started a model farm and produced a book on farming methods for the Kildare Place Society.[137] Under the Board of National Education, a model farm was founded to train teachers in 1837 and model agricultural schools were opened from the 1840s.[138] Revd Sillery visited France in the 1840s where a Protestant orphan institution was working under the same principles. 'A large farm of ground belongs to it in which the boys took turns in learning and practising improved agriculture … they learn trades and many acquire the business of florist and agriculturalists in a large garden adjoining'.[139] The Limerick POS started a model farm on land donated by Lord Guillamore in 1848; the children learned valuable agricultural methods, and produced crops on the land which were distributed among the poor in Limerick.[140] In 1848 Poor Law Guardians were permitted to buy land to instruct workhouse children in agricultural work.[141]

DPOS apprenticeships

The DPOS believed that, 'manifestly it was doing nothing or worse than nothing for a child to support him in comparative comfort for a few years and then return him to the destitution from which he had been taken'.[142] Apprenticeships were, therefore, considered imperative to the children's future progress. As discussed in chapter 2, no provisions were made for the apprenticeship of workhouse children when the Poor Law was extended to Ireland.[143] DPOS orphans were generally bound out at the age of twelve or over[144] for three to seven years depending on the trade while Poor Law Guardians in England bound out orphans from the age of seven until the age of twenty-one.[145]

The DPOS introduced a number of measures to ensure that children were not exploited by their masters; for example, in some cases at least two apprentices were bound out to the same employer and, where possible, children served their time in the same parish or county in which they had spent their childhoods:

> Most of the children previously apprenticed having been bound in Dublin, your committee consider that it would be advantageous that they should be apprenticed when practicable in the country where they have been reared, and are known and have formed friendships. Exclusive of the advantage to the apprentices themselves in respect both of health and morals, your committee cannot forbear remarking, as a secondary benefit of this arrangement that thereby a permanent addition will be made to the Protestant population of the country parishes.[146]

In an annual report dated 1839, the committee resolved that the character and the circumstances of employers necessitated their utmost vigilance. The children also required 'peculiar watching' as clergymen claimed that 'whilst the orphans are young, their management is comparatively easy, but when they grow up and begin to act and think for themselves they occasion increased trouble'.[147] In numerous cases children ran back to their nurses, which suggests they had formed strong bonds with them during their formative years.[148] In fact the incidence was so high that the DPOS committee sent a circular to nurses warning them not to permit the orphans to return to their homes, for it would both unsettle them and hinder their progress.

The same year the Society invested in a home located near St Stephen's Church in Dublin. The Society House, or Percy Place as it was better known, was used for the reception of nurses and orphans prior to annual meetings; as a collection point for the orphans' clothing and shoes; but, primarily, it served as a training home or 'boarding school' for apprentices where potential employers could make arrangements to meet the children.[149] The children were sent to Percy Place from their nurses for further training and remained there for periods ranging from a few weeks to a year depending on the availability of apprenticeships. Fewer than thirty apprentices resided there during the 1840s. Initially, extended kin could visit freely; however, shortly afterwards the committee required visitors to seek sanction from the office. The relatively flexible system reflects the efforts made to preserve family ties. The Tipperary POS also founded an apprentice training home in Clonmel in 1841 for 'the reception of 14 children master and mistress and committee of ladies to regulate its affairs'.[150] Training homes generally came under the management of ladies' committees. A number of orphans were sent to the Providence Home, founded in Dublin in 1839, which trained respectable homeless girls in domestic skills and was managed by a ladies' committee. The Home's motto was 'prevention is better than cure'.[151]

The DPOS set up an 'Apprentice Relief Fund' in 1842 to assist any orphan who 'shall have served his or her apprenticeship satisfactorily, or who has lost his or her place without fault on the part of such apprentice'.[152] The committee claimed that by helping the orphans in this way, it was 'acting the parents' part'.[153] The fund was hugely beneficial: it gave apprentices who were considered in 'urgent need' the chance to emigrate or secure another apprenticeship and it gave those who had served their time well the means to purchase the necessary tools for their trade. In the same year, Revd Minchin, secretary to the DPOS, assisted an apprentice boy when his master, a ship's carpenter, to whom the Society had paid an apprentice fee, neglected to train him:

> Mr Minchin proceeded to state that his only object was to see that the boy was done justice to, that the society being supported by subscription, depended on public opinion for its well-being, and it was his duty to see that all masters to whom apprentices were sent from that institution should treat them properly, otherwise all confidence would be withdrawn from the society.[154]

The judge in this case applauded Revd Minchin's support of the boy: 'his conduct was praiseworthy in the extreme. It was his duty to look after the children entrusted to the society'.[155] The case was closed in favour of the DPOS.

Revd Dr Joly founded the 'Premium Fund' in 1844 which provided the committee with sufficient resources to give children who 'in addition to general good conduct, exhibit the greatest proficiency at stated examinations', small rewards, known as 'good conduct premiums'.[156] The committee allocated a portion of Dr Joly's fund to encourage 'improvement in needlework' and girls who made 'satisfactory proficiency' received rewards.[157] Revd Thomas Gregg, former DPOS secretary, left a bequest in 1846 which was added to the fund.[158] In the same year, the DPOS committee arranged a 'Protestant Orphan Tea' for the apprentices, held biannually thereafter, in order to keep them in close sight and monitor their progress.[159]

With a decline in applications for apprentices during the famine and its aftermath, it became necessary to seek out apprenticeships in England and elsewhere.[160] For example, a family who intended to emigrate to Canada in 1847 applied to the Society for two orphans. The Society agreed to the arrangement, 'in consideration of the advantages to the children and the difficulty of providing suitable places in this country at present'.[161] In another case, a Reverend and his wife brought a female orphan with them when they emigrated to Australia in September 1847.[162] The DPOS also sent a small number of children to the Cape of Good Hope. As mentioned in chapter 2, the Children's Friend Society sent orphans and destitute children to Canada and the Cape of Good Hope as part of an early emigration scheme.[163] Charlotte Neff suggests that the charity organisers introduced measures to prevent, or at the very least reduce, the incidence of child exploitation as cheap labour.[164]

The DPOS also sent children to sea. For example, in March 1848 it was noted that 'three boys having expressed their wish to go to sea [are to] be sent to Portsmouth with some careful person in order, if possible, to have them apprenticed in the Royal Navy and that Dr M'Clintock [is to] be requested to procure any further information as might be useful'.[165] The committee resolved to do their utmost to 'get them into the Merchant Service in the event of disappointment'.[166] Seamanship is discussed in more detail in chapter 6.

In September 1849, Revd Shore investigated the Society's legal position with respect to apprenticeship indentures and discovered, through the gratuitous help of an attorney, that employers could not cancel indentures unless the apprentice had committed a felony.[167] Although apprentices had always been inspected, Shore also recommended the appointment of an inspector to deal specifically with apprentices to ensure their 'constant and vigilant superintendence'.[168] The committee appointed an 'Apprentice Superintendent' who was 'well acquainted' with trades and tradesmen and the 'reciprocal duties' of masters and apprentices.[169] (Revd Shore, who was chaplain to the Newgate prison and familiar with the causes of criminality, later founded a Protestant reformatory school.)

Conclusion

The DPOS was responsible for the placement of children with 'suitable' families, inspections, medical care, and education. Where possible, children were placed with their siblings, and nurses were made accountable to the authority of the clergymen in their own parish and to the DPOS committee in Dublin, which were innovative and child-oriented policies. Moreover, given the general absence of state provisions, invest-ment in an apprenticeship scheme in the 1830s, hinging on the idea that prevention was better than cure, was both a progressive and ambitious undertaking. The DPOS apprenticeship system was a vital component of its overall commitment to family support, for children who were equipped with skills became useful members of society; but more practi-cally, they became useful members of the families to whom they were likely to return, bringing with them an education and earning power. As discussed in the next chapter, despite the apparent progress made by PO Societies in the area of child and family welfare, there was considerable opposition to its work.

Notes

1 Extract from tenth annual general meeting held at Rotunda, Dublin on Friday 5 April 1839.
2 DPOS annual report, 1844, NAI, POS papers, 1045/1/1/11–17, p. 13
3 For full rules see DPOS annual report, 1831, NAI, POS papers, 1045/1/1/1–7, pp. 6–7.
4 *Ibid.*, 1834, p. 12.
5 Enright, '"Take this child"'.
6 Evidence that Roman Catholic applications were refused on the basis of strict admission criteria; see unregistered applications (refused and post-poned applications), NAI, POS papers, 1045/5/4.
7 DPOS annual report, 1831, NAI, POS papers, 1045/1/1/1–7, p. 10.
8 TPOS minutes, 5 Jan. 1836, NLI, County Tiperary POS papers, MS 32,521.
9 *Ibid.*, 20 Jan. 1836.
10 J. F. McEldowney, 'Policing and the administration of justice in nine-teenth-century Ireland', in C. Emsley and B. Weinberger (eds), *Policing Western Europe: Politics, Professionalism, and Public Order, 1850–1940* (Westport, CT: Greenwood Press, 1991), pp. 18–35, p. 18.
11 Hill, 'Protestant ascendancy challenged', p. 165.
12 See TPOS annual report, 1862, County Tipperary POS papers, MS 32,521(1).
13 Kilkenny POS annual report, 1849, p. 5, RIA.
14 Massy, *Footprints of a Faithful Shepherd*, p. 326.
15 ARDP annual report, 1841, pp. 10–11, RIA.
16 Registers of applications, 1829–50, NAI, POS papers, 1045/5/2.
17 *Third Report of the Commissioners for Inquiring into the Condition of the Poorer Classes*, p. 101.
18 Milne, *Protestant Aid*, p. 5.
19 L. M. Geary, *Medicine and Charity in Ireland, 1718–1851* (Dublin: UCD Press, 2004), p. 193.

20 Parochial Visitors Society annual report, 1843, pp. 20–1, NLI.

21 *Ibid.*, p. 25.

22 Registered application files, 1840s, NAI, POS papers, 1045/5/3.

23 *Ibid.*

24 Register orphan histories, 1834, NAI, POS papers, 1045/5/1/1.

25 Registered application files, 1842, NAI, POS papers, 1045/5/3.

26 *Ibid.*

27 *Ibid.*, Mar. 1841.

28 *Ibid.*, Apr. 1841.

29 Register orphan histories, 10 Jan. 1842, NAI, POS papers, 1045/5/1/2.

30 *Ibid.*

31 Minutes, 1838, NAI, POS papers, 1045/2/1/1.

32 *Ibid.*

33 Registered application files, 1841, NAI, POS papers, 1045/5/3.

34 *Ibid.*

35 *Ibid.*, 1849.

36 *Ibid.*, letter in registered application file.

37 Registered application files, NAI, CPOU papers, 1045/11/2.

38 V. George, *Foster Care: Theory and Practice* (London: Routledge and K. Paul, 1970), p. 6.

39 DPOS annual report, 1830, NAI, POS papers, 1045/1/1/1–7, p. 10.

40 *Ibid.*, 1841.

41 Davidoff, 'Kinship as a categorical concept', p. 412.

42 Minutes, 4 Dec. 1835, NAI, POS papers, 1045/2/1/2.

43 Massy, *Footprints of a Faithful Shepherd*, p. 327; see also, Enright, '"Take this child"'.

44 See ministers' brief description of clergymen's care of orphans in *Minutes of proceedings of Dundalk Union, relative to pauper children*, 1842, p. 3.

45 Minutes, 30 Jan. 1835, NAI, POS papers, 1045/2/1/2.

46 TPOS annual report, 1840, NLI, County Tipperary POS papers, MS 32,530/A(5), p. 12.

47 *Ibid.*

48 *Ibid.*, p. 6.

49 Prunty, *Dublin Slums*, p. 246.

50 DPOS annual report, 1843, NAI, POS papers, 1045/1/1/11–17, p. 25.

51 *Ibid.*

52 Reference to 1837 LPOS annual report, Massy, *Footprints of a Faithful Shepherd*, pp. 346–65, p. 347, p. 365; see also Enright, '"Take this child"', p. 42.

53 Massy, *Footprints of a Faithful Shepherd*, p. 332; see also, Enright, '"Take this child"', p. 42.

54 Luddy, *Women and Philanthropy*, p. 72.

55 TPOS, annual report, 1840, NLI, County Tipperary POS papers, MS 32,521, p. 15.

56 Minutes, 22 June 1849, NAI, POS papers, 1045/2/1/4, p. 288.

57 Register orphan histories, NAI, POS papers, 1045/5/1.

58 DPOS annual report, 1830, NAI, POS papers, 1045/1/1/1–7, p. 41.

59 Minutes, 4 Dec. 1835, NAI, POS papers, 1045/2/1/2.

60 'Constitution and rules of a proposed Protestant Orphan Society submitted by committee to general meeting; with amendments as passed in 1828', NAI, POS papers, 1045/6/2/1./.

61 Minutes, 8 July 1836, NAI, POS papers, 1045/2/1/2.

62 Minutes, 2 Sept. 1836, NLI, County Tipperary POS papers, MS 32,521.

63 Revd T. R. Shore, *Case of Rev. Thomas R. Shore, and the Protestant Orphan Society with a statement of the circumstances under which he was removed from the Society* (Dublin: William Leckie, 1851), p. 4.

64 Minutes, 23 Dec. 1836, NAI, POS papers, 1045/2/1/3.

65 DPOS annual report, 1841, NAI, POS papers, 1045/1/1/1–7, p. 13.

66 Minutes subcommittee nurses and education, Oct. 1843, NAI, POS papers, 1045/2/3.

67 *Ibid.*, 1838–43.

68 See Shore, *Case of Rev. Thomas R. Shore, and the Protestant Orphan Society*, p. 5.

69 Minutes, 15 Aug. 1851, NAI, POS papers, 1045/2/1/5, p. 23.

70 Minutes subcommittee nurses and education, 1838–43, NAI, POS papers, 1045/2/3.

71 L. M. Geary, *Medicine and Charity in Ireland, 1718–1851* (Dublin: UCD Press, 2004), p. 67.

72 *Ibid.*

73 *Ibid.*, p. 66.

74 *The Treble Almanack*, p. 189.

75 *Dublin Temperance Gazette*, 1:1 (1830), p. 90.

76 *Slater's National Commercial Directory of Ireland* (Manchester and London: I. Slater, 1846), p. 234.

77 *Irish Times* (29 March 1869).

78 Minutes, 3 Apr. 1846, NAI, POS papers, 1045/2/1/4, p. 68.

79 See full details of Dr Ringland's notable achievements in H. Andrews, 'John Ringland', *Dictionary of Irish Biography*.

80 *Irish Times* (25 January 1864).

81 *Ibid.*

82 Minutes, 22 Oct. 1847, NAI, POS papers, 1045/2/1/4, p. 168.

83 H. Andrews, 'Alfred Henry McClintock', *Dictionary of Irish Biography*.

84 See Anonymous, *The Dublin Examiner in Anatomy, Physiology, Surgery Practice of Physic, and the Lateral branches of Medicine* (Dublin: Fannin & Co, 1846).

85 Minutes subcommittee nurses and education, 13 Oct. 1843, NAI, POS papers, 1045/2/3/1 (1834–67).

86 Minutes, 8 Feb. 1850, NAI, POS papers, 1045/2/1/4, p. 326.

87 *Ibid.*

88 Anonymous, *The Dublin Examiner in Anatomy*.

89 A. Drurie, 'Medicine, health and economic development: promoting spa and seaside resorts in Scotland c. 1750–1830', *Medical History* (2003), pp. 195–216, p. 198.

90 *Ibid.*

91 DPOS annual report, 1843, NAI, POS papers, 1045/1/1/11–17, p. 25.

92 J. Robins, *The Miasma: Epidemic and Panic in Nineteenth Century Ireland* (Dublin: Institute of Public Administration, 1995), p. 234.

93 Registered application files, 1830s, NAI, POS papers, 1045/5/3.

94 3 & 4 Vic., c. 29.

95 R. D. Cassell, *Medical Charities, Medical Politics: The Irish Dispensary System and the Poor Law, 1836–1872* (Woodbridge: Boydell Press, 1997), p. 119.

96 Minutes, 21 Nov. 1845, NAI, POS papers, 1045/2/1/3, p. 33.

97 *Ibid.*, 28 Nov. 1845, p. 37.

98 *Ibid.*, Feb. 6, 1846, p. 51.

99 Register incoming letters, 1846, NAI, POS papers, 1045/3/1/3.

100 *Ibid.*

101 Minutes subcommittee nurses and education, 17 Aug. 1855, NAI, POS papers, 1045/2/3.

102 Minutes, 24 Apr. 1846, NAI, POS papers, 1045/2/1/4, p. 67.

103 Register incoming letters, 1846–47, NAI, POS papers, 1045/3/1/3.

104 *Ibid.*

105 *Ibid.*

106 *Ibid.*

107 *Ibid.*

108 Minutes, 1846, NAI, POS papers, 1045/2/1/4, p. 106.

109 *Ibid.*

110 *Ibid.*, 1847, p. 149.

111 Register incoming letters, 1847, NAI, POS papers, 1045/3/1/3.

112 Minutes, 16 Apr. 1847, NAI, POS papers, 1045/2/1/4, p. 134.

113 *Ibid.*, 25 Sept. 1846, p. 97.

114 *Ibid.*, 2 July 1847, p. 149.

115 *Ibid.*, 24 Apr. 1846, p. 66.

116 *Ibid.*, 29 Nov. 1850, p. 378.

117 *Ibid.*

118 *Ibid.*

119 See D. McLoughlin, 'Workhouses and Irish female paupers', in Luddy and Murphy (eds), *Women Surviving*, pp. 117–47, pp. 136–41; see also Robins, *Lost Children*, p. 193.

120 DPOS annual report, 1843, NAI, POS papers, 1045/1/1/11–17.

121 Register orphan histories, 1841, NAI, POS papers, 1045/5/1/2.

122 Minutes, 12 Sept. 1845, 1045/2/1/4, p. 15.

123 *Ibid.*, 26 Sept. 1845, p. 18.

124 *Ibid.*, 13 Mar. 1846, p. 57.

125 *Ibid*, 5 June 1846, p. 77.

126 *Ibid.*, 16 Apr. 1847, p. 134.

127 'Address to the British public on behalf of the Protestant Orphan Society for Ireland', *Church of England magazine, Church Pastoral-Aid Society*, 29 (1850), p. 334.

128 Parkes, *Kildare Place*, pp. 18–20.

129 *Ibid.*, p. 27.

130 H. Pim, 'On the importance of reformatory establishments for juvenile delinquents', *Journal of the Statistical and Social Inquiry Society of Ireland*, 3:7 (1853/54), pp. 1–20, p. 9.

131 S. Parkes, 'The Reverend Canon Henry Kingsmill Moore, DD, Ball. Coll. Oxon., FLS, and Church of Ireland Education, 1880–1927', in S. Gilley (ed.), *Victorian Churches and Churchmen: Essays Presented to Vincent Allan McClelland* (Catholic Record Society, monograph ser., 7) (Woodbridge: Boydell, 2005), pp. 279–91, p. 282.

132 Minutes, 1850, NAI, POS papers, 1045/2/1/5, p. 383.

133 Robins, *Lost Children*, p. 128.

134 *Ibid.*; Milne, *Protestant Aid*, p. 3.

135 Pim, 'On the importance of reformatory establishments', p. 9.

136 Robins, *Lost Children*, p. 296.

137 N. O'Ciosain, 'Oral culture, literacy, and reading, 1800–50', in J. H. Murphy, *The Oxford History of the Irish, Volume IV: The Irish Book in English, 1800–1891* (Oxford: Oxford University Press, 2011), pp. 173–92, p. 187.

138 J. Coolahan, *Irish Education: Its History and Structure* (Dublin: Institute of Public Administration, 1981), p. 23.

139 *Penny Journal*, 4:90 (Summer 1847).

140 See Enright, '"Take this child"', p. 32.

141 Robins, *Lost Children*, p. 238.

142 DPOS annual report, 1846, NAI, POS papers, 1045/1/1/11–17.

143 Robins, *Lost Children*, p. 159.

144 Minutes, 22 May 1835, NAI, POS papers, 1045/2/1/2.

145 P. Gregg, *A Social and Economic History of Britain, 1760–1950* (London, Toronto, Wellington, Sydney: George G. Harrap and Co., 1950), p. 136.

146 Annual report, 1838, NAI, POS papers, 1045/1/2–10, p. 12.

147 *Ibid.*, 1839.

148 Minutes, 1840s, NAI, POS papers, 1045/2/1/3–4.

149 See minutes apprentice subcommittee, 1836–55, NAI, POS papers, 1045/2/4/1.

150 TPOS annual report, 1841, NLI, County Tipperary POS papers, MS 32,530/A(6), p. 13.

151 Luddy, *Women and Philanthropy*, p. 84.

152 DPOS annual report, 1846, NAI, POS papers, 1045/1/1/11–17, p. 16.

153 *Ibid.*

154 *Freeman's Journal* (20 October 1842).

155 *Ibid.*

156 DPOS annual report, 1844, NAI, POS papers, 1045/1/1/11–17, p. 16.
157 Minutes, 13 Mar. 1846, NAI, POS papers, 1045/2/1/4, p. 57.
158 DPOS annual report, 1846, NAI, POS papers, 1045/1/1/11–17, p. 16.
159 Minutes, 21 Aug. 1846, NAI, POS papers, 1045/2/1/4, p. 93.
160 *Ibid.*, 29 Oct. 1847, p. 169.
161 *Ibid.*, 7 May 1847, p. 139.
162 *Ibid.*, Sept. 1847.
163 Neff, 'The Children's Friend Society in Upper Canada', pp. 236–7.
164 *Ibid.*
165 Minutes, 3 Mar. 1848, NAI, POS papers, 1045/2/1/4, p. 197.
166 *Ibid.*, 14 Sept. 1849, p. 296.
167 *Ibid.*
168 *Ibid.*, 21 Sept. 1849, p. 301.
169 *Ibid.*

4

Opposition and support, 1850–98

The success of these societies is unquestioned.[1]

Introduction

Dr Paul Cullen replaced Daniel Murray as Roman Catholic Archbishop of Dublin in 1852, which was followed by a new phase of extensive church building and parish reorganisation. During Archbishop Cullen's episcopate (1852–79; cardinal from 1866), criticisms of, and opposition to, the Church of Ireland and its associated charities, including PO Societies, escalated in the lead up to disestablishment. Concurrently, social reformers dealt with vital issues such as public health, workhouse children, juvenile delinquency and cruelty to children which eventually led to the introduction of crucial reforms. This chapter examines the two directly opposing views of PO Societies which emerged in the second half of the nineteenth century. At one end of the spectrum of opinion were Archbishop Cullen and Margaret Aylward who investigated the charity on the grounds of suspected proselytism while at the other were social reformers who regarded the POS boarding-out scheme as an ideal child welfare model worthy of imitation.

Missionary work in Ireland

In 1850, after the influx of Irish Catholics during the Great Famine, the full Roman Catholic hierarchy was restored in England in line with Roman Catholic countries, and known as the 'Papal aggression',[2] which provoked anti-Catholic sentiment throughout England. The presence of 'continental religious orders', and reports of Protestant persecution in Europe[3] alerted Protestants to the potential threat. The missions of the Fathers of Charity in Dublin unsettled the 'Protestant party', which was 'annoyed at these missions and the city was often placarded all over with the announcements of controversial sermons'.[4] Reportedly, one-hundred Protestants had been converted. In 1851 the Redemptorist Mission in Dublin was allegedly 'attended by many Protestants' and 'some few of them were received into the church'.[5] According to the priests, the mission attracted such attention when it came to light that Fr Lockhart was an Oxford convert.

Archbishop Cullen called for unity among Catholic bishops against ICM missionary progress in the west of Ireland. Growing Catholic strength in Europe and the 'invasion of popery'[6] sparked extensive English Protestant enthusiasm for the ICM as a means of defence from 'the Romish priesthood who seek the subversion of the Protestant Established Church of Ireland'.[7] Reports from Prussia claimed that Jesuit priests were 'among the Protestant population'.[8] In 1852 Archbishop MacHale, Tuam diocese, assisted by Frs Lockhart and Rinolfi, endeavoured to thwart the progress made by the ICM.[9] In Lyons, France, in the 1850s, there were reports that two English Jesuit priests had been drafted in to seek out English residents 'with a view to their conversion to the Romish faith'.[10] The Protestant poor were thought particularly vulnerable.[11] In the 1840s the DPOS referred to a school in Lille founded for the purpose of 'preserving the children of Protestant parents from the destructive precepts of Romish instructors'.[12] Redemptorist and Jesuit missions were set up in County Wicklow, Londonderry, Fermoy and Antrim in the 1850s and 1860s which were countered by the ICM.[13] By the mid-1850s the ICM had established 125 mission stations primarily in the west and south west of Ireland.[14] As well as its activity in the west, the ICM also had a strong presence in Dublin.

Ellen Smyly, née Franks, had been dedicated to her church and to philanthropy from a young age.[15] Mrs Smyly was a close affiliate of Alexander Dallas, the ICM, and married to Josiah Smyly, medical officer to the DPOS. Archbishop Whately's wife and daughters assisted Mrs Smyly in her work which included the management of a network of schools; however, the archbishop is said not to have supported the mission.[16] Other Protestants linked to both the ICM and the DPOS included, for example, Revd John Gregg, the Earl of Roden, and Joseph Napier Esq. M.P.

A number of Irish Protestants disapproved of providing aid in conjunction with scriptural education[17] and publicly criticised the methodologies used by the ICM. Miriam Moffitt argues that after the 1861 census which exposed the weak Protestant position and the failure of the ICM, and in the lead up to disestablishment, Irish Protestants who had previously backed the ICM turned their attention away from the conversion of Catholics to concentrate instead on defending the faith of

Protestants;[18] however, the preservation of Protestantism had been of major concern since before Catholic emancipation was granted.

PO Societies and religious rivalry

Following Archbishop Cullen's 1856 pastoral on proselytism, which denounced the ICM in particular, there were a number of altercations between the Ladies of Charity (Margaret Aylward founded a branch of the Ladies' Association of Charity of St Vincent de Paul for Spiritual and Temporal Relief of the Sick Poor in St Mary's parish Dublin in 1851),[19] and the ICM in Dublin.[20] In addition, Margaret Aylward, with the assistance of Fr John Gowan, founded St Brigid's boarding-out orphanage in 1856 to defend the faith of Roman Catholic children under threat of Protestant proselytism.[21] (The first child was received in January 1857.) St Brigid's boarded out children to small farmers in north Dublin, and counties Wicklow and Kildare who had been recommended by parochial clergy and worked in direct competition with the ICM, and the CPOU.

PO Societies also came under close scrutiny in the same year. Revd David Moriarty, who Cullen appointed coadjutor to Cornelius Egan, Ardfert, Kerry, in 1854, and who counteracted much of the Dingle peninsula missionary activity,[22] wrote to the Kerry POS on 18 July 1856, enclosing £1:

> As I perceive that a meeting is called this day, in aid of your Orphan Society, may I trouble you to hand in this very small offering of mine. Allow me to express a regret that in advocating the claims of these dear little innocents, sentiments are expressed which cast on the institution a suspicion of proselytism, and prevent a more extensive co-operation of the charitable of all classes on its behalf. Under your direction I feel the fullest security it seeks only, as its name implies, to protect and educate the orphan children of Protestant parents. – With great respect, I am, sir, yours very faithfully, David Moriarty.[23]

In reply, Revd A. Denny, Rector, Tralee, thanked Bishop Moriarty for his contribution, claiming that there had never been any grounds for suspicion. Moriarty's public display of support for the Kerry POS did not go unnoticed by Archbishop Cullen.[24] (Religiously indiscriminate charitable donations were not particularly unusual – Protestants also donated to Catholic charities.[25]) A year later Dr Cullen stated that while allegations of this kind against Protestant institutions had caused offence they would encourage Catholics 'to take care of their children'.[26] There were also outcries that Catholic children were at risk of proselytism in workhouses.[27] (Cullen presented these grievances to the Select

Committee on the Irish Poor law in 1861.) It has been suggested that the Catholic church seized upon the flaws in the Poor Law and the issue of boarding out as it vied for political power in Ireland.[28]

In 1860 the *Catholic Telegraph* featured a report from the Ladies of St Vincent de Paul on the alleged proselytising activity of the DPOS. Henry H. Joy Esq. responded on 14 April 1860:

> Why was it that especially the Catholic brethren had so much representa-tion within the present year not only from the dignitaries and priests of that church but from the laity of the Church and gentlewomen. What had they [the DPOS] done to call down this storm of misrepresentation. The Protestant Orphan Society was not a proselytising agency one of its cardi-nal rules being to admit no children no matter how poor, however destitute that were not the orphans of Protestant parents.[29]

Mr Joy referred to the report and stated that Protestants believed Archbishop Cullen was 'responsible for such misrepresentation'.[30]

The Ladies' Association of St Brigid's carried out intensive surveillance of Protestant activities[31] and its 'obviously partisan'[32] annual reports regularly featured the DPOS among many other Protestant institutions:

> Undoubtedly, many of them are the children of Protestant parents, but strangely enough we find one third of them bearing names that are in Ireland eminently Catholic such as Kelly, McCann, O'Flaherty, Geraghty. The truth is that several adults who live as hypocrites upon the bribes of the proselytisers are sometimes taken away in their sins and then the orphans become the prey of the society.[33]

DPOS case files record the applicants' religion and, at least in the cases examined by the author, applicants were from traditional Protestant back-grounds – Church of Ireland and England, Methodist and Presbyterian (Presbyterians and Methodists founded separate boarding-out schemes in 1866 and 1870 respectively) – and converts of long-standing. Protestants also converted to Roman Catholicism, some of whom were received into the church when they intermarried. A convert to Roman Catholicism of sixteen years was assisted by St Brigid's in the 1860s.[34] Moreover, one of St Brigid's most ardent supporters was a German convert.[35] DPOS inspectors recorded the parents' religion and, in many cases, provided a brief description of their family histories. The DPOS required marriage certificates, birth certificates and burial certificates from every applicant. The committee had asserted in 1830:

> As the sole object of the society is the relief of the most wretched and deserving objects of *our fellow Protestants*, in order to guard against any imposition being practised upon them, they have agreed that the petition

of each child for admission into this society shall be accompanied by certificates of marriage of the parents and baptisms of the children, or, if this cannot be conveniently procured, such other documents as shall appear satisfactory.[36]

This rule was adhered to until 1898 when the Protestant Orphan Refuge Society (PORS) and DPOS amalgamated, after which the Protestant orphans of Protestant parentage and of mixed marriages were admitted. If these certificates were not lodged with the committee, cases could be deferred for months or refused altogether. Applications were also refused and postponed due to limited funds and age restrictions, and if applicants were judged 'undeserving'. Managers of the DPOS continued to exert caution with the outlay of funds, which led to fewer admissions, even in more prosperous times. The DPOS provided orphans with long-term care, if required, which was extremely costly: in many cases children were cared for from infancy to adulthood.

In 1862, the Belfast auxiliary stated, 'be it remembered that it is a defence association, not in any way connected with the controversies now agitating the church, its object being that the orphans of our Protestant brethren should be educated in the faith of their fathers, and trained up in habits of industry'.[37] The Westmeath POS refused admission of orphans from mixed marriages, declaring that it received only the orphans of Protestant parentage.[38] In 1863 the DPOS reiterated that 'it was called the Protestant Orphan Society merely to show that it was Protestant orphans who were assisted by it and surely the first duty incumbent on Protestants was to assist those belonging to that class'.[39] In response to further allegations, the DPOS stated in 1890, 'the charges of proselytism which had been brought against them were all nonsense, because they never accepted any child except from the legal guardian or the surviving parent'.[40] St Brigid's also publicly condemned the work carried out by the Charitable Protestant Orphan Union (CPOU).

The CPOU

The CPOU, later known as the Protestant Orphan Refuge Society, had a clear purpose, 'to preserve the Protestantism of the orphans of mixed marriages'.[41] At the Synod of Thurles, 1850, described as a 'display of ecclesiastical triumphalism',[42] it was announced that papal dispensations had to be granted before mixed marriages could take place; marriage partners were required to pledge in writing that all children would be raised in the Roman Catholic church.[43] In 1855 there were 103 children under the CPOU's charge. From a sample of two-hundred application files, dating from 1850 to 1860, in 62 per cent of cases, Protestant women had married outside their church; Protestant men had intermarried in 38 per cent of cases.[44]

The CPOU claimed that to provide for the orphans of mixed marriages was not proselytising for surely if that were so, orphans of mixed marriages raised in Catholic institutions were also victims of the same religious interference; 'unless, therefore, you bring these children up as heathens, it is impossible to bring them up by any means unless what will be liable to the charge of being a proselytising society'.[45] The CPOU also acknowledged that the Protestant public favoured the DPOS: 'I have heard and no doubt you have heard people speak very favourably of the Protestant Orphan Society, and very depreciatory of ours, although they are the same in principle. People say, "I do not like your society, it is a proselytising society"'.[46] Owing to its strict admission criteria, the DPOS was not involved in disputes over orphans' religious upbringing to the same extent as the CPOU.[47] DPOS and CPOU application files and associated correspondence differ considerably: while CPOU files refer to priests' or Catholic relatives' interference in the children's placements, references of this kind are not typically found in DPOS files.

In 1859 the CPOU committee requested an amalgamation with the DPOS[48] as it could not 'obtain a hearing' among those who already supported the DPOS.[49] However, the DPOS opposed amalgamation as, 'it would imperil the interests of the Society, prove unsatisfactory to its best friends, and involve a departure from the principle on which the Society was formed, namely to provide for destitute orphans of Protestant parents'.[50] It also confirmed that the CPOU was entirely separate from the DPOS, 'the two Societies, which have had a separate and independent action for twenty-nine years, each occupying a totally distinct sphere of usefulness'.[51]

It was stated in St Brigid's annual reports that Catholics who intermarried would not allow their children to be raised Protestant: 'A Catholic parent cannot under pains of eternal separation from God give his children to be reared in heresy. Besides we must charitably believe, what in fact almost always happens, that the Catholic parent has had his children baptised in the Catholic Church'.[52] In March 1864, a Protestant widower wrote to the CPOU to apply for the admission of his four children. In his letter he informed the committee that he was a convert to Protestantism. He explained that almost ten years earlier, he had had misgivings with the Roman Catholic church for some time and that he had attended no place of worship until after his marriage to a Protestant woman. He attended church regularly with his wife and became a Protestant in 1854, greatly against his parents' wishes. His wife died in

November 1863[53] and the parish priest had encouraged the widower's mother to place her grandchildren with St Brigid's: 'Revd Mr. Murphy called to hear her confession and took the names and ages of the four children and they were to be taken in on the following board day'.[54] The widower explained that 'his wife's mother having heard of it went to the Revd Mr. Jordan and that gentleman got them sent to Haddington Road'.[55] The widower informed the CPOU of the situation as he had applied to the CPOU not St Brigid's. In this case both father and mother and children were Protestant. The father was alive and expressly wished his children to be raised Protestant.

The well-documented Mary Mathews case was another example of the tug of war between St Brigid's and a Protestant family over children's religious upbringing. In 1860 Margaret Aylward was found innocent of kidnapping but imprisoned for six months for contempt of court.[56] St Brigid's dismissed allegations of proselytism and reaffirmed its defensive stance.[57] PO Societies, such as the Longford POS, which accepted the Protestant orphans of mixed marriages, also reported similar cases. In 1857, for example, a Protestant father requested that after his death his wife, a Roman Catholic, would raise his son a Protestant. His widow, who was 'afflicted with paralysis and in very poor circumstances'[58] admitted the child to the Longford POS where he remained for six years. Press reports state that in 1863 the child was 'seized by a carman',[59] that his mother was present during her son's removal, and that the Longford POS sought the child's return. The case was settled in court when it was decided that, as in the Mary Mathews case, the mother's guardianship rights should be upheld.[60]

PO Societies: further development

In the 1850s, the Vicar of Mullingar stated that Protestant workhouse children lived under 'perpetual insult and petty persecution', and had 'apostatised from their religion in order that their lot would be easier'.[61] Archbishop Richard Whately founded the Society for the Protection of the Rights of Conscience for the Benefit of Poor Protestants and Converts in 1850.[62] The Society for the Protection of Converts was formed to protect 'in the exercise of Christian liberty, those converts from Romanism who had been deprived of all former means of earning a livelihood on account of their change of religion'.[63] The Society assisted converts to secure employment though it stated that, 'no money shall be given except as wages for work actually done (and at the lowest rate in the neighbourhood for similar)'.[64] Whately shared the Vicar of Mullingar's concerns in 1858 when he claimed that a Protestant housed with Roman Catholics in workhouses was akin to a 'slave in South Carolina'.[65] By 1851 there were 106,000 children in workhouses of whom 40 per cent were orphans.[66] The DPOS also drew attention to the perceived dangers of placing Protestant orphans in workhouses:

> It was a principle of philosophy that when two bodies, one large and the other small are floating on any fluid, the large body always attracts the smaller; and so they should take care that the relative numbers of the Roman Catholics in workhouses, which are the larger body, do not absorb the Protestant portion, which is the smallest.[67]

Persistent reports that Protestant children were under threat as well as the mounting influence of the Roman Catholic church in Ireland prompted the further development of PO Societies. Cholera reappeared in Cork city, Belfast and Newry, and Dublin[68] from 1853 to 1855 when 2,606 deaths were reported.[69] A DPOS auxiliary meeting at Ballymena, County Antrim, in September 1854 was poorly attended as were meetings in Belfast due to the 'cholera being very bad in this place'.[70] The outbreak resulted in higher POS admission rates, particularly in Dublin, and was likely to have encouraged the foundation of additional local PO Societies.

The Donegal POS was founded in 1857 by a clergymen in the Gweedore district. Initially, due to limited funds the committee elected the most destitute applicants only; however, Mr John Boyd, of Ballymacool, objected and 'carried a resolution that no destitute orphan who was Protestant should be refused and the society increased and strengthened, and became equal to the support of them all'.[71] The Donegal POS was referred to as 'purely defensive' and a 'lifeboat for Protestant orphans'.[72] It had also always maintained that 'it was not a proselytising society'

Table 4.1 Foundation of county PO Societies, 1850–70

PO Societies	Year founded
Donegal	1857
Galway	1857
Fermanagh	1859
Mayo	1861
Waterford	1862
Londonderry	1865
Antrim and Down	1866
Armagh	1867
Monaghan	1870

Source: DPOS annual reports.

but rather a mechanism to ensure that Protestant orphans were raised by Protestant families.[73]

The inaugural meeting of the County Mayo POS was held in the school-house of the Church Education Society, Castlebar in November 1861. Although not directly responsible for its establishment, the Bishop of Tuam, Thomas Plunket, hoped the Society would prove an important symbol of the Church of Ireland's worth as disestablishment loomed: 'as a Protestant institution, it deserves the support of all Protestants, especially when there are parties at the present day, who are loudly calling out for the spoliation of the church in this land, who think it is a lifeless corpse which it is time to bury'.[74] While the 1859 Ulster Revival had reinvigorated the Protestant churches, leading to a rise in church and Sunday school attendance, the Bishop of Tuam's words attest to the Church of Ireland's attempts to justify its place in Ireland: 'He thought that this meeting having for its object the formation of a Protestant Orphan Society, spoke volumes for the vitality of the church, as well as that it afforded them an opportunity of preserving that vitality'.[75] Robert McDowell identifies the various attacks made against the pre-disestablished Church of Ireland and the motivations for doing so while also noting its 'virtues'.[76]

In 1864 and 1865 Jesuit and Redemptorist missioners were active in Antrim and Londonderry.[77] In 1866, there was a reoccurrence of cholera with 2,308 deaths in Wexford, Donegal, Wicklow, Roscommon and Queen's County with Dublin most affected reporting close to 1,000 deaths within six months.[78] The Londonderry POS was founded in 1865 and the Antrim and Down POS on the 28 June 1866. Formerly an auxiliary to the DPOS, it separated from the parent society as, 'widowed mothers were often unwilling and refused to give up their children to be sent so far away from them as Wicklow and Wexford, where the greater number of the children under the care of the parent society were located'.[79] The newly formed Society aimed to serve Belfast and 'such parts of the counties of Antrim and Down, and the county of the town of Carrickfergus, as shall connect themselves with the Society'.[80]

In the same year, the DPOS reaffirmed its position as a defensive society: 'Let it not be imagined that the faith of Protestant orphan children in Ireland is in less danger of being tampered with now than it was eight and thirty years ago, when this society first started upon its mission of mercy'.[81] Founded in 1867, the Armagh POS opening ceremony was held in the Tontine Rooms in Belfast. The Lord Primate and Mrs Beresford, Sir Capel Molyneux, John Vance Esq. and a number of ladies were present. The Lord Primate called attention to the serious neglect of Protestant orphans in the area; the need to protect them from the 'cold mercies of the workhouse'; and 'putting them in such a position as they might have occupied had their parents lived'.[82] The Armagh POS also promoted education in order to ensure the orphans 'go through future life with respectability'.[83] Moreover, it was said that the 'generations yet to come' would be grateful for the legacy of charity left behind as, 'the orphans and the widows of this county were not forgotten'.[84] Revd Thomas Ellis, honorary secretary, claimed, 'They do not believe in the workhouse system as a nursery for their children, and they made a laudable effort to carry the better system in which they do believe'.[85] In line with other PO Societies, the Armagh POS aimed to limit the number of Protestant children dependent on workhouses. The Monaghan POS was founded in 1870.

The Church of Ireland was disestablished by the Irish Church Act, 26 July 1869, which came into effect on 1 January 1871. The Meath POS expressed trepidation in its annual report:

> Our society, in common with other charitable institutions must bear its part in contending against the waves of the sea of troubles on which we have been launched. The ancient Irish Church has been disestablished and disendowed by the act of legislature. This momentous crisis, fraught, we believe, with danger to the whole kingdom, now hangs like a storm on our horizon.[86]

In 1870 the DPOS committee stated that, 'the altered position of the Irish Church renders it more imperative than ever upon its members to make full provision for the maintenance and education of the destitute orphans of our communion'.[87] Despite the embrace of evangelicalism by the lower clergy and the laity of the Church of Ireland, and its growth in the mid-nineteenth century, the church did not become fully committed to evangelicalism until after disestablishment.[88] The DPOS upheld the same defensive stance post-disestablishment as it had done since its foundation:

> The Protestant Orphan Society still maintains its ground, the prosperity of the institution is intimately connected with that of the entire church in our land. Every agency, which tends to unite the members of our church in close fellowship with one another, is most valuable at the present time. Every effort to keep the young of our communion and to educate them in the fear and love of god, is now specially required, and the committee venture to claim for the Protestant Orphan Society a foremost place in promoting these great objects.[89]

PO Societies continued to serve the Protestant population in counties throughout Ireland, see figure 4.1.

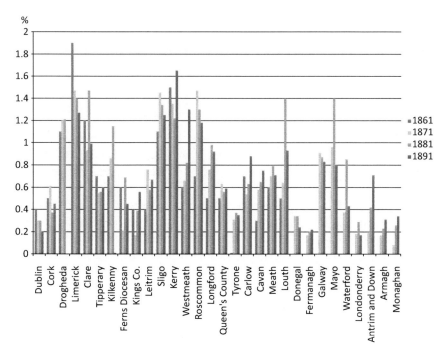

Figure 4.1 Percentage of Protestant population served by PO Societies, 1861–91.
Source: DPOS annual reports, 1861–91, NAI, POS papers, 1045/1/1/29-65.

Following disestablishment, Church of Ireland clergy eventually accepted the church's independence, with some viewing it as freedom from 'political trammels'.[90] William Conyngham Plunket, who has been described as a 'natural diplomat and a seeker of peace'[91] wrote in the early 1870s of the moderate character of the 'great majority of Irish Churchmen, including the ablest and most influential of our clergy and laity'.[92] Disestablishment also resulted in the empowerment of the laity.[93]

One way in which the laity contributed to the church and its affiliated charities including PO Societies was through legacies and donations. In 1872 Joseph Kinsey Esq., Balcorris House, County Dublin, 'an old subscriber of the Society',[94] bequeathed part of his estate to the DPOS. The money was donated to finance The Kinsey Marriage Portion Fund Charity. The scheme, which was devised by Kinsey, offered marriage portions to POS orphans.[95] He also bequeathed an additional sum for the establishment of a Protestant Orphan Society in Auckland, New Zealand and 'for the support of clergymen of the English Episcopal Church in Auckland. The Newry POS, Westmeath POS and the Belfast

POS also received bequests'.[96] It perhaps illustrates the extent to which lay members of the church influenced the management of PO Societies while also showing their commitment to the preservation of the Church of Ireland and Protestant posterity.

'I shall work away *in the shade*'[97]: women and PO Societies

Church of Ireland women, who were heavily involved in bible societies, Sunday schools, the Mothers' Union, the Young Women's Christian Association and the Girls' Friendly Societies, also played an important role in ensuring the longevity of PO Societies and were among its most stalwart supporters. In the second half of the nineteenth century women continued to organise bazaars, which were often grand two day events requiring extensive and effective planning. A lady who organised the Limerick bazaar in the early 1850s stated the following in the weeks leading up to the event:

> I proceeded to Limerick to canvass Mrs – for our benevolent object. However I was replied by such a tirade against the vanity, frivolity, and dis-honesty of Bazaars in general, that I was afraid it would extend to the poor Protestant Orphan Bazaar in particular ... The receipt for making a good stall-holder comprises a certain proportion of energy, ditto gracefulness, ditto popularity, ditto steadiness ... Perhaps I may be wrong in wishing to keep our list aristocratic ... But I am so afraid of affronts and jealousies amongst the Mrs-s. No one can say a word to my Lady Dunraven, or to my Lady Clarina, but I dread a murmur of, 'Well! I think I am as good as Mrs. D. or Mrs. Any-one-else. I don't see why I am not made a Patroness', and that would be endless ... We must have a preparatory meeting, without it all the pens, ink, and paper extant would not suffice for the knotty point of tables, tickets, and so forth.[98]

On its first day 700 people attended the bazaar.[99]

Embroidery and other 'fancy works' were typically displayed at bazaars. PO Societies and convent schools continued to support domestic industry after the manufacture revival of the early 1850s.[100] Crochet pieces were also sold to raise funds for the DPOS and in the 1860s pieces of 'ornamental needlework' were sold in 'orphan baskets'.[101] In 1867 the Armagh POS noted that ladies had raised two-thirds of the funds for all Protestant orphans in Ireland through 'cards, concerts, bazaars and orphan baskets'.[102] In 1888 the ladies of the Armagh POS held a bazaar in Lurgan from which close to half of the annual income was derived. At the 1890 Armagh POS annual bazaar, Indian embroidery, Indian brass work and hand painted items were sold.[103] Indian embroidery had been displayed for many years in Ireland, for example, in 1853 at the Irish Industrial Exhibition.

Women also used poetry, music and art to generate interest in the Society's work. The Limerick POS reported that its lady supporters produced poetry 'in aid of the bazaar'.[104] In 1854, Mrs William Crofton published *Eight Views, for the Benefit of the Leitrim Protestant Orphan Society*. The book contained pictorial works from Mrs Crofton's original drawings. Music, particularly hymns, was another important fundraising strategy. Generally, individual PO Societies featured distinct 'orphan hymns' in their respective annual reports. A few lines from the Cavan POS orphans' hymn gives a sense of the sympathy expressed for the orphans and the spirit behind 'good deeds':

Look mildly on the fatherless!
Ye may have power to wile
Their hearts from saddened memory
By the magic of a smile
Deal gently with these little ones
Be pitiful, and he
The friend and father of us all
Shall gently deal with thee.[105]

Evangelical clergy introduced hymn-singing in favour of metrical psalms.[106] Cecil Frances Humphreys (1818–95) who married Revd Alexander, also an acclaimed poet, and later Archbishop of Armagh,[107] was one of the most famous composers of children's hymns. While the writers of the 'orphan hymns' are not documented, it is likely that clergymen and their wives were perhaps inspired by Mrs Alexander's *Hymns for Children* (published in 1848).[108]

In Galway Henry D. Stanistreet Esq. led the Ballinasloe Choral Society, of which many members were women, and arranged 'very successful Concerts in aid of the Galway Protestant Orphan Society in 1865 and 1866'.[109] Amateur concerts were held in aid of the Fermanagh POS in the 1860s. In 1863 an amateur concert was held on behalf of the Cavan POS. Mrs Whyte Venables composed one piece of music played on the 'pianoforte' on the night; a piece that was shortly due for publication.[110] The Cavan Choral Society also contributed to the night. 'The quality of Mrs. Wolfe's singing, there can be no second opinion. The kindness that induced her to lend her service is only equalled by the excellence of her performance. Her management of her voice we have seldom, if ever, heard equalled by an amateur'.[111]

Mrs Beresford arranged a concert on behalf of the Armagh POS in 1876, which was held at the Tontine Rooms, Belfast. The programme for the concert included: Duet, Rondo in F, clarinet and piano (Beethoven), Mr Strangways and Dr Marks; part song, 'The Fairest Flower' (Sir R. B. Stewart), 'Wake, my love' (Loder), 'Hark, the curfew' (Attwood), 'The Mill Wheel' (Kreutzer), 'Zampa' (Laberre), the Irish ballad, *Norah, the Pride of Kildare*, among many others. The harp featured in some of the arrangements.[112] In 1890, a concert was held in the evening after the first day of the annual bazaar in the Town Hall, Lurgan, and ladies performed 'pianoforte' and violin solos.[113]

Women were also involved in more practical aspects of the Society's management; for example, they assisted the clothing subcommittees. The Antrim and Down POS reported in 1868 that, 'during the past year the sub-committee, aided by the ladies has spared no exertion in providing not only a suitable but a comfortable outfit for all the orphans elected by our society, as well as for the apprentices'.[114] The Tyrone POS committee recorded its appreciation for a recently deceased lady subscriber and collector in 1877:

> The mention of the latter name can only awaken feelings of the greatest regret for her loss in all who wish well to the Protestant orphans of the county. Indefatigable in her exertions on behalf of the Society she persevered to the last as the Orphan's friend in the task of gathering contributions, and by her very successful efforts she added materially to the Society's yearly finances.[115]

Tributes of this kind feature in the annual reports of the DPOS and local PO Societies throughout the second half of the nineteenth century and bear testament to the commendable work of so many Church of Ireland women who had fundraised on the Society's behalf for much of their adult lives.

Additional fundraising strategies: the language and visual expression of transformation

Revd John Gregg, renowned for his oratory abilities, delivered annual sermons on behalf of the DPOS. In 1850 he preached a sermon entitled 'Misery and Mercy' which emphasised the stark difference between the children's lives before and after they had received assistance.[116] Known as 'good John Gregg' (Archdeacon of Kildare 1857), he was extremely well liked, and had a special affinity with the orphans as his own father had died when he was nine; he referred to himself as 'the orphan child of the only Protestant family in one of the obscurest parishes in the most neglected county in Ireland'.[117] Gregg also wrote a number of sermons for children which he preached 'on an early Thursday in the month of January',[118] such as 'Plain teaching for little children', 'Wisdom unto salvation: a sermon to children', and 'The way to be good'. Gregg was thanked for his 'untiring interest' in the DPOS and for the 'steady increase in the contributions so liberally supplied by the congregation in Trinity Church'.[119]

Other clergymen also expressed a sense of empathy for the orphans; for example, in a sermon preached on behalf of the County Leitrim POS in 1864, Revd C. Adams stated that 'he [Adams] had a solemn and peculiar feeling attached to it which reminded him of friends whom he had lost. In the year 1839, he understood the society was formed, and in that year he lost his mother, being then only two and a half years old. He could speak in some measure from experience that that was an incalculable loss'.[120] Moreover, after his mother's death, Revd Godfrey Massy, Limerick POS, became responsible for his younger brothers and identified well with parental loss.

As discussed in chapter 3, children were put on display at annual meetings, a practice which continued into the second half of the nineteenth century. Nurses were responsible for escorting the children to Dublin while clergymen's wives, daughters and other supporters of the Societies dressed them in their best clothes and prepared the children's 'tea' after the event. In 1865, the Fermanagh POS committee commented on 'the appearance of the children on the platform' as 'abundant proof of the good effected by the Society'.[121] The language of transformation was utilised by other charities and missionary societies. The ICM, for example, produced hymns that told of converts' transition from the darkness of 'popery' into the light.[122] In the 1850s the Limerick POS referred to the children's appearance at its annual meeting: 'They display before us vividly the fact that there is an intimate connection between ours and the other state'.[123] The orphans acted as a reminder of the uncertainty of life.

Born in 1845 in Upper Gardiner Street, Dublin, and christened in St Andrew's Church, Thomas Barnardo was deeply inspired by the late 1850s evangelical revival and became an active member of the Young Men's Christian Association. In the 1860s he attended meetings at the home of Mr and Mrs Henry Grattan Guinness in Dublin and opened his first refuge in London in 1870.[124] Lydia Murdoch identifies Barnardo's use of song, dance and dramatic scenes to emphasise the 'before and after'.[125] He stated in 1890 that, 'people believe in what they see'.[126] PO Societies and Thomas Barnardo used language and visual proof to stress the transformative power of their respective work which evoked an emotive response from subscribers.

Family support

Workhouses continued to represent often the only source of relief for destitute widows and their dependents. In a north Antrim town, for example, it has been observed that 'up until the late 1860s, the main role of the Ballymoney workhouse seems to have been as a longer-term shelter for the most vulnerable in society: the elderly, deserted or widowed women and their children, and the vast majority of them were to remain in the workhouse for a significant length of time'.[127] In 1861 William Neilson Hancock, credited with the foundation of the Dublin Statistical Society in 1847, identified the negative impact of workhouse dependency for artisans in reduced circumstances: 'how much greater must it be in the poor labourer's or artisan's family, where a hus-band's and a father's death means not only the withdrawal of comfort, care, protection, and guidance, but also the stoppage of the means of support'.[128] Despite widows' (with two or more legitimate dependents) eligibility for outdoor relief, Hancock claimed, 'whether these classes get out-door or in-door relief is a matter left entirely to the discretion of the guardians'.[129] Hancock pointed out the vast difference between the provision of outdoor relief in England and that in Ireland: 'on the 25th of April, 1857, there were only 957 persons receiving out-door relief or less than a fiftieth part of the number receiving indoor relief'.[130]

Thus, the DPOS and local PO Societies retained an appeal among respectable but reduced widows who welcomed an alternative to indoor relief provided in workhouses in the north and south of the country. Isabella Tod, the renowned social reformer, emphasised the ill-considered policy of offering respectable people in reduced circumstances only the option of workhouse relief.[131] In workhouses 'respectable' and 'unre-spectable' women tended to be separated to 'prevent moral contamina-tion'.[132] PO Societies, which continued to support 'the family system' as opposed to the placement of orphans in workhouses,[133] therefore met a specific demand for relief from the lower middle class who invested in their children's futures by subscribing to the charity.

In 1879 the Antrim and Down POS reminded its subscribers that it served those children who 'might otherwise have been degraded amid the associations of the workhouse, or have grown up a nuisance to society ... Under the parental care of this Society the children do well, and come out well in the end'.[134] PO Societies also asserted that widows should be 'respected and respectable', which were core artisa-nal values.[135] The avoidance of the 'dreaded workhouse stigma' meant that widows could maintain their respectability which in turn lessened the likelihood of downward social mobility leaving them in better stead to remarry: remarriage was used as a strategy by many widows to re-establish themselves and reunite their families.[136] Class boundaries[137] and levels of respectability determined women's suitability for marriage. While there is evidence that women availed themselves of indoor relief or private charity from sources such as PO Societies it was, neverthe-less, typically a last resort. Despite an increase in the provision of public outdoor relief in Ireland from 6,263 cases in the 1860s to 56,619 in the 1890s,[138] the number of widows in receipt of outdoor relief remained relatively low due to the stigma associated with the acceptance of any form of poor relief.[139]

Child welfare reforms

In 1850 there were 119,628 children in Irish workhouses and by 1853 there were 82,434 under the age of fifteen[140] of whom 5,710 were ille-gitimate and 93 per cent were orphans and deserted children. While there were regular reports of dismal mortality rates among workhouse children, the DPOS boasted consistently low mortality rates, which fell on average below two per cent of the total children on the Society roll in any given year. As discussed in chapter 2, since the passage of the Poor Law, 1838, the DPOS and local PO Societies had endeavoured to draw the public's attention to its successes particularly in relation to the chil-dren's good health and repeatedly held up its system as a superior alter-native to workhouse provision for widows and children. In 1860, for example, the *Christian Examiner* referred to the DPOS recommenda-tion for 'a family system of rearing orphans rather than workhouses'.[141] St Brigid's also advocated the 'family system', compared its system to workhouses, and objected to children's placement in workhouses on medical grounds.[142] However, by the mid-1850s, other Catholic lay orphan associations that boarded out children had been taken over by various religious congregations, after which the institutional model was generally used. In the next twenty-five years, for example, the Sisters of Mercy went on to establish thirty orphanages.[143]

Octavia Hill and Mary Carpenter campaigned to improve conditions for destitute children in England. From the 1850s onwards, the Dublin Statistical Society provided a vital platform for debates on child welfare reforms. Ingram, Hancock, O'Hagan and O'Shaughessy all approved of boarding out for workhouse children. In 1856, Mr Norward, a guard-ian in the North Dublin Union, attempted unsuccessfully to introduce a boarding-out scheme described as an 'enlightened and benevolent proposal'.[144] The North Dublin Union had refused to admit children 'at present in the hands of the police' because 'it would be nearly certain death to receive them into this house'.[145] In its 1857 annual report the DPOS referred to the North Dublin Union case and reminded its subscribers that destitute Protestant orphans 'would have no shelter to fly to but the poorhouse, if the Protestant Orphan Society did not exist!'.[146]

In the late 1850s, Mrs Hannah Archer argued that the placement of children under the age of two in workhouses was detrimental to their health and that such an environment was unsuitable for children due to the long-term negative effects of institutionalisation,[147] conclusions which echoed points raised in DPOS reports from the pre-famine years. Following an examination of the work carried out by PO Societies and St Brigid's, Neilson Hancock concluded that, 'with such an amount of Irish opinion, both Protestant and Roman Catholic, against the workhouse system, the difficulty is to conceive what is to be said in its defence'.[148] Hancock sought the opinion of Revd Eugene O'Meara, DPOS Secretary, on whether the 'family system' implemented by PO Societies would prove useful for workhouse children.[149] O'Meara reported that children's health would be greatly improved if sent to 'the salubrious air of the country', which he considered far more advantageous to bodily health than years spent in union workhouses. He also assured Hancock that many of the children helped by the Society 'have raised themselves to positions of respectability'. Only 5 per cent 'turned out badly' and only 'very few' became criminals. While unable to guarantee that the same system could be successfully applied to workhouses, O'Meara believed that 'the children themselves' and the 'community at large' would benefit.[150] Sir John Arnott, Mayor of Cork, in an investigation into the condition of the Cork workhouse children a year earlier recommended the Cork POS as a model system on which workhouse reform could be based, particularly in relation to the health benefits for children and in light of 'shocking' workhouse child mortality rates.[151] Children were found in deplorable conditions suffering from scrofula and ophthalmia.[152]

At the Social Science Congress held in 1861, lady attendees visited the homes of DPOS nurses and orphans. Greatly impressed by the good care taken of the children, they duly praised the Society's work, which is thought to have 'considerably influenced the introduction of boarding-out arrangements for workhouse children in Ireland and in Britain'.[153] Reformers were able to present a solid argument in favour of boarding out by referring to the DPOS, a reputable charity with almost fifty years of experience, as a tried and tested model.

When asked in 1861 whether he thought it wise to board out work-house children, Mr Nicholas Mahony, Cork Poor Law Guardian, replied, 'Yes; just the same as the Protestant Orphan Society in Cork do, with very good results; the children all turn out very well'.[154] In 1862 the Poor Law (Ireland) Amendment Act was passed,[155] which introduced boarding out for children under five years of age.[156] Archbishop Cullen and the Royal College of Physicians called for amendments and submitted petitions to appeal.[157] Consequently, guardians were empowered to exceed the age limit from five to eight years if children's good health depended on such an extension.[158] However, the Board of Guardians were not compelled to board out children; rather the decision to do so was discretionary.[159]

In 1862, the Earl of Roden restated that the DPOS aimed to encourage independence rather than dependence for children.

> I need hardly suggest to you that whether the child is reared and educated in the workhouse or in the Protestant Orphan Society, the money that supports it comes equally out of our pockets, and the only option you have to choose is whether you will pay poor rates for the bad education of the workhouse and the perversion of its objects, or give a subscription to the Protestant Orphan Society, for good objects and for beneficial results.[160]

The Earl of Roden went on to say that he had witnessed children who had remained in workhouses for numerous years without any hope of a future as 'respectable, independent citizens'.[161] Through the DPOS, Protestants laid the groundwork for an alternative to workhouses for Protestant widows and children, one which did not perpetuate stigma but rather promoted respectability, social mobility and independence.

In 1868 Florence Davenport Hill commended the DPOS for its careful supervision of the orphans whilst boarded out and drew attention to the many health benefits of its system.[162] St Brigid's also received considerable praise:

> Confraternities in the City voluntarily collect the subscriptions; and the inspection is performed by the ladies connected with St. Brigid's. In this latter respect it may even be superior to the Protestant orphanage, for, able and devoted as are the gentleman who visit the little Protestants in their homes, it cannot be disputed that women are, by virtue of their sex, more competent to judge the well-being of children.[163]

As discussed in chapter 3, although DPOS clergymen and committee members acted as local superintendents and official inspectors, clergymen's wives were also expected to take an interest in the orphans' welfare. Moreover, the Limerick POS organised parish ladies' visiting committees from the 1830s.[164]

The 1871 DPOS annual report noted the Statistical Society's acknowledgement and support of its system:

The plan adopted by the Society of locating its orphans in respectable families in the country has received the approval of one of our highest statistical authorities and has by the same authority, been pronounced to be greatly superior to the assembling of children together in one building, under the boarding school system.[165]

In December 1875, the DPOS welcomed further support. The Vice-President of the Statistical and Social Inquiry Society of Ireland, John Ingram, recommended the DPOS system: 'The success of these societies is unquestioned, and is to me the standing and conclusive evidence, that in spite of all allegation to the contrary, the boarding-out system, if properly worked, can be carried out effectively, and made to produce the happiest results'.[166] Ingram recommended an extension of the age limit for boarding out children to thirteen years, which led to legislative reform in 1876.[167]

Two years later, Isabella Tod presented a paper to the British Association for Advancement of Science in August 1878. The paper referred to the report made by Mrs Senior to the Right Hon. James Stansfield, President of the Local Government Board on the district schools that housed girls from London workhouses.[168] (Tod had founded the North of Ireland's Women's Suffrage Association in 1872 and from 1874 Anna and Thomas Haslam, Quakers, began to draw attention to women's suffrage using the *Women's Advocate* as their platform for debate.) Haslam went on to form the Dublin Women's Suffrage Society in 1876. In 1878 Tod called for reforms in the area of outdoor relief and acknowledged the DPOS in her report:

Warned by the errors of the old charter schools, which had just been closed, the Protestant Orphan Society from the first eschewed large buildings and mechanical arrangements, and placed the children in families in the country. The success of this institution is beyond dispute, and as it deals with hundreds at a time, the scale is sufficiently large to be an excellent test of efficiency.[169]

Impartial in her assessment of Catholic and Protestant boarding-out schemes, Tod also praised the work of the Presbyterian Orphan Society, St Brigid's and St Joseph's, 'who have constantly boarded the children in the care among farmers and others in the country, with the best results'.[170] The Presbyterian Orphan Society was indebted to the DPOS for its assistance and advice when the charity first began its charitable work.

In 1889 Florence Davenport Hill put into perspective the true extent of the DPOS's social influence.

The careful organisation of this Society, to which its success is doubtless largely owing, has special interest for the advocates of Boarding-out as now pursued for State children. It was accepted as an example by Mr Greig when more than 40 years ago he modelled the system for the city parish of Edinburgh; and its main features are reproduced in the English Boarding-out Orders of 1870 and 1877.[171]

Mr George Greig, Inspector of the Poor for the city parish of Edinburgh, detailed the 'family system' he had implemented, which was 'chiefly modelled by him upon those devised by the Irish Protestant Orphan Society'.[172] Greig referred to careful nurse selection, the importance placed on inspections, and the removal of children in cases of neglect.[173] Florence Davenport Hill noted 'the success of Scotland in boarding out the children of the state has become proverbial'.[174] By 1869 almost all Scottish workhouse children were boarded out to respectable families.[175] The publicity surrounding the *Orphans of Glenbirkie* raised the Society's profile outside Ireland and perhaps even reached reformers such as Greig in Scotland. The DPOS and local PO Societies were recognised by the highest authorities as having pioneered an outstanding large-scale boarding-out system which became the blueprint for workhouse reforms in Scotland, Ireland and England.

Anti-child cruelty legislation and the Dublin Aid Committee

Dr Curgeven founded the Infant Life Society in 1870 and following a number of 'baby farming' scandals the Infant Life Protection Act[176] was introduced in 1872,[177] under the terms of which people who accepted money for the care of more than one infant were obliged to register their name with the authorities. The Children's Dangerous Performances Act, which prevented children under fourteen from participation in dangerous exhibitions, was passed in 1879. Following continued baby farming scandals, the Prevention of Cruelty and Protection of Children Act[178] was introduced in 1889.[179] The begging clause empowered the police to transfer children to safety. The act was amended in 1897 following a number of high profile cases of criminal baby farming in England and Wales.

The Dublin Aid Committee, which was founded in 1889 by Rosa Barrett, raised public awareness of anti-cruelty legislation and acted as an authority on child welfare issues. Rosa Barrett, social reformer and founder of the Cottage Home for Little Children and the first crèche in Ireland, also had a working relationship with the DPOS: children elected to the DPOS were occasionally sent to Barrett's cottage home.[180]

The Roman Catholic church was initially distrustful of the Dublin Aid Committee, later known as the National Society for the Prevention of Cruelty to Children.

Mrs Elizabeth Leeper, sister of Dr Isabella Mulvany, the renowned long-standing headmistress of Alexandra College, and her husband, Richard Robert Leeper, became prominent members of the NSPCC committee.[181] There was a special fund named the Elizabeth Leeper Clothing Guild, which was still in use in the 1970s. Richard Robert Leeper MD, St Patrick's Hospital, was a progressive force in the field of mental illness: he greatly improved patients' quality of life in a multitude of ways, from rebuilding patient accommodation to nurse training.[182] Richard Leeper was closely related to Revd Canon Alexander Leeper, discussed in the last chapter as being an active member of the Dublin POS and Church Education Society in the 1850s.

In addition, for example, Mrs Black, Blackheath, Clontarf, is listed as a contributor of 'toys, clothes and fruit' and was a member of the NSPCC committee in the early 1890s.[183] Better known as Mrs Gibson Black, Mrs Cecilia Black's husband was the wealthy wine merchant, Mr Gibson Black.[184] His father was Revd Gibson Black, a former secretary of the DPOS, and a highly regarded figure in the 1830s and 1840s. These close connections perhaps provide some insight into the legacy of charitable work which can be traced back to a number of Church of Ireland clergymen, their wives, and to some extent the DPOS.

In a paper presented in 1892, Rosa Barrett raised the issues of parental duties and 'children's rights' in light of the recently carried Prevention of Cruelty to Children bill: 'by means of this law, a parent or guardian if convicted of cruelty endangering the life or health of a child, may be deprived of its custody until the child is fourteen years of age, if a boy, or sixteen years, if a girl. Previously a parent might beat, starve, ill treat, or neglect his child with impunity, and even by neglect kill it, so long as the murder was committed slowly enough, and no one had the power to interfere'.[185] This statement constitutes a firm basis for advancing the argument that the DPOS and local PO Societies acted as private child protection enforcers in the absence of public anti-cruelty measures. Prior to the 1889 act, as Barrett argues, parents could treat their children as they wished without punishment.

If children were neglected, exploited, beaten by their own parents, to whom could they turn? POS orphans were inspected, clergymen and their families were responsible for their care; they were monitored in school and Sunday school, and more likely to receive medical attention. The committees comprised both religious and lay representatives and all were accountable to the subscribers, and to the children's relatives.

Conclusion

Local PO Societies were founded in the second half of the nineteenth century because Protestants opposed the placement of Protestant widows and children in workhouses for three main reasons: first, the likelihood that Protestant orphans would change their religion rather than endure persecution; second, widows' respectability was compromised; and, third, on medical grounds: children's physical development was stunted, fresh country air was medically recommended to improve health, and workhouses reported high infant and child mortality rates. Archbishop Cullen and Margaret Aylward also publicly objected to the placement of children in workhouses. Social reformers commended the DPOS and St Brigid's boarding-out orphanage in equal measure, and from a social perspective and in spite of allegations of proselytism and the religious competition which divided them, both charities were convinced of the advantages of boarding out and both undoubtedly contributed to workhouse reforms. The next chapter analyses the DPOS system in practice to determine whether it merited such widespread support.

Notes

1 J. Ingram, 'The organisation of charity and education of the children of the state', *JSSISI*, 40:57 (Winter 1875), pp. 449–73, p. 462.
2 O. Rafferty, *The Catholic Church and the Protestant State* (Dublin, Portland: Four Courts Press, 2008), p. 70.
3 Moffitt, *Irish Church Missions*, p. 20.
4 *Missions in Ireland: Especially with reference to the Proselytising Movement* (Dublin: J. Duffy, 1855), p. 34.
5 *Ibid.*, p. 70.
6 Moffitt, *Irish Church Missions*, p. 20.
7 'Popery, abroad and at home', *Belfast News-letter* (24 September 1852).
8 *Belfast News-letter* (8 October 1852).
9 Moffitt, *Irish Church Missions*, p. 98.
10 E. Maguire, *Roman Catholic Proselytisers Met and Answered: Recollections of a Visit to Lyons in 1858* (Dublin: Curry, 1858), p. 8.
11 *Ibid.*
12 See introduction of *The Orphans of Glenbirkie*, p. 19.
13 See J. Prunty, 'Battle plans and battlegrounds: Protestant mission activity in the Dublin slums, 1840–1880', in C. Gribben and A. Holmes (eds), *Protestant Millennialism, Evangelicalism and Irish Society, 1790–2005* (Basingstoke: Palgrave Macmillan, 2006), pp. 119–43, p. 132.
14 Kinealy and MacAtasney, *The Hidden Famine*, p. 135.
15 D. Bryan 'Ellen Smyly', *Dictionary of Irish Biography*.
16 Acheson, *History of the Church of Ireland*, p. 199.

17 Moffitt, *Irish Church Missions*, p. 149.
18 *Ibid.*, p. 152.
19 Prunty, *Margaret Aylward*, p. 22.
20 Prunty, 'Battle plans and battlegrounds', p. 136.
21 *Ibid.*, p. 119.
22 D. Bowen, *Paul, Cardinal Cullen and the Shaping of Modern Irish Catholicism* (Wilfrid Laurier University Press, 1983), p. 175.
23 *Freeman's Journal* (18 July 1856).
24 D. A. Kerr, *A Nation of Beggars? Priests, People, and Politics in Famine Ireland, 1846–1852* (Oxford: Oxford University Press, 1998), p. 324.
25 Prunty, *Dublin Slums*, p. 305.
26 Robins, *Lost Children*, p. 127.
27 Prunty, *Margaret Aylward*, p. 59.
28 A. Clarke, 'Orphans and the Poor Law: rage against the machine', in V. Crossman and P. Gray (eds), *Poverty and Welfare in Ireland, 1838–1948* (Dublin: Irish Academic Press, 2011), pp. 97–114, pp. 103–4.
29 *Irish Times* (14 April 1860), book of press cuttings, NAI, POS papers, 1045/6/1.
30 *Ibid.*
31 K. D. McCarthy, *Women, Philanthropy, and Civil Society* (Indiana: Indiana University Press, 2001), p. 21.
32 See Prunty, 'Battle plans and battlegrounds', p. 135.
33 St Brigid's Orphanage annual report, 1864, TCD, OLS B3 744 no. 1, p. 18.
34 J. Prunty, 'Mobility among women in nineteenth century Dublin', in D. J. Siddle (ed.), *Migration, Mobility, and Modernization* (Liverpool: Liverpool University Press, 2000), pp. 131–63, p. 147.
35 Prunty, *Margaret Aylward*, p. 75.
36 Minutes, 27 Mar. 1830, NAI, POS papers, 1045/2/1/1.
37 *Irish Times* (5 April 1862).
38 Registered application files, NAI, CPOU papers, 1045/11/2 (284–99).
39 *Irish Times* (12 June 1863).
40 *Irish Times* (6 March 1890).
41 *Irish Times* (27 July 1861).
42 Bowen, *Protestant Crusade*, pp. 264–5.
43 S. J. Connolly, *Religion and Society in Nineteenth-century Ireland* (Dundalk: Dundalgan Press, 1985), p. 27; see also, O. P. Rafferty, *Catholicism in Ulster, 1603–1983: An Interpretative History* (Columbia: University of South Carolina Press, 1994), p. 139.
44 Registered applications, 1850–60, NAI, CPOU papers, 1045/11/2.
45 *Irish Times* (8 April 1863).
46 *Ibid.*
47 Prunty, *Dublin Slums*, p. 243.
48 Minutes, 16 Sept. 1859, NAI, POS papers, 1045/2/1/6, p. 285.
49 *Ibid.*, p. 284.

50 *Ibid.*, p. 287.
51 *Ibid.*
52 St Brigid's Orphanage annual report, 1864, TCD, OLS B3 744, no. 1, p. 18.
53 Registered applications, NAI, CPOU papers, 1045/11/2 (423–50).
54 *Ibid.*
55 *Ibid.*
56 See for a full account of the case, Prunty, *Margaret Aylward*, pp. 91–101.
57 St Brigid's Orphanage annual report, 1863, TCD, OLS B3 744, no. 1, p. 6.
58 *Freeman's Journal* (18 April 1863).
59 *Ibid.*
60 *Ibid.*
61 Robins, *Lost Children*, pp. 252–3.
62 Acheson, *History of the Church of Ireland*, p. 199.
63 *Irish Ecclesiastical Gazette* (15 Aug. 1860).
64 *Ibid.*
65 Robins, *Lost Children*, pp. 252–3.
66 *Ibid.*, p. 193.
67 DPOS report, *Irish Times* (23 November 1861).
68 Robins, *The Miasma: Epidemic and Panic*, p. 204.
69 *Ibid.*
70 Minutes, 29 Sept. 1854, NAI, POS papers, 1045/2/1/2, p. 291.
71 'Donegal POS', *Belfast News-letter* (26 June 1896).
72 'Donegal POS', *Belfast News-letter* (27 August 1864).
73 'Donegal POS', *Belfast News-letter* (16 August 1882).
74 *Irish Times* (23 November 1861).
75 *Ibid.*
76 R. B. McDowell, *The Church of Ireland: 1869–1969* (London: Routledge, 1975), p. 25.
77 Prunty, 'Battle plans and battlegrounds', p. 135.
78 Robins, *The Miasma: Epidemic and Panic,* p. 206.
79 *Belfast News-letter* (7 March 1868).
80 DPOS annual report, 1866, NAI, POS papers, 1045/1/1/37–42, p. 15.
81 *Ibid.*, p. 18.
82 *Belfast News-letter* (8 November 1867).
83 *Ibid.*
84 *Ibid.*
85 'Armagh POS', *Belfast News-letter* (27 October 1876).
86 Athey, 'A short history of the Meath Protestant Orphan Society', p. 8.
87 Minutes, 1 Apr. 1870, NAI, POS papers, 1045/2/1/8, p. 209.
88 Acheson, *History of the Church of Ireland*, p. 132.
89 DPOS annual report, 1873, NAI, POS papers, 1045/1/1/43–9, pp. 16–17.
90 R. Clarke, 'The clergy and disestablishment', in Bernard and Neely (eds), *The Clergy of the Church of Ireland*, pp. 169–85, p. 170.
91 *Ibid.*, p. 182.

92 *Ibid.*

93 K. Milne, 'Disestablishment and its lay response', in Gillespie and Neely (eds), *The Laity and the Church of Ireland*, pp. 226–49, p. 249.

94 Minutes, 1867–72, NAI, POS papers, 1045/2/1/8, p. 365.

95 Documents relating to the Kinsey Marriage Portion Fund, NAI, POS papers, 1045/4/8/7.

96 'A Windfall for Auckland', *Auckland Star* (15 July 1872), p. 2.

97 This quote refers to a Limerick POS lady subscriber, see Massy, *Footprints of a Faithful Shepherd*, pp. 429–33, p. 430.

98 *Ibid.*, pp. 429–33.

99 *Ibid.*, p. 432.

100 See M. Cronin, '"You'd be disgraced!": middle-class women and respectability in post famine Ireland', in F. Lane (ed.), *Politics, Society and the Middle Class in Modern Ireland* (Basingstoke, New York: Palgrave Macmillan, 2010), pp. 107–29, p. 111; see also, Enright, '"Take this Child"'.

101 'Fermanagh POS', *Irish Times* (9 August 1865).

102 *Belfast News-letter* (12 November 1867).

103 'Armagh POS Bazaar', *Belfast News-letter* (4 December 1890).

104 Massy, *Footprints of a Faithful Shepherd*, p. 438.

105 Cavan POS annual report, 1855, NLI.

106 J. Crawford, *St Catherine's Parish Dublin, 1840–1890: Portrait of a Church of Ireland Community* (Dublin: Irish Academic Press, 1996), p. 43.

107 See L. Lunney, 'William Alexander', *Dictionary of Irish Biography*; see also N. Vance, *Irish Literature since 1800* (London: Longman Publishing Group. 2002), p. 258.

108 W. G. Neely, 'The laity in a changing society', in Gillespie and Neely (eds), *The Laity and the Church of Ireland*, pp. 196–225, p. 214.

109 *Tuam Herald* (27 April 1867).

110 'Cavan POS', *Irish Times* (6 July 1863).

111 *Ibid.*

112 *Belfast News-letter* (9 March 1876).

113 'Armagh POS Bazaar', *Belfast News-letter* (4 December 1890).

114 *Belfast News-letter* (7 March 1868).

115 Tyrone POS annual report, 1877, p. 11, NLI.

116 Revd J. Gregg, *Misery and Mercy: A Sermon Preached in Trinity Church on Sunday, January 13, 1850 in aid of the Protestant Orphan Society* (Dublin: William Curry, 1850), p. 12.

117 H. Andrews, 'Gregg, John', *Dictionary of Irish Biography*.

118 R. S. Gregg, *Memorials of the Life of John Gregg, D.D.* (Dublin: George Herbert, 1879), p. 100.

119 DPOS annual report, 1859, NAI, POS papers, 1045/1/1/29–33, pp. 14–15.

120 *Irish Times* (30 July 1864).

121 'Fermanagh POS', *Irish Times* (9 August 1865).

122 See Moffitt, *Irish Church Missions*, p. 87.

123 Massy, *Footprints of a Faithful Shepherd*, p. 334.

124 Williams, *Barnardo*, pp. 22–5.

125 L. Murdoch, *Imagined Orphans: Poor Families, Child Welfare, and Contested Citizenship in London* (New Brunswick, NJ: Rutgers University Press, 2006), p. 41.

126 *Ibid.*, p. 41.

127 O. Purdue, 'Poverty and power: the Irish Poor Law in a north Antrim town, 1861–1921', *Irish Historical Studies*, 37:148 (2011), pp. 567–83, p. 578.

128 W. N. Hancock, 'The difference between the English and Irish Poor Law as to the treatment of women and unemployed workmen', *JSSISI*, 3:18 (1861), pp. 217–34, p. 228.

129 *Ibid.*, p. 224.

130 W. N. Hancock, 'On the importance of substituting the family system of rearing orphan children for the system now pursued in our workhouses', *JSSISI*, 2:13 (1859), pp. 317–33, p. 329.

131 See V. Crossman, 'Welfare and nationality: the poor laws in nineteenth-century Ireland', in S. King and J. Stewart (eds), *Welfare Peripheries: The Development of Welfare States in Nineteenth and Twentieth Century Europe* (Bern: Peter Lang, 2007), pp. 67–96, p. 89.

132 M. Luddy, '"Angels of mercy": nuns as workhouse nurses, 1861–1898', in Jones and Malcolm (eds), *Medicine, Disease and the State in Ireland*, pp. 102–17, p. 107.

133 *Christian Examiner* (December 1860), book of press cuttings, NAI, POS papers 1045/6/1.

134 *Belfast News-letter* (18 October 1879).

135 J. R. Farr, *Artisans in Europe, 1300–1914* (Cambridge: Cambridge University Press, 2000), p. 283.

136 Cases in registers orphan histories, NAI, POS papers, 1045/5/1/1–13.

137 Cronin, '"You'd be disgraced!"', p. 112–13.

138 V. Crossman, *Politics, Pauperism and Power in Late Nineteenth-Century Ireland* (Manchester: Manchester University Press, 2006), pp. 11–18, p. 12.

139 M. Cullen, 'Widows in Ireland, 1830–1970', in Bourke (ed.), *Field Day Anthology of Irish Writing*, pp. 609–18, p. 610.

140 Robins, *Lost Children*, p. 193.

141 *Christian Examiner* (December 1860), book of press cuttings, NAI, POS papers 1045/6/1.

142 Prunty, *Margaret Aylward*, p. 64.

143 Robins, *Lost Children*, p. 294.

144 Hancock, 'On the importance of substituting the family system', p. 326.

145 *Ibid.*

146 *Ibid.*

147 George, *Foster Care*, p. 7.

148 Hancock, 'On the importance of substituting the family system', p. 328.
149 *Ibid.*, p. 329.
150 *Ibid.*
151 Sir J. Arnott, Mayor of Cork, *The Investigation into the Condition of the Children in the Cork Workhouse with an Analysis of the Evidence* (Cork: Guy Brothers, 1859), p. 41.
152 Clarke, 'Orphans and the Poor Law', p. 101.
153 Robins, *Lost Children*, p. 272.
154 *Report from the Select Committee on Poor Relief (Ireland) 1861*, HC 1861 (408), vol. xx.
155 Robins, *Lost Children*, p. 273.
156 J. K. Ingram, 'A comparison between the English and Irish Poor Laws with respect to the conditions of relief', *JSSISI*, 4:27 (1864), pp. 43–61, p. 57.
157 Robins, *Lost Children*, p. 273.
158 Ingram, 'Comparison between the English and Irish Poor Laws', p. 57.
159 Robins, *Lost Children*, p. 275.
160 *Irish Times* (5 April 1862).
161 *Ibid.*
162 Davenport Hill, *Children of the State* (1st edn 1868), pp. 132–5.
163 *Ibid.*, p. 137.
164 Reference to 1837 LPOS annual report, Massy, *Footprints of a Faithful Shepherd*, pp. 346–65, p. 347, p. 365; see also Enright, '"Take this child"', p. 42.
165 DPOS annual report, 1871, NAI, POS papers, 1045/1/1/37–42.
166 Ingram, 'The organisation of charity and education', p. 462.
167 Robins, *Lost Children*, p. 280.
168 I. Tod, 'Boarding out of pauper children', *Journal of the British Association for Advancement of Science*, 54 (1878), pp. 293–8.
169 *Ibid.*, p. 295.
170 *Ibid.*
171 F. Davenport Hill, F. Fowke (ed.), *Children of the State* (London: Macmillan and Co., 1889), p. 148.
172 *Ibid.*, p. 156.
173 *The Medical Record*, 7 (1872), p. 487.
174 Davenport Hill, Fowke (ed.), *Children of the State*, p. 155.
175 R. Parker, *Uprooted: The Shipment of Poor Children to Canada, 1867–1917* (Bristol: The Policy Press, 2010), p. 30.
176 35 & 36 Vic., c. 38
177 Luddy, *Women and Philanthropy*, p. 92.
178 52 & 53 Vic., c. 44.
179 R. M. Barrett, 'Legislation on behalf of neglected children in America and elsewhere', *JSSISI* 9:72 (1892), pp. 616–31, p. 618.
180 Minutes, 1890s, NAI, POS papers, 1045/2/1/13.
181 NSPCC annual reports, NLI.

182 L. Lunney, 'Richard McClelland-Leeper, Richard Leech', *Dictionary of Irish Biography*.
183 *Irish Times* (15 April 1893).
184 'Will of Mr. Gibson Black', *Irish Times* (23 March 1889); parish records; Lunney, 'Richard McClelland-Leeper, Richard Leech'.
185 Barrett, 'Legislation on behalf of neglected children', p. 618.

5

Bereaved families and boarded-out children, 1850–98

They were put into families where they found another father and another mother, and had an opportunity of mixing with children of their age. They were not drilled like soldiers, as they would be in an institution; they were simply treated like members of the family.[1]

Introduction

Despite the general rise in living standards, widowhood remained a defining period for women and their families due to poorly paid and often scarce employment, and the burden of dependents. While some widows managed to find work, remarried or emigrated, for others the heavy responsibility of providing for their families alone, and often unexpectedly, caused mental and physical decline; children were also deeply affected by bereavement and separation from their mothers. Through case history analysis, this chapter closely examines the difficult period of bereavement, the chain of circumstances that led widows to seek relief from PO Societies, which by 1870 had a presence in every county in Ireland, and the effects of such upheaval for children. It assesses the boarding-out environment in which children were placed, and, using the Dublin POS as a case study, establishes whether the system was as effective in practice as in theory.

Bereaved families: applicants

PO Societies generally received applications from the families of professionals, artisans, and semi-skilled and unskilled workers. During the period from 1877 to 1894, the Tyrone POS received applications from widows of labourers (44 per cent), farmers (10 per cent), shoemakers (7 per cent), weavers (5 per cent), soldiers (almost 3 per cent), school masters (2 per cent), blacksmiths (2 per cent), and servants (2 per cent).[2] Other occupations included bakers, coopers, plumbers, scutchers and sawyers.

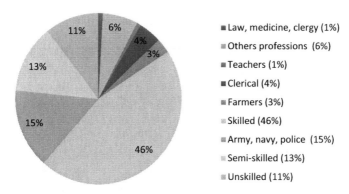

Figure 5.1 DPOS applicants' occupational profile, 1850–98.
Source: Register of applications, 1850–98, NAI, POS papers, 1045/5/2/2–4.

The DPOS received applications from the widows of soldiers, labourers, shoemakers, carpenters, weavers, tailors and servants; clerks, farmers, artists, architects/civil engineers, chandlers, chemists, Church of Ireland clergymen, Presbyterian ministers, dairymen, hatters, lawyers, and japanners, violinists and band masters. Just as in the first half of the nineteenth century, there is evidence to suggest that a number of families had experienced a reduction in circumstances prior to bereavement due to declines in their husbands' trades.[3] The children of high ranking policemen – acting inspector of police, the inspector of the Metropolitan Police, and police sergeants – as well as police constables were among those also admitted. See figure 5.1.

There was a strong military presence in Dublin throughout the nineteenth century and the DPOS served a percentage of these families, many of whom originated from England, Wales and Scotland.[4] The 1863 return of judicial statistics in Ireland states that there were 12,337 members of the constabulary in Ireland with 1,079 in the Dublin Metropolitan Police, 538 in Tipperary and 152 in Londonderry.[5] By 1870 Catholics represented almost three-quarters of the police force, primarily in the lower ranks.[6]

The records of the Monaghan, Cork, Belfast, Tipperary, Londonderry, Tyrone and Dublin PO Societies[7] suggest that with few exceptions, widows were left 'unprovided for' and 'utterly destitute'. The seeming lack of provision was largely attributable to the sudden deaths of their often very young husbands. Causes of death ranged from duty in the Crimean War (1854–56) to work-related accidents; for example, an engine driver was killed in the 'Trillick Outrage', on the Derry and Enniskillen Railway, Friday 15 September 1854 which left four orphans.[8] (The Employer's Liability Act was passed in 1880 and the Workmen's Compensation Act in 1897.)

The incidence of consumption (TB) in Ireland had exceeded English and Scottish figures in 1866; fevers, and the cholera epidemics of 1853 and 1866 also produced many young widows. In one such case, a slater and plasterer by trade, resident of Kingstown, Dublin, who had kept his wife and two daughters 'in comfortable circumstances' during his lifetime, died 'after a very few hours illness'.[9] Other causes of death included general ill health, in a minor number of cases improper medical care, and age. In 1861 it was reported that in Dublin, the average life expectancy for the artisan class was twenty years and the wealthier classes forty-eight years.[10]

Work for widows

The female industrial movement, which was particularly active in the early 1850s, increased employment for women; for example, in Dublin women produced embroidery and plainwork, and sewed muslin,[11] work which was intended to have a moralising effect on the lower classes.[12] Mrs Jellico, a Quaker, and founder of the Queen's Institute, 1861, and Alexandra College, Dublin, 1866, and committed campaigner for women's inclusion in university education,[13] reported on Dublin factories in 1862, noting that one factory alone employed 400 women and girls.[14] Jellico concluded that needlework in all its forms was a substantial source of employment for women 'from the tradesman's daughter ... to the reduced gentlewoman, striving to eke out a meagre existence'.[15] Women with dependents tended not to engage in home-work, and those who did were scarcely able to survive on the wages which were considerably lower than those in factories.[16] However, as it was socially unacceptable for middle-class women to work outside the home, taking up homework helped to preserve the respectability of widows in reduced circumstances at least in the short term.[17] In the years after 1871 there was a decrease in the number of women recorded in census returns as having a separate occupation from their husbands; they were accounted for as 'non-productive'.[18]

By admitting their children to the DPOS, widows from Dublin, and other parts of the country including the north, where the textile trade was booming and needle work 'very remunerative', could obtain higher paid factory work. (Until the foundation of local PO Societies in the north, children were placed under the guardianship of the DPOS.) A number of widows who applied to the DPOS recorded their occupations as plainworkers, needlewomen and dressmakers.[19]

In many DPOS applications, widows were recorded as having no occupation; for example, the entries read 'mother' or 'mother, no occupation', while in other cases, women shared the same occupation as their husbands – father's occupation 'umbrella maker' and mother's occupation 'mother and umbrella maker'.[20] Domestic service was a highly represented occupation among widows at the time of their application to the DPOS. Widows also worked as housekeepers, nurses, teachers, charwomen and laundresses, albeit in fewer numbers.

As discussed in chapter 3, the DPOS, those who applied on behalf of widows, and the widows themselves recommended that if the youngest dependents were admitted to the Society, widows would be free to 'earn their bread'. Records from emigration schemes such as Barnardo's contain numerous cases in which widows sent their children to the homes because they could not secure day care.[21] By admitting one or all of their children to the DPOS,[22] or local PO Societies, particularly their youngest dependents, whether temporary or long term, overburdened widows could work, migrate or emigrate. As Maria Luddy suggests for women, 'in order to engage in remunerative and rewarding work they had to leave the country'.[23]

The following cases support the view that if relieved of their youngest dependents, widows could re-establish themselves with a certain degree of independence. A Cork widow was assisted by local people to 'open up a little shop' after her husband, a soldier, died of consumption in the trenches of Sebastol during the Crimean War (1854–56).[24] The Cork POS admitted her younger dependents.

In 1880 a widow admitted her two daughters, aged eight and five, and one boy aged six to the DPOS. At the time of her application she recorded her occupation as a stewardess on the SS *Lady Olive*. Mrs – had two addresses, one in London and one in Dublin, depending on where the ship was anchored – 'SS *Lady Olive*, North Wall, Dublin or SS *Lady Olive*, Millers Warf, Smithfield, London'.[25] The DPOS case file register documents the widow's employment history while her children were under its care, first as a nurse in the Adelaide Hospital in 1881, then in 1883 as a nurse in Sir Patrick Dun's Hospital, and finally in 1885 as a nurse in the North Dublin Union.[26] In cases of this kind, PO Societies represented a substitute for, or an extension of, kin support networks. Furthermore, other widows admitted their children to a local PO Society on a temporary basis until they could afford to emigrate with the whole family. The Newry POS reported a case of this kind in September 1874 when a widow removed her daughter from its care and emigrated to America.[27]

Widows as nurses to their own children

While many widows requested that the Dublin POS (DPOS) admit their youngest dependents, in other cases widows refused to part with any of their children. As early as 1855, a lady subscriber to the DPOS advised, 'it may perhaps be as well to mention that the Monkstown Protestant Orphan Society has consented in several cases, to permit the surviving parent to have charge of the child'.[28] Other local PO Societies also permitted children to remain with their mothers in specific cases. The Cork POS stated in 1859 that 'in former years the committee felt it their duty not to commit the care of the orphans in any case to their mothers. It was, no doubt, a sure way of testing their destitution. The harsh and painful course is no longer pursued by the Society; if the mother be a member of the Church, of unexceptionable character, and possessed of some means of livelihood, she is intrusted with the care of her own child'.[29] However, it soon encountered difficulties and though it continued to provide widows with grants, at times it doubted the propriety of its decision, particularly in light of the inferior housing, and unhealthy surroundings in which some widows lived.

Nevertheless, the Cork POS also reported excellent results; for example, in 1888, it told of a widow who was given charge of her children, 'a most industrious woman' who was 'paying off some debts',[30] and 'making a hand first to retain her farm for her boys; she has taught her elder child to milk and make butter'.[31] The widow later stated that 'the Society's help is what kept her on her farm and she is deeply grateful for it'.[32] The Tyrone POS confirmed in 1877 that mothers could nurse their children until they were three years old and in other 'peculiar circumstances'.[33]

A DPOS subscriber argued against the policy change adopted by local PO Societies, claiming that widows would be prevented from finding employment and that bereaved families in poor circumstances could not provide their children with adequate care if dependent solely on the relatively small grants provided. The DPOS had always allowed children to remain with their mothers in infancy (the length of their stay depended on the widow's individual circumstances and the children's health). Moreover, the committee granted 86.6 per cent of written requests from mothers and extended kin to visit with their children during the period 1 July 1868 to 23 December 1869,[34] and allowed children to remain with their mother in certain cases. In 1883 the DPOS indicated that it had temporarily relaxed the rule on children's removal from their mothers but later reverted to the 'old rule' which it adhered to until the late nineteenth century.[35]

The Donegal POS debated the possible rule change at an annual meeting in 1890, at which many ladies were present. One speaker claimed the existing system was unfair to mothers and to children: 'it very seriously loosened the ties that should bind a mother to her child'.[36] The committee subsequently agreed to rescind the rule; however, in 1892, following a number of difficulties, the committee revised its policy again. Thereafter, discretionary powers were given to the committee to decide on a case-by-case basis whether children should be left in the care of their mothers or relatives and paid an allowance, a decision which proved unpopular with subscribers as evidenced in the decline in support reported the following year.[37] By 1896 the Donegal POS had placed 45 out of 61 children with their mothers and grandmothers and boarded out the remaining orphans.[38]

Widows' physical health

There were a number of advances in public health which improved life expectancy in the second half of the nineteenth century: the Medical Charities (Ireland) Act, 1851 (also known as the Dispensary Act), under the terms of which the Poor Law Commission became the central authority for a countrywide system of dispensaries; the Medical Registration Act, 1858; the first Medical Officer of Health, 1864; the Sanitary Act, 1866; Public Health (Ireland) Acts 1874 and 1878; and compulsory registration of births, deaths and marriages, introduced in 1879.[39]

It was relatively common for widows to become physically and mentally ill following the death of their husbands, the major breadwinners, which thwarted the best efforts of otherwise willing and able mothers to provide for their families. The esteemed doctor, William Wilde, ophthalmic surgeon of St Mark's Hospital, whose name features on the Dublin POS collections lists, reported in the 1851 census that 'over 53,000 women, or 1 in 63, of the total female population, were classed as sick'.[40] Women were also underrepresented as hospital patients. Despite women's ill health, it was also likely that women were generally the primary care-givers to their husbands when sick and that they were reliant on state medical care and charity whilst men had better means to access superior medical care if required.[41]

A widow in Cork cared for her husband until he passed away and just as she herself was close to death. He had worked as 'confidential clerk and manager' and died of consumption.[42] The Cork POS inspector visited the widow: 'she is now in very delicate health with a young family thrown upon her for support while she is quite unable to do anything for them and is rapidly hastening toward her end being in

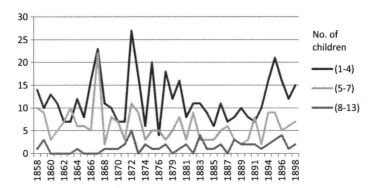

Figure 5.2 Children in household at time of bereavement, DPOS applicants, 1858–98.
Source: Register of applications, 1858–98, NAI, POS papers, 1045/5/2/2–4.

consumption'.[43] In his report, the inspector referred to the fact that this
widow had herself been raised by the Cork POS; she had completed
training as a dressmaker, and received a good conduct premium and a
marriage portion.

While many widows were in a position to work in some capacity, for
those with many dependents, no support networks, in poor physical
or mental health, there were limited options and thus more tragic outcomes. On average, at the time of bereavement there were four children
in every family who applied to the DPOS from 1858 to 1898; records
also show that in certain cases there were between eight and thirteen
children in the family at the time of bereavement.[44] In larger families,
elder siblings, if old enough to work, were viewed as contributors rather
than dependents. The children's age determined their usefulness in the
family. These figures shed light on the level of burden under which
widows struggled. See figure 5.2.

The available evidence suggests that many widows endured great
hardship rather than accept charity and often neglected their own health
to provide for their families. In 1855 the DPOS received a letter from a
clergyman in Wicklow which stated, 'The destitution of the mother is as
great as it was. The poor creature's illness was brought on by exposure
and overwork in walking to Wicklow, nine miles off, and returning
with fish generally carried on her head. By the sale of eggs and fruit she
earned a few pence for her family'.[45] The rector stated as the weather
had been 'very cold and wet', he had 'forewarned' her to slow down
and that she would become ill if she persisted. He said 'during the late
snow the family would have starved except for some aid I supplied and I
am now employing one of the girls about the yard'.[46] The same year,

another Protestant widow was 'in consumption scarcely able to leave her bed'. She was 'hardly able to procure them bread, being from illness neither capable of needle or the necessary household work'.[47] In many similar cases widows did not seek assistance unless compelled to do so out of urgent necessity.

A widow admitted her infant daughter to the DPOS in May 1881 and updated the secretary, Mr Jepps, of her circumstances on 14 January 1882:

> I write to let you know that I have changed my residence I left my situation in Spencer Hill, Eglinton Park on the first of December and have obtained the present situation this month. I hope you are quite well and all your family. I saw you one day in Dublin and I waited a long time to get to speak with you, but you were engaged speaking with a gentleman at the corner of Grafton Street and you walked on with him, so I was disappointed. Dear sir, it is rather late for me, but I must wish you a happy new year. P.S. I am happy to hear that Mrs – has another orphan she will be a good comrade for my little – I hope soon to be able to go see her. I am sure she has grown very tall.[48]

At the time the letter was written, Mrs – was healthy enough to work; however, four years later, by 20 January 1886, her circumstances had deteriorated dramatically. The committee noted, 'mother in Baggot Street Hospital suffering from cancer'.[49] Just under two weeks earlier, the widow's daughter had been sent to lodge in Dublin. Less than three months later, by 9 April 1886, the widow had passed away in the South Dublin Union. The DPOS arranged for her daughter's admission to the Female Orphan House on 7 June 1886.

Depending on their individual circumstances, widows were often overwhelmed to the point of mental as well as physical collapse by the pressure to provide for their families alone.[50] In 1861 it was reported that there were 554 married, 1,617 unmarried, and 204 widowed women in Irish lunatic asylums.[51] The Inspectors of Lunacy observed that in widowhood, 'the woman, deprived of her natural support, and thrown perhaps on the world, must feel her position more acutely than a man correspondingly situated'.[52]

A number of widows who were with child or who had recently given birth applied to the DPOS for assistance. The *Dublin Journal of Medical Science* contains references to widows whose husbands' deaths caused a corresponding decline in their health. 'M.D., aged 30; second pregnancy; admitted in very low spirits and extremely weak, her husband having died a week before, leaving her in a state of great privation'.[53] The widow delivered a baby girl but died twenty-five days later.[54]

In the early 1890s the DPOS admitted four siblings under the age of nine, the youngest just months old. The children's mother, aged forty, was unwell at the time and subsequently admitted to the Richmond District Lunatic Asylum after she threatened 'to destroy herself'. (Mrs – had been admitted to the Richmond for the first time four years earlier.) 'Domestic trouble and heredity' were the supposed causes of insanity. On her admission the widow was described as having a 'sorrowful face':

> idiotically laughing, worn features, sunken eyes, dishevelled appearance are presented by this woman, as she sits gazing vacantly with mouth parted and vacuous smile. Her story is a sad one, of a marriage to a drunkard, large family, [and] hard work … [Her husband] died here about two months ago, and she considers that a good riddance. But she is anxious about the children who are left in poverty and neglect consumed with evil sights and smells. Whilst she felt herself inclined to commit suicide, urged by some irresistible influence, and she confesses she often said she would do it.[55]

(In addition to the younger children admitted to the DPOS, Mrs – also had older children who were likely to have been beyond the DPOS age limit. She appears to have been most concerned for the welfare of these older children who could not be admitted to the Society and who were therefore left unprovided for.) Within weeks of her admission, the medical officer reported that the widow began to 'realize the isolation of her position amongst people whom she calls "unreasoning idiots", but her language follows no coherent order, her judgement in no way improved'.[56] The following year she attacked a matron, which was considered out of character for a woman generally regarded as 'harmless'. In the months that followed, the medical officer noted that after the widow was informed of her eldest son's death, she became 'dull and depressed' and refused food for a time. DPOS records also state that her youngest daughter died of 'convulsions'. (The child's death was likely to have occurred during teething.) The widow, who 'was constantly in bed', died in the asylum of suspected phthisis less than a year later.[57]

There seems little doubt that the practical rather than emotional implications of her husband's death caused a rapid deterioration in the widow's health and exacerbated a pre-existing illness. The birth of her youngest daughter in the months before her husband's death was also likely to have been a contributory factor in her decline. Moreover, the widow clearly expressed acute anxiety over her children's future wellbeing given the family's reduced circumstances. The consequent separation from her children and the later death of her eldest son and youngest daughter also caused her immense distress. Following the widow's own death, a relative adopted her other young daughter and her two young sons remained with their DPOS nurse until apprenticed. Without the assistance of the DPOS and a relative, the children would most probably have become dependent on the union workhouse.

Boarded-out children

In 1869 Florence Davenport Hill, social reformer, outlined the system of 'modern boarding out':

> boarding-out seeks before all things to preserve life ... the foster-parent is invited to share in a benevolent action ... profit, if considered at all, is a minor object, and the payment is so regulated as to prevent the children being taken as a source of gain ... boarding-out challenges the utmost publicity ... boarding-out is entrusted to those alone whose character is above suspicion ... boarding-out involves, as an essential feature, close and constant supervision ... the boarded-out child must daily attend school, and thus come under the constant notice of persons who would not hesitate to proclaim any sign of ill-treatment they might observe.[58]

As discussed in chapters 3 and 4, PO Societies laid the foundations for this model and continued to improve its system.

The idea of 'domestic bliss' in the middle-class family was enshrined in evangelical Protestant teaching influenced by the romantic era and espoused by preachers such as Revd John Gregg. In a sermon he preached on behalf of the DPOS in 1850, Gregg observed:

> Was there ever yet painted a perfect scene of pure domestic bliss, whether with pencil or with pen, in poetry or in prose, in which children did not form part of the picture? Would not every family scene be imperfect without them? I need not tell the virtuous brother and the affectionate sister, grown up to mature life, how the happiness of the home and the attraction of the fireside is owing to engaging and playful children. Many a harsh tone is arrested and corrected by their joyous voices ringing through the house. The saddest scene will be relieved by their playfulness, and the brow of care relaxed by their smiles. This is so in the families of the rich. But children have, in my mind, a peculiar interest and charm in lowly and virtuous life. I do not know that I enjoy anything more than to visit, as I am sometimes called upon to do, an humble dwelling where I know that peace and truth reside. In such the little children have their places, they are loved as tenderly, and watched as carefully, as in more wealthy homes.[59]

Gregg's words shed light on mid-nineteenth century attitudes toward children and the family.

Figure 5.3 DPOS nurse and orphan c. 1880s to 1890s.

PO Societies aimed to provide the orphans with the ideal concept of family life as described by Gregg. To this end, the Dublin POS continued to approach the entrustment of children to nurses with great caution. A DPOS inspector reported in 1853, 'the people seem kind and I am sure the children would be treated as members of the family and well fed'.[60] An inspector said of one applicant, 'I believe that she would pay special attention to their moral and religious training and take the place of a mother to the orphans as far any one could do so'.[61] Another observed, 'she is a careful motherly woman'.[62] Other nurses were referred to as 'decent', 'respectable', 'pious people'.[63] There is also evidence that the same 'good nurses' were kept on by the Society for a number of years; letters of recommendation shed light on the committee's gradual development of trust for nurses: 'she has taken very good care of the two already entrusted to her, I can with confidence recommend her'.[64] Over time, the inspectors came to depend on a network of reliable and respectable families.

Clergymen closely observed the manner in which prospective nurses treated their own children. However, given that many of the children retained ties with their mothers and extended kin,[65] the nurses and their families were not typically expected to form permanent bonds with the children leading to informal adoption apart from in cases of full orphanhood.[66]

DPOS nurse inspection reports, dating from the 1850s and 1860s, suggest that owing to the general rise in living standards, nurses in the second half of the nineteenth century were in better stead to receive children into their homes. The Society paid the nurses annually, provided the orphans with an annual supply of clothing and shoes and paid the schools a sum for each orphan in the neighbourhood who attended.

While a number of the DPOS's nurses were tenant farmers' wives, the wives of fishermen and blacksmiths also sought nursing positions. (Farmers' wives were generally in charge of milking, unless they had servants to carry out these duties, and continued in this role for the domestic use of milk while men milked commercially from the late nineteenth century following the establishment of cooperative creameries.[67]) Described as 'a very respectable looking woman about 36 years of age', the nurse in one report had four young children and employed 'a servant to mind them'. The family lived on a farm with 'two houses joining each other – one is a shop in which she sells tea, tobacco'.[68] Her husband was noted as a 'decent man' who 'keeps cows and goes to fish sometimes'. The inspector also indicated that 'the house is situated on the strand – it would be a good place for delicate children. I am sure they would be comfortable'.[69] The home was highly sought after not least because it was close to the sea.

In most other cases the children were sent to women who cared for the children themselves. For the most part, the DPOS tended to appoint relatively young nurses with their own small children as the aforementioned case attests; however, in other instances, it appointed much older women, many of whom were widows themselves. In the 1890s the Cork POS employed nurses who were between thirty and forty years of age as well as a minor number of women in their seventies who had served the Society throughout their married lives.[70]

Inspections

As discussed in chapter 3 DPOS orphans were visited unannounced once in summer and once in winter by committee members, and supervised in their local parish by parochial clergymen and their wives, as well as the community at large. DPOS inspection reports from the 1870s indicate that the children were visited quarterly. At the Antrim and Down POS inaugural meeting, 1868, attendees were reminded that, 'A child is placed in a certain parish. The clergyman's family, and indeed all the families, take an interest in it'.[71] Occasionally, concerned neighbours informed the DPOS committee that orphans were being mistreated by their nurses; for example, on 28 October 1869, the DPOS committee received an anonymous note stating, 'the orphans located at Cappa and Shauna are very badly treated'.[72] Similar concerns were raised about another nurse on 21 June 1869.[73] Visiting kin, including siblings, also detected cases of neglect and, in some cases, asked the DPOS committee to inspect the home or transfer the children.[74] In the second edition of *Children of the State*, published in 1889, Florence Davenport Hill restated her support for the DPOS system, particularly its safeguards to protect boarded-out children.[75]

As shown in chapter 3, the Limerick POS arranged 'ladies' committees' to visit the orphans. The Cork POS also reported in 1859 that 'several ladies have kindly signified their intention to the committee to undertake this interesting and important duty [the supervision of nurses and orphans in every parish]'.[76] In 1869, the Cork POS noted that Mrs Woodroffe, the wife of the secretary, Revd Woodroffe, was requested to help persuade a young orphan to reside with another nurse for health reasons: 'Mrs. Woodroffe to try and induce her to go'.[77] The Mayo POS reported in 1866 that no child had died that year and the 'nurses have, in general, fulfilled their duties to the satisfaction of the Committee, who are gratified in being able to report most favourably of them. Some changes, on account of removal, have taken place, and other nurses appointed, but except in one instance this did not arise from any fault found with the nurses'.[78] The Mayo POS inspectors kept detailed records of the children's circumstances and progress,[79] which were particularly useful for monitoring the children's health.

The Donegal POS awarded prizes to 'deserving nurses' and included their names in reports of its annual meetings published in local newspapers, both of which were innovative ways to encourage nurses to meet the required standards of care. In 1892 Revd Crookshank, the inspector, having visited all the orphans 'without previous notice' awarded prizes to the most deserving nurses'.[80] The Donegal POS committee remarked in 1896 that 'a very real attachment which existed between the orphans and their foster mothers was pleasant to behold'. The bonds between nurses and their foster children were demonstrated through 'little gifts from the children from America' and 'affectionate remembrances of old and happy connections'.[81] Equally important were the bonuses or gratuities that most PO Societies gave nurses for the effective care of sick children.

DPOS orphans: a case study

Revd Thomas Shore, noted in chapter 3 as a driving force behind the DPOS in the first half of the nineteenth century, was appointed Protestant chaplain to the North Dublin Union in 1852. The DPOS committee considered that given his appointment to a new position, he would no longer have sufficient time to devote to the Society and recommended his dismissal. One committee member also noted that when he had visited County Wicklow, where the majority of orphans were placed, he had heard his name (Revd Shore's) 'in every one's mouth, and they seemed to think and speak of no one in the Society, but Rev. Shore'.[82] Another committee member remarked that Shore had 'had too much administrative power in the Society'.[83] Following Shore's departure, the newly appointed inspectors formed a subcommittee to arrange children's placements.

In its first year, the subcommittee found the children in good circumstances, overall, however, 'although they saw much to their satisfaction, they also saw problems'.[84] In one case, children lived in overcrowded accommodation, had inadequate bedding, and suffered from the 'itch',[85] the medical treatment of which is discussed later in the chapter. The subcommittee subsequently warned all the nurses that such neglect was unacceptable.[86] In June 1853, the subcommittee reported a dreadful account of neglect and physical mistreatment against two orphans who were 'not fed or treated in any respect like her own family'.[87] The children were overworked before and after school and given no time for recreation and the nurse regularly sent the children for whiskey and beat the children;[88] the children were removed immediately, and the nurse dismissed.[89] While undoubtedly a troubling account, the very existence of any detailed evidence of neglect was most reassuring, for it confirmed the effectiveness of surprise visits and the inspection process as a whole. Furthermore, it invited crucial discussion on how best to guard against similar mistreatment in the future.

The aforementioned cases of neglect and mistreatment led to the revision of the original 1837 nurse guidelines. The honorary secretaries, Revd Beaver H. Blacker and Revd Thomas Kingston, former committee member of the Irish Daughters' Clergy School, which assisted orphans and curates' daughters, modified the rules:

1 No relative shall be allowed to visit the orphans at the nurse's home without written permission from this office.
2 Nurses are to pay particular attention to train the orphans in habits of personal cleanliness and to report infirmities in any of them which the nurses' care may not be able to correct. Their hair should be kept cut rather short, and the daily use of the comb enforced.
3 The committee require that the orphans be supplied with three comfortable meals each day, that they sit and eat with the family, and the food be freshly made and warm.
4 The committee require that the orphans, after their return from school, be allowed a reasonable time for recreation and preparing their lessons for the next day.
5 The committee expect that the nurse, or some member of her family, will attend church with the orphans so as to have an eye to them and set them a good example; and that she will also send her own children in the company of the orphans to Sunday school.
6 In case of any nurse having a complaint to make of the conduct of an orphan, or an orphan having reason for complaint about anything, the clergyman of the parish in all cases is to be applied to.
7 Every nurse shall be responsible, that no orphan shall ever go without shoes, or wear broken ones; and the practice of mending the old shoes too often, when they have become too small for the orphans, cannot be allowed. Any nurse who neglects attending to the above regulations must expect that all the orphans will be immediately removed from under her care.
8 It is expected that the nurse will have family prayer daily at which the orphans should attend. [90]

The DPOS insisted that the orphans wore shoes to give the appearance of respectability and to maintain their general health; however, inspectors later reported that nurses did not always comply while in other cases children's shoes were found in disrepair. The Fermanagh POS provided orphans with clogs rather than shoes which was objected to by subscribers at an annual meeting in 1861.[91] In the 1870s, the Belmullet Board of Guardians supplied workhouse children with clogs.[92]

Transferrals

In 1855 twenty-three children were transferred to alternative nurses, twenty-one children in 1856 and nine children in 1857[93] from a total of approximately four hundred children. They were almost invariably removed from nurses on the grounds of ill health, neglect – moral, physical and religious, death of nurse, and poor schooling. PO Societies considered the children's moral well-being as important as their physical health. As discussed in chapter 3, respectability was central to the Society's ethos and any infractions of the rules which undermined the Society's moral authority were not tolerated. In May 1856 DPOS orphans were removed from a nurse in Newcastle, County Wicklow, because the committee was given notice that 'a young unmarried woman resident in the house of a Nurse – of Newcastle has given birth to a child; that Nurse – be informed that the committee have heard with great regret of the above occurrence and desire to know whether the young woman has left or shall immediately leave or the children shall be forthwith removed'.[94] The rector subsequently told the committee that the nurse was 'anxious now to send away the young woman whose presence in the nurse's house induced the committee to order up the orphans there from'.[95] Following the assurance of another clergyman that the 'young woman in question' had been removed from the nurse's home, the children were permitted to stay. The discovery of drunkenness on the part of the nurses or any members of their families was also considered just cause for the orphans' immediate removal.

Nevertheless, despite the relatively minor number of transferrals, inspectors continued to detect isolated cases of neglect which led the DPOS committee to revisit the issue of nursing standards in 1858. In a 'special address to the nurses', the committee urged nurses to adhere to the following rules:

1 That the orphans shall never be kept from school or church, except in case of illness, or extreme inclemency of weather, or by special leave applied for to, and given by the Teacher of the School.
2 That they shall not be allowed to be without shoes and stockings at any time, either when at home or at school.
3 That they shall partake of the same food, and be treated in all respects as the Nurses' own children, and if the Nurse have no children of her own, that Breakfast and Tea be taken with the Nurse, and Dinner as far as possible.
4 That they shall never be put to any kind of work at which the Nurses' own children of the same age are not usually employed.

5 That no more than two children shall be allowed to sleep in the same bed.

[Note: When the issue of overcrowding was raised in a workhouse hospital in the late nineteenth century, the guardians, who were increasingly represented by labourers, were unconcerned as their own children slept four to a bed.[96]]

6 That special attention be paid to the general cleanliness of the Orphans by daily washing and also by daily combing of their heads, and that their clothes be kept clean and in repair: particular attention is to be given to keep good shoes on the Orphans.

7 That the Orphans be allowed reasonable time for recreation, and for the preparation of their school business, at least one hour each evening.

8 That the Nurses shall have family prayer daily, with reading of the Holy Scriptures.

[Note: The nurses were provided with a book of prayers 'The Tent and the Altar' in 1858 for family use.]

9 That the Nurses and their families shall be careful in all things to set the Children a good example, by a conscientious regard to truth, and by carefully abstaining from the appearance of evil: i.e., remaining at home when summoned to Divine Worship on Sunday evening.[97]

The DPOS also forbade nurses from putting children to work instead of school: 'No boy or girl shall be kept from school to do work at a farm, or go for messages, nor at all, except during sickness or under peculiar circumstances, such as the clergyman of the parish would approve'.[98] However, in September 1859 inspectors reported that specific children were absent from school for long periods: 'Rev. Halahan spoke very severely to the nurses and they promise to send them regularly'.[99] The committee suggested at a meeting dated 24 July 1869 that 'nurses who keep the orphans from school will get no gratuity'.[100]

A selection of surviving inspection reports for the year 1872 indicate that, overall, the orphans received a satisfactory standard of care. Inspectors visited nurses' homes located in Baltinglass, Dunlavin, Carnew, Killiskey, Kiltegan, Inch, Shillelagh and Tinahely. The reports confirmed that 56 per cent of cases were 'satisfactory'; 21 per cent 'fairly satisfactory'; 15 per cent 'very satisfactory'; and, 6 per cent 'unsatisfactory'.[101]

For the years 1890 to 1892, 70 per cent of cases were satisfactory; 13 per cent of cases were transferred; 8 per cent 'very satisfactory'; and 5 per cent 'fairly satisfactory'.[102] In 1894, the secretary of the committee concluded that he had not in seventeen years of service, 'found matters on the whole more generally satisfactory'.[103] The report of that year stated 'a full and minute inspection of the orphans has been made, and we have to express our gratification generally with the appearance, health and cleanliness and manners of the orphans and in exceptional cases the nurses were instructed or reprimanded'.[104] Broadly speaking, the Society's enforcement of stricter nursing instructions and regular unannounced visits gradually improved nursing standards and the general care of orphans.

Children's mental health

Children were likely to have suffered immense grief at both the loss of their fathers and separation from their mothers;[105] the transition

Figure 5.4 DPOS nurse and orphans c. 1880s to 1890s.

Figure 5.5 DPOS nurse and orphan c.1880s to 1890s.

was extremely difficult with attendant emotional effects as mani-
fested in behaviours such as running away, bed wetting and disruptive
behaviour.

As discussed in chapter 3, PO Societies prioritised the placement of
siblings together. St Brigid's Catholic boarding-out institution (founded
in 1856) also introuduced this policy. In a study of middle-class siblings
in nineteenth-century England, it was found that 'elder siblings provided
care, leadership and control using a range of behaviour from autocratic
bullying to loving guidance and practical help, often in lieu of ailing or
dead parents'.[106] Boarded-out siblings became each other's confidante,
source of support and a stabilising force in their lives.

Figure 5.6 DPOS orphans, siblings c.1880s to 1890s.

In August 1885, a brother and sister, aged thirteen and eleven respectively, 'eloped' from their nurse's home in Donoughmore, Donard in West Wicklow and arrived the same day at their maternal grandmother's home in Northumberland Road, Ballsbridge, Dublin. When the children were found their clothing was described as being 'in a wretched state';[107] however, no account was given of how they managed to reach their grandmother's home. While there was also no mention of ill-treatment on the part of their nurse, which might have explained their decision to run away, the committee was informed that the children's mother, who had left Ireland in January 1883, was 'now in a dying state in America'.[108]

Figure 5.7 DPOS orphans, siblings c.1880s to 1890s.

After a young boy ran away from his nurse because of alleged mis-treatment, he wrote to the DPOS committee to apologise.[109] He did so to avoid being separated from his younger sister: 'I feel heartily sorry for what I committed through my own foolishness running off. I will never do such a thing again. I have never been ill-treated since I came to Mrs – in any way. I hope the committee will forgive me for what I did and to please leave me with Mrs – on account of my little sister'.[110] The com-mittee later noted, 'There has been no serious ill treatment, at the same time I think the boy must have been a good deal frightened and expected to be well punished or he would not have stayed out all night'.[111] The children were sent 'to another nurse who is known for having a very

Figure 5.8 DPOS orphans, siblings c.1880s to 1890s.

good reputation as a kind nurse'.[112] The inspectors concluded that his original nurse was a respectable woman but entirely unsuited to the role.

Bed wetting

Enuresis, or bed wetting, though not particularly common, was nonetheless mentioned at DPOS committee meetings and in inspectors' reports. Generally, bed wetting is recognised in some instances, not all, as an emotional response to trauma particularly 'separation from the mother, the loss of a parent or inadequate care on the part of the parents'.[113] However, in the nineteenth century it was stigmatised and viewed as

Figure 5.9 DPOS orphans, siblings c.1880s to 1890s.

a weakness that many believed needed to be beaten out of children. Moreover, personal testimonies of Irish industrial school life reveal that children were frequently beaten for bed wetting well into the twentieth century.[114]

In the 1840s, Dr Robert L. M'Donnell, Licentiate of the King and Queen's College of Physicians and the Royal College of Surgeons Ireland, referred to the case of an eight-year-old boy, a habitual bedwetter; every remedy had been tried to no avail; a doctor had recommended 'a "whipping" to be administered every morning', which the child's mother had 'rigidly followed'.[115] M'Donnell disapproved of the 'cure'. The DPOS gave nurses practical and child-oriented directions for the prevention of the 'infirmity at night',[116] which did not include punishment. It advised against drinking too much in the evening; urinating excessively during the day; sleeping on their back; and recommended having 'every convenience close to the bed'.[117] 'Marine medication' – sea air and sea bathing – was recommended by doctors in France and London in the 1860s to cure children of 'nocturnal incontinence of urine'.[118] Nurses were held responsible if reports of such cases were not promptly conveyed to the office in Dublin. Attributing blame to mothers/nurses for the continuation of nightly infirmities was commonplace in the nineteenth century.[119] The possible emotional causes were not generally acknowledged.

A child aged ten was found to suffer a 'nightly infirmity' in 1852. The nurse was 'warned to attend to the child. Last Spring he was reported in the same state, and in April, the attention of the nurse was again urgently directed to this matter'.[120] DPOS inspectors discovered that the boy was 'put in a miserable place to sleep by himself' and when the inspectors spoke to both the nurse and her husband on the subject, they answered, roughly, 'they could do no more'.[121] The inspectors 'advised *immediate* removal' of the boy.[122]

Additional evidence of children's emotional responses to bereavement included destructive behaviour. In June 1898, the DPOS committee was informed that despite a nurse's best efforts to settle a young orphan on his arrival by accommodating him in 'a room next to her own' as she worried that he 'would feel lonely in the lower part of the house',[123] the boy 'took her [the nurse's] nice little gold watch and her marriage present ring ... he lost the gold ring and he smashed her nice watch'.[124] The boy had not been with the nurse for very long before the incident happened and there was no question of mistreatment on the nurse's part.

Children's health

As discussed in chapter 3, the DPOS consistently emphasised the health benefits of placing children with farming families in the 'pure air' of the country where they would be provided with 'pure milk'. Where possible, it sent orphans to nurses who resided in Killiney, Delgany and Greystones for the benefit of sea bathing and sea air. In the second half of the nineteenth century, 'marine medication' continued as a cure-all for children's ailments.[125] Private nurses advertised sea-side accommodation for children during the summer months in the *Irish Ecclesiastical Gazette*.

A widow (a respectable Protestant) who has a young family would take charge of a few children during the summer months, who would have the advantage of sea bathing, and be treated as their own. Unquestionable references as to character and circumstances. Residence on the coast, twenty-five miles North of Dublin – railway. Terms moderate.[126]

The *Gazette* also advertised a hydropathic establishment at Malvern House, Delgany, County Wicklow, encouraging Dublin clergy and medical men to partake in the 'water cure'.[127] Archbishop Whately remained a keen supporter of homœopathy into the 1860s. From the 1860s fresh air as a 'climatic treatment' for consumption became popular.[128] A Protestant home for sick children was also opened in Delgany. Children were sent to the home after time spent in hospital.[129]

During the workhouse reform debates of the 1860s, discussed in chapter 4, children's health was identified as a major concern for both opponents and proponents of a boarding-out system for workhouse children. In 1862 the Dublin College of Physicians submitted a report to the Chief Secretary for Ireland regarding the physical effects of workhouse life, in which several key points were raised: children required special care up to the age of five after second dentition; a combination of good nutriment, 'good air and healthful locality' were required for the formation of bones; ophthalmia and scrofula were more likely to develop in children who were removed too early from the 'pure air of the country' to the confines of workhouses.[130] In the 1860s the chairman of the North Dublin Union stated that after analysis its milk supply was deemed 'not pure'. 'Bad milk', he claimed, 'showed seven or eight degrees of cream', while good milk 'showed twelve to thirteen'.[131] There were several ways to adulterate the milk and in this case the milk had been watered down considerably.[132]

Opponents of the system argued against boarding out on the basis that children were carriers of disease. 'Opponents of boarding-out express terror lest the pauper child should spread disease in his foster parent's home; but there is such virtue in dispersion that maladies absolutely invincible when concentrated in the workhouse become manageable if the cases are isolated, and a free open-air life strengthens the constitution'.[133] DPOS medical officers had raised many of the same points in favour of boarding out twenty years earlier.

The Country Air Association was formed in Dublin in 1886; its objective was to send the Protestant poor of Dublin, both adults and children, 'away from their crowded and unhealthy homes' to the country air 'and the thousand and one pleasant, health giving associations that the country life affords'.[134] Its supporters regarded the work as 'preventative medicine' for those who without such intervention would 'break down from overwork, fall into permanent ill health, and pauperism'.[135] In many respects it was an extension of the work which had already been carried out by PO Societies from the 1840s. There was an associated home in Bray, County Wicklow.[136] A Catholic Fresh Air Association was also founded.

Provision of medical care

The DPOS, local superintendents, the nurses with whom the children were placed, and surviving kin were jointly responsible for the maintenance of the orphans' health and the provision of medical care. This following section asks whether the children ever became ill due to general and medical neglect whilst boarded out, whether they became ill due to ordinary children's ailments or whether they were weak and sick prior to admission. The DPOS medical examiner made observations on the children's health on admission in 1855 as shown in table 5.1. Children could have suffered neglect or physical mistreatment prior to their admission or while in their mothers' care prior to their transferral to the nurses in the country. After the famine, up until 1853, a number of reports were made regarding the children's weak state of health when admitted.

Table 5.1 Children's health on admission, DPOS, 1855

Age	State of health	General appearance
n/r	Delicate	Dirty badly fed
4	Good	Clean looking – small
8	Good	Dirty slight appearance kernels in the neck
7	Good	Rough small for his age
6	Delicate	Bald on the head
3	Good	Head scruffy
3	Delicate after measles	Hair coming off eyes weakly scruff in head
7	Delicate	Eyes delicate, sore in neck, very dirty, rather simple in mind
n/r	Good	But has a cough
8	Delicate	Very weak not fit to be taken into the society
2	Healthy	Deformed head
n/r	Healthy	Stupid and short sighted – defect in eye lids
8	Healthy	But not very stout
5	Good	Robust but not fat; eyes have a slight squint
n/r	Good	A very nice little boy robust, slight appearance of scruff on face

Source: Register of state of health and education of newly elected orphans, March 1855.

While the principle epidemic diseases, measles, scarlet fever, typhus, whooping cough, diphtheria and diarrhoea along with everyday ailments were the primary causes of children's sickness, there is evidence to suggest that children also fell ill as a direct result of neglect. As discussed earlier, in 1852 inspectors found children in a delicate state with the 'itch'. Nurses were reprimanded for the outbreak, the secretary, George Jepps, stated, 'Now this is a serious matter and the committee have therefore determined upon enforcing such a regard for cleanliness in the nurses' families including the orphans as shall effectually prevent a continuance or recurrence of this disease amongst the children'.[137] Jepps circulated instructions on the appropriate medical care of the children:

> With respect to the treatment in this disease, it may be well first to observe that the daily use of yellow soap will, in nine cases out of ten, prevent persons taking the itch and in slight cases the rubbing of a little hog's lard to the parts affected and washing some time after with soap around the wrists, arms and about the legs, if affected. It may be necessary to use a stronger remedy … apply to me for a box of ointment and the printed instructions for using which you can have without charge and this ointment, if properly applied will affect a cure in a short time. Of course it will be necessary to take great care that the child does not take cold while the rubbing in be done last thing at night before a good fire. Then let the child or children go immediately to bed into sheets and the first thing the next morning let the children be well washed all over with soap and warm water using a bit of flannel, then dried with a clean towel.[138]

These were child-oriented directions which took the children's general health into account.[139]

In a second case, a widow found that her daughter 'fell into delicate health'[140] while at nurse. Rather than discuss the matter with the DPOS committee, the widow applied to the Monaghan POS for her daughter's admission. The Monaghan POS committee referred to the case: 'Her mother is most anxious to take the child from the care of the Dublin society but as she was unable to provide proper nourishment for the child she applied to this society for an allowance'.[141] While the widow's request suggests possible neglect on the nurse's part, the widow may have applied to the Monaghan POS because it permitted widows care of their own children with an allowance which was not typically possible under DPOS rules.

Moreover, there is evidence that in other cases the DPOS committee heeded widows' warnings and investigated their complaints. For example, in January 1876, inspectors were directed to inquire into a case of alleged neglect in which a widow had complained about a nurse's treatment of her children. The inspectors reported the 'specially healthful' appearance of the children. They noted 'the appearance of a recent boil on the child's arm but according to the opinion of the doctor present this was of no consequence, the more so as the child had two such boils when placed under the nurse's care'.[142] The inspectors concluded that in consideration of the children's 'state of weakness' when admitted that they were 'fully of the opinion that the children were well cared for'.[143] However, as a precaution, they agreed to transfer the children to another nurse 'to try if any benefit will come'.[144]

There is abundant evidence that 'good nurses' were largely responsible for the Society's record of consistently low mortality rates.[145] Local PO Societies also reported low mortality rates: in 1860 the Cork POS – one death out of 256 children (190 were at nurse); the Limerick POS also only one death. (In 1860 only four children died while under the care of St Brigid's boarding-out orphanage, which did not apply a 'health test' when admitting children.[146])

The containment of disease and access to medical care were equally important factors which resulted in low mortality rates. The effects of smallpox had been felt in Ireland throughout the nineteenth century. Under the Medical Charities Act, 1851, dispensary medical officers did not require payment for vaccinations. However, the uptake was not as high as predicted due to concerns over possible contagion at the dispensaries; in many cases, even those who did take their children to be vaccinated, declined to return as requested for the second visit to ensure the vaccination had 'taken'.[147] After the Vaccination Act, 1853,

Table 5.2 DPOS child mortality rates, 1850–98

Year	%	Year	%	Year	%	Year	%
1850	0.27	1862	0.69	1875	0.57	1887	0.52
1851	0.8	1863	0.46	1876	1.35	1888	0.53
1852	0.77	1864	0.46	1877	0.27	1889	0
1853	0.75	1865	1.16	1878	0.54	1890	0
1854	0.75	1866	0.92	1879	1.36	1891	0.63
1855	0.75	1867	0.69	1880	1.2	1892	3.1
1856	1.25	1868	1.44	1881	0.3	1893	1.9
1857	0.47	1869	n/r	1882	1.91	1894	2
1858	0.71	1871	1.53	1883	0.69	1895	0.66
1859	0.47	1872	1.54	1884	0	1896	0.39
1860	0.24	1873	1.17	1885	1.32	1897	2.14
1861	0.46	1874	0.3	1886	1.44	1898	1.3

Source: Annual reports; registers of orphan histories, 1850–98.

and the Compulsory Vaccination (Ireland) Act, 1863, deaths from smallpox fell considerably.[148] Yet despite initial optimism, there was a smallpox epidemic in 1871 and 1872 which caused 4,000 deaths in Ireland.[149]

The DPOS committee made every effort to contain its spread among orphans already under its care. For example, it advised that children with smallpox or other illnesses should be sent to Percy Place where they could be isolated in a 'separate dormitory'.[150] The committee stated that 'every exertion had been made to provide proper care for these orphans'.[151] In 1872 the children were not permitted to attend the annual meeting because 'smallpox is in Dublin'.[152] In December of that year there were also two cases of measles and one of fever.[153] There is evidence that DPOS nurses gave children who were suffering from whooping cough hippo-wine and syrup of squills,[154] which were recommended treatments for respiratory complaints, such as whooping cough and croup. In a rare glimpse into the administration of medicine in the domestic setting, the case suggests that nurses treated the orphans with well-known and readily available remedies as mothers would have done for their own children.[155] Scarlatina or scarlet fever, which was extremely contagious and associated with childhood, was also reported. Without effective medication, it was life-threatening for children in the nineteenth century. In some cases, children who had received adequate medical care for one illness were struck down with another whilst in hospital.

The Monaghan POS reported a minor number of cases of ophthalmia and consumption in the 1870s and 1880s.[156] The Dean of Cloyne inspected cases for the Cork POS and in October 1880 he showed concern for a widow who had the charge of her own children: 'this widow is a most respectable woman yet very delicate in health and I fear the orphans are delicate also; she has no farm and I suspect they do not get enough milk'.[157] 'Delicacy of health' was also recorded by Monaghan, Cork and Dublin PO Societies.[158] In these cases doctors recommended 'good new milk and an otherwise nutritious diet and ... cod liver oil daily'.[159] Despite public health reforms, medical care was not always available to the children. In 1889, the Monaghan DPOS reported that the parson was forced to arrange medical treatment for a young girl under his superintendence: 'The secretary reported the case of – and Revd Wilson's claim for £1.5.0 for medical attendances. Wilson being called in when the locum of Ballybay Dispensary District neglected to attend to – when seriously ill with measles and bronchitis'.[160] This case provides evidence that clergymen often played a highly significant role in the ongoing maintenance of the children's health. In one of the cases mentioned in table 5.3 a child was admitted to hospital with measles but contracted scarlatina and died while in hospital, the occurrence of which calls for caution when analysing children's charities' mortality rates: in these cases children's deaths were beyond the control of the charities' managers.[161]

In its 1896 annual report, the NSPCC referred to the 'many deaths of infants, particularly as at the present time, when epidemics of measles,

Table 5.3 Children's medical care, DPOS, 1855–98

Age	Ailment	Year	Treatment	After care
n/r	Scrofula	1855	To nurse beside the sea in August	Sea air and sea bathing
n/r	Bad eyes	1862	Adelaide hospital from Cork POS	To nurse in Dublin, back to Cork
n/r	Bad eyes	1867	Baggot Street Hospital	To be sent to St Mark's for advice
n/r	Weak limb	1867	City of Dublin Hospital	Extra nourishment, change of air, crutch
n/r	Measles	1871	Steven's Hospital	To lodge with mother
n/r	Small pox	1872	James Street Smallpox Hospital	Killiney, change of air
12	Measles	1873	Cork St Hospital	Recovered contracted scarlatina in hospital, died
10	Eye treatment	1877	To mother, then to Adelaide	Recovered
n/r	Ulcer on eye lid	1878	St Mark's Hospital	Open air and check up as weak general health
12	Eye treatment	1878	Medical treatment and to mother	Recovered
8	Psoriasis	1879	Kept with mother	Recovered
n/r	Scarlatina	1879	Adelaide Hospital	2 months
8	Rash	1879	Doctor Tweedy	Recovered
4 m.	Whooping cough	1880	Adelaide Hospital	Died
9	Typhoid fever	1880	Adelaide Hospital	To convalescent home
6	Scarlatina	1881	Died at nurse's home	Died
9	Sore eye	1882	St Mark's Ophthalmic Hospital	Recovered
4	Eye treatment	1882	St Mark's Ophthalmic Hospital	Recovered
6	Measles	1882	n/r	Recovered
3	Scarlatina	1883	Under nurse's care	Died

Table 5.3 (Continued)

Age	Ailment	Year	Treatment	After care
12	Broken Leg	1883	Surgical aid at once procured	Leg cured
5	Eczema	1884	Dublin medical treatment	Recovered
7	Squeezed fingers in mangle	1885	Extra nourishment, cod liver oil	(not serious) recovered
1 m.	Diarrhoea	1886	Under mother's care	Died
13	Scarlatina	1886	Newtown Fever Hospital	Killiney for sea air
8	Tonsillitis	1887	Adelaide Hospital	Killiney for sea air
14	Itch	1888	Shillelagh Union	Killiney for sea air
13	Itch	1888	Shillelagh Union	Killiney for sea air
11	Itch	1888	Shillelagh Union	Killiney for sea air
12	Tubercular sore	1888	Richmond Hospital	To mother in Limerick for 3 months
15	Dog bite	1889	Whitworth Hospital	Recovered
14	Curvature of spine	1890	Whitworth Hospital	One month's treatment
n/r	Lungs not quite sound	1890	Dr Tweedy	Cod liver oil and change of air
12	Scarlatina (Bethseda)	1892	Cork St Fever Hospital	Sent to nurse for change of air
13	Consumption	1893	Whitworth Hospital Drumcondra	Died

Source: Register of orphan histories; minutes subcommittee on nurses, 1850–98.

scarlatina, and whooping cough are raging'.[162] The DPOS also reported higher mortality rates in 1897 and 1898.[163] NSPCC annual reports also contain numerous references to 'medical neglect', which perhaps highlight DPOS achievements in the area of medical care; for example, 'Neglect of a child by failing to procure medical aid for a loathsome skin disease, which was rapidly disfiguring its face and eating into its eyes. The mother did not seem to attach the slightest importance to the matter'.[164] The DPOS record of consistently low mortality rates and good health was stressed in earlier workhouse reform debates. Referring to the Cork POS, it was noted that, 'They grow up strong, cheerful, red-cheeked, and spirited; and disease, much less death seldom thins their numbers ... They are attended to on the first signs of illness'.[165]

Conclusion

The extent to which widowhood caused destitution or a reliance on private or public poor relief depended on several factors: the number and age of dependents in the household; the mother's health – mental and physical; and, the availability of support networks. PO Societies gave widows the freedom to work and preserved their respectability by providing an alternative to workhouses. It was considered a form of respite or, if required, a longer term solution. Widows found work, remarried, or emigrated; once re-established their children were generally returned to them on request unless the committee deemed such a move inadvisable. Certain local PO Societies provided widows with grants to care for their own children in individual cases. The doctors associated with the DPOS who promoted the importance of good hygiene, adequate nourishment, fresh air and access to medical care, the nurses who followed these instructions, and the inspectors who monitored the children's progress all contributed to the Society's consistently low mortality rates. Though DPOS boarding-out placements were not all successful, overall, the children appear to have been well cared for. The Society invested in the children's education, recommended reasonable time for recreation and limited work; the next chapter examines the subject of child labour and child training in greater detail.

Notes

1 'Meath POS', *Irish Times* (30 September 1893).
2 Tyrone POS, annual reports, 1877–94, NLI.
3 Registered application files, NAI, POS papers, 1045/5/3; see also register orphan histories, 1850–95, 1045/5/1/3–6.
4 Prunty, 'Mobility among women', p. 135.
5 *Return of judicial statistics of Ireland (part I, police; criminal proceedings; prisons) (part II, common law and equity; civil and canon law)* [3418] HC 1863, vol. lvii, p. 11.
6 T. Bartlett, *Ireland: A History* (Cambridge: Cambridge University Press, 2010), p. 313.
7 Annual reports; minutes; registers of applications.
8 The Protestant Orphan Society Record, 1855, NLI, p. 12.
9 Letter in register, 15 June 1855, NAI, POS papers, 1045/5/3.
10 T. E. Jordan, *Victorian Childhood: Themes and Variations* (New York: SUNY Press, 1987), p. 85.
11 Cronin, 'The female industrial movement'.
12 Cronin, '"You'd be disgraced!"', p. 111.
13 See Neely, 'The laity in a changing society', p. 215.

14 M. Luddy, *Women in Ireland, 1800–1918: A Documentary History* (Cork: Cork University Press, 1995), pp. 181–5.

15 *Ibid.*

16 M. Luddy, 'Women and work in nineteenth and early twentieth-century Ireland: an overview', in Whelan (ed.), *Women and Paid Work*, pp. 44–56, p. 51.

17 E. Breathnach, 'Charting new waters: women's experience in higher education, 1879–1908', in M. Cullen (ed.), *Girls Don't do Honours: Irish Women in Education in the 19th and 20th Centuries* (Dublin: Argus Press, 1987), pp. 55–78, p. 57.

18 Luddy, 'Women and work', p. 45.

19 Registered application files, NAI, POS papers, 1045/5/3.

20 Register orphan histories, NAI, POS papers, 1045/5/1/3–6.

21 J. Parr, *Labouring Children: British Immigrant Apprentices to Canada, 1869–1924* (London: Croom Helm, 1980), p. 14.

22 See registered application files, NAI, POS papers, 1045/5/3.

23 M. Luddy, 'Women's History', in L. M. Geary and M. Kelleher (eds), *Nineteenth Century Ireland: A Guide to Recent Research* (Dublin: UCD Press, 2005), pp. 43–60, p. 51.

24 Scrapbook, 1855, RCBL, CPOS papers, PRIV MS 519.16.1.

25 Register orphan histories, 1880, NAI, POS papers, 1045/5/1/6, p. 128.

26 *Ibid.*

27 'Newry POS', *The Belfast News-letter* (3 September 1874).

28 Letter with registered application form, NAI, POS papers, 1045/5/3.

29 M. S. O'Shaughnessy, 'On the rearing of pauper children out of workhouse, and the legislative provisions necessary for their protection', in G. W. Hastings (ed.), *Transactions of the National Association for the Promotion of Social Science* (London: J.W. Parker and son, 1862), pp. 652–9, p. 652.

30 Minutes, Sept. 1888, RCBL, CPOS papers, PRIV MS 519.3.

31 *Ibid.*

32 *Ibid.*

33 Tyrone POS annual report, 1877, p. 7, NLI.

34 Register incoming letters, 1868–69, NAI, POS papers, 1045/3/1/13.

35 DPOS annual report, 1883, NAI, POS papers, 1045/1/1/50–54.

36 'Donegal POS', *Belfast News-letter* (5 June 1890).

37 'Donegal POS', *Belfast News-letter* (27 June 1892).

38 'Donegal POS', *Belfast News-letter* (26 June 1896).

39 See Prunty, *Dublin Slums*, pp. 72–82, p. 72.

40 Malcolm, 'Hospitals in Ireland', p. 709.

41 *Ibid.*

42 Letter in scrapbook, 1863, RCBL, CPOS papers, PRIV MS 519.16.2.

43 *Ibid.*

44 Registers of applications, 1850–95, NAI, POS papers, 1045/5/2.

45 Registered application files, 1855, NAI, POS papers, 1045/5/3.

46 *Ibid.*
47 *Ibid.*
48 Letter in DPOS register orphan histories, NAI, POS papers, 1045/5/1/6.
49 *Ibid.*
50 E. Ross, *Love and Toil: Motherhood in Outcast London, 1870–1918* (New York, Oxford: Oxford University Press, 1993).
51 *Tenth Report on the District, Criminal, and Private Lunatic Asylums in Ireland, 1861,* p. 245, HC 1861 [2901], vol. xxvii.
52 *Ibid.*
53 G. Johnston, 'A report of the Rotunda Lying-in Hospital for the year 1873', *Dublin Journal of Medical Science,* 57:26 (Winter 1874), pp. 177–204, p. 195.
54 *Ibid.*
55 Female case-book, 1890–91, NAI, PRIV 1223 (RDLA papers), p. 354.
56 *Ibid.*
57 *Ibid.*
58 F. Davenport Hill, 'The boarding-out system distinguished from baby farming and parish apprenticeship', A paper read before the National Association for the Provision of Social Science, October 1869, pp. 4–5.
59 Gregg, *Misery and Mercy,* p. 12.
60 Applications for employment as nurse, 1853, NAI, POS papers, 1045/5/6/8 (1847–62).
61 *Ibid.,* 1856.
62 *Ibid.*
63 *Ibid.*
64 *Ibid.,* 1857.
65 Mothers/extended kin or an appointed guardian escorted the children to the nurses' homes after they were admitted in order to settle them and, as mentioned earlier, widows could also visit their children while boarded out, see register of orphans' movements, NAI, POS papers, 1045/5/6.
66 See Enright, '"Take this child"' for examples from the Limerick POS.
67 Luddy, 'Women and work', p. 48.
68 Applications for employment as nurse, 1856, NAI, POS papers, 1045/5/6/8.
69 *Ibid.*
70 Minutes, 1890s, RCBL, CPOS papers, PRIV MS 519.3.
71 *Belfast News-letter* (7 March 1868).
72 Register incoming letters, NAI, POS papers, 1045/3/1/13.
73 *Ibid.*
74 *Ibid.,* 2 Aug. 1869.
75 Davenport Hill, Fowke (ed.), *Children of the State.*
76 O'Shaughnessy, 'On the rearing of pauper children out of workhouses', p. 658.
77 Minutes, 2 Aug. 1869, RCBL, CPOS papers, PRIV MS 519.1.
78 Mayo POS, annual report, 1866, NLI.

79 *Ibid.*
80 *Belfast News-letter* (27 June 1892).
81 *Belfast News-letter* (26 June 1896).
82 Shore, *Case of Rev. Thomas R. Shore*, p. 11.
83 *Ibid.*
84 Minutes subcommittee nurses and eduction, Dec. 1852, NAI, POS papers, 1045/2/3/2.
85 *Ibid.*
86 *Ibid.*
87 *Ibid.*, 3 June 1853.
88 *Ibid.*
89 *Ibid.*
90 Revised nursing directions, Oct. 1854, NAI, POS papers, 1045/5/6/14.
91 'Fermanagh POS', *Irish Times.*
92 V. Crossman, 'Middle-class attitudes to poverty and welfare in post-famine Ireland', in Lane (ed.), *Politics, Society and the Middle Class*, pp. 130–47, p. 138.
93 See DPOS annual reports 1855–57, NAI, POS papers, 1045/1/1/24–28; see also register orphan histories 1855–57, NAI, POS papers, 1045/5/1/4.
94 Minutes, May 1856, NAI, POS papers, 1045/2/1/6, pp. 10–13.
95 *Ibid.*
96 Crossman, 'Middle-class attitudes', p. 143.
97 Minutes, 1858, NAI, POS papers, 1045/2/1/6, p. 195.
98 Directions to nurses by the committee, Oct. 1854 NAI, POS papers, 1045/5/6/14.
99 Minutes subcommittee nurses and education, Sept. 1859, NAI, POS papers, 1045/2/3/1.
100 Minutes 24 July 1869, NAI, POS papers, 1045/2/1/8.
101 Minutes subcommittee nurses and education, NAI, POS papers, 1045/2/3/2 (1867–96); inspection (nurses) reports, NAI, POS papers, 1045/5/6/13; parish inspection reports, 1872, NAI POS papers, 1045/5/6/15.
102 Minutes subcommittee nurses and education, NAI, POS papers, 1045/2/3/2 (1867–96); inspection (nurses) reports, NAI, POS papers, 1045/5/6/13; register orphan history, NAI, POS papers, 1045/5/1/4–6.
103 Minutes subcommittee nurses and education, 1894, NAI, POS papers, 1045/2/3/2 (1867–96).
104 *Ibid.*
105 See G. S. Frost, *Victorian Childhoods* (Westport, CT: Praeger Publishing, 2009), p. 20.
106 Davidoff, 'Kinship as a categorical concept', p. 412.
107 Register orphan histories, 1879, NAI, POS papers, 1045/5/1/6, p. 107.
108 *Ibid.*
109 Bound volume of incoming letters, 1898, NAI, POS papers, 1045/3/1/25.
110 *Ibid.*
111 *Ibid.*

112 *Ibid.*
113 J. Bollard and T. Nettelback (eds), *Bedwetting: A Treatment Manual for Professional Staff* (London: St Edmondson Press, 1989), p. 12.
114 M. Raftery and Eoin O'Sullivan, *Suffer the Little Children: The Inside Story of Ireland's Industrial Schools* (Dublin: New Island Books, 1999).
115 R. L. MacDonnell, 'Observations on the nature and treatment of various diseases', *Dublin Medical Press*, 16:311 (1846), pp. 306–8, p. 307.
116 Directions given to nurses, Oct. 1854, NAI, POS papers, 1045/5/6/14.
117 *Ibid.*
118 T. Brochard, physician to the sea-bathing establishment La Tremblade, S.W. of France, W. Strange, tr. (ed.), *Sea Air and Sea Bathing for Children and Invalids* (London: Longman, Green, 1865), p. 125.
119 Bollard and Nettleback (eds), *Bedwetting: A Treatment Manual*, p. 12; see also Murdoch, *Imagined Orphans*, p. 158.
120 Minutes, 1850–56, NAI, POS papers, 1045/2/1/5, p. 213.
121 *Ibid.*
122 *Ibid.*
123 Bound volume of incoming letters, 1898, NAI, POS papers, 1045/3/1/25.
124 *Ibid.*
125 Brochard, *Sea Air and Sea Bathing*, p. 125.
126 *Irish Ecclesiastical Gazette* (15 August 1860), p. 362.
127 *Irish Ecclesiastical Gazette* (15 September 1860), p. 403.
128 See G. Jones, 'Women and Tuberculosis in Ireland', in M. Preston and M. Ó'hÓgartaigh (eds), *Gender and Medicine in Ireland, 1700–1950* (Syracuse: Syracuse University Press, 2012), pp. 33–48, p. 40.
129 Luddy, *Women and Philanthropy*, pp. 94–5.
130 *Letter by Dublin College of Physicians on physical effects of rearing children in workhouses 1862*, HC 1862 (348), vol. xlix.
131 'North Dublin Union', *Irish Times* (15 March 1860).
132 *Ibid.*
133 F. Davenport Hill, 'The family system for workhouse children', *Contemporary Review*, 15 (1870), pp. 240–73, p. 263.
134 'Country Air Association', *Irish Times* (6 May 1899).
135 *Irish Times* (27 May 1887).
136 See Walsh, *Anglican Women*, p. 94.
137 Found in papers re. rules and schemes governing the Society, NAI, POS papers, 1045/6/2.
138 Nurse instructions, Oct. 1854, NAI, POS papers, 1045/5/6/14.
139 *Ibid.*
140 Minutes, 6 Aug. 1874, RCBL, MPOS papers, PRIV MS 692.1.
141 *Ibid.*
142 Minutes subcommittee nurses and education, 30 Jan. 1876, NAI, POS papers, 1045/2/3/2 (1867–96).
143 *Ibid.*
144 *Ibid.*

145 Minutes general committee, registers orphan histories, subcommittee nurses and education.

146 O'Shaughnessy, 'On the rearing of pauper children out of workhouse', p. 658.

147 Cassell, *Medical Charities, Medical Politics*, p. 125–6.

148 *Ibid.*

149 D. Brunton, 'The problems of implementation: the failure and success of public vaccination against smallpox in Ireland, 1840–1873', in Jones and Malcolm (eds), *Medicine, Disease and the State in Ireland*, pp. 138–57, p. 140.

150 Minutes, 24 May 1872, NAI, POS papers, 1045/2/1/8, p. 371.

151 *Ibid.*

152 *Ibid.*

153 *Ibid.*, 22 Dec. 1872, p. 330.

154 DPOS miscellaneous papers, 1872.

155 In one recorded case dated 1872 a widow visited her sick child at nurse and expressed her disapproval at the way the nurse cared for the child while ill. She subsequently reported the matter to the DPOS secretary who investigated the case but found that the nurse had treated the child the same as her own children.

156 Minutes, 10 Aug. 1887, RCBL, MPOS papers, PRIV MS 692.1.

157 Minutes, 20 Oct. 1880, RCBL, CPOS papers, PRIV MS 519.3.

158 DPOS minutes, Cork POS minutes, Monaghan POS minutes.

159 Register orphan histories, 1880–85, NAI, POS papers, 1045/5/1/6, p. 115.

160 Minutes, 7 Nov. 1889, RCBL, MPOS papers, PRIV MS 692.1.

161 See similar accounts in M. Cruickshank, *Children and Industry: Child Health and Welfare in the North-west Textile Towns during the Nineteenth Century* (Manchester: Manchester University Press, 1981), p. 138.

162 NSPCC annual report, 1896, p. 8, NLI.

163 DPOS annual reports, 1897–98, NAI, POS papers, 1045/1/1/66–93.

164 NSPCC annual report, 1890, p. 11, NLI.

165 Arnott, *The Investigation into the Condition of the Children in the Cork Workhouse*, p. 41.

6

Child training or child labour? 1850–98

It is nobler far to set the beacon over the sunken rock as a warning to the vessel that she may not be shipwrecked, than to send out the life-boat when the vessel is shattered to pieces, and to save perhaps the struggling mariner. Make the children independent, and they would be blessed themselves as well as blessings to others.[1]

Introduction

PO Societies regarded the term of apprenticeship as a key stage of the growing-up process, one that if successfully completed drastically reduced the incidence of juvenile delinquency and the likelihood of associated adult criminality, and produced hard working, law-abiding citizens. The escalating problem of juvenile delinquency among homeless children in the post-famine years and the idea that workhouse children, numbering 104,000 in 1850,[2] had few prospects added weight to the Society's argument in favour of a preventative approach. The DPOS laid the foundations of an apprenticeship system in the first half of the nineteenth century; this chapter examines its progress in the second. Despite the Society's best intentions, the provision of effective training was not always possible; therefore, the main consideration is whether Protestant orphans were bound out as cheap labour or provided with valuable apprenticeships. The chapter also focuses on employers' treatment of apprentices and the increasing role assumed by surviving parents and elder siblings in shaping the children's futures.

Juvenile delinquency

The POS apprenticeship scheme was viewed as a means of reducing juvenile delinquency; 'they [subscribers] should support an institution such as the Protestant Orphan Society, which takes under its care those children who are otherwise likely to become vagrants and criminals'.[3] There was a considerable rise in orphanhood, associated vagrancy and juvenile delinquency in the post-famine years. Children up to the age of seven were viewed as adults and punished accordingly.[4] Harvey Pim reported in 1852 that a quarter of the prisoners in the Richmond Bridewell, Dublin, were juveniles – 315 children under ten years of age and 1,874 children under fifteen years of age were committed for vagrancy and criminal offences. He also claimed that there were high reoffending rates particularly among orphans, abandoned children and runaways.[5] The Metropolitan Police revealed that it had taken into custody 1,679 children under ten and 3,259 juveniles aged between ten and fifteen years of age. In 1853, the Committee of the House of Commons on juvenile delinquency reported that in Cork some of the children tried for serious offences were 'so small that a turnkey was obliged to hold them up in the dock in order that he might see them', while others as young as six were imprisoned for begging.[6]

Social reformers and Quakers, John Howard and Elizabeth Fry, initially informed public debate on the issue of child imprisonment in adult gaols; however, Mary Carpenter, who highlighted the issue in 1851,[7] is credited with bringing about reforms in England. The Youthful Offenders (Reformatory Schools) Act, 1854 was extended to Ireland in 1858.[8] In the succeeding decades, reformatory schools were opened throughout Ireland.[9] Nevertheless, the imprisonment of children in gaols continued in certain parts of the country throughout the 1870s.[10] Despite being sentenced to reformatory schools, in some cases due to overcrowding children were instead sent to gaol. Sir John Lentaigne stated that in one such case a boy committed suicide in his cell.[11] Revd Benjamin Waugh, founder of the London branch of the NSPCC, wrote *The Gaol Cradle, Who Rocks It?* in 1873, which focused on the urgent need for juvenile courts.[12]

Revd T. R. Shore, former General Superintendent of the DPOS, assisted in the foundation of the Protestant Reformatory School for Boys at Rehoboth Place, South Circular Road, Dublin, which was certified on 18 November 1859 and had charge of eighteen inmates.[13] A Protestant Reformatory for girls was also founded, in Cork Street, Dublin, in the same year. By 1865 ten reformatory schools had been established in Ireland and by 1870 there were 740 child inmates. The schools were subject to inspection and the children's maintenance was publicly funded.[14] In 1875 there were 101 Protestant boys detained in schools, 3 in prison, and 20 Protestant girls in reformatory schools.[15] Orphans and juvenile offenders were otherwise housed in workhouses or maintained by private charity.

After the reformatory schools act and the later Industrial Schools (Ireland) Act, 1868, fewer children were placed in workhouses and gaols.[16] Industrial schools were state funded, operated along denominational lines, and were mainly intended 'for the little waif or arab whose relatives or associates are vicious or criminal; that is to say, children who appear to have no chance in life but that of growing up corner-boys or disreputable women'.[17] Protestants in the north objected to the scheme on the grounds that proselytism was likely to become an issue.[18] Catholic industrial schools included St Joseph's, which was founded in 1862 and accommodated 145 boys, and the Artane Industrial School established in 1870 with accommodation for 830 boys. Protestant industrial schools included the Training Home Industrial School for Protestant girls, Union-quay, Cork (1870); the Meath Industrial School for Protestant boys, Blackrock, Dublin (1871); and the Cork Industrial School for Protestant boys (1892).[19]

The Intermediate Education (Ireland) Act, 1878,[20] extended education to secondary level and by 1901 35,306 children attended 500 schools.[21] Technical schools were opened throughout Ireland following the Local Government (Ireland) Act, 1898 and the Roman Catholic church warned against any 'Protestant interference', forbidding Catholics to attend residential homes which Protestants attended.[22] By the end of the nineteenth century the number of industrial schools had increased to seventy-one, nine of which were Protestant.[23] The NSPCC reported that from 1885 to 1888 2,621 children under the age of fifteen years were committed for offences in the Dublin Metropolitan Police District.[24] In 1896, out of the 451 children taken from Dublin Police courts to the schools, it was found that only eight cases were on the basis of 'criminal surroundings'; the remainder were identified as 'non-criminal destitute poor'. Many of these children were 'orphans or children of disabled parents, and with no one able or willing to take care of them'.[25] As discussed in chapter 3, PO Societies admitted children whose fathers were alive but 'incapacitated bodily or mentally'.

PO Societies and child labour

While industrialisation in the north placed new demands on child workers, in other parts of the country employment was agriculturally based. According to the 1851 census, 23,356 children were employed in labouring and domestic service.[26] Agricultural training was considered an effective means of reducing the high number of workhouse children (68,402 in 1852); however, as many of the children had ophthalmia and 'sore heads', employers were reluctant to give them work. Moreover, as the children could not be apprenticed, Poor Law Guardians were powerless to assist those who were sent to 'unsuitable masters'.[27] The 1861 census recorded that 35,000 boys worked as farm labourers[28] while girls were highly represented in domestic service and textiles in the same year.[29] Though model farms had been a major training initiative, the scheme gradually declined from 1870 to 1900. There were a number of training colleges such as the Munster Model Farm and the Albert National Agricultural Training College, Glesnevin; there were also farms attached to national schools, nineteen out of 228 of which were regarded as model agricultural schools.[30]

In a number of cases presented to the DPOS, the elder siblings of the admission candidates were the sole earners in their families. Women in labouring families who had had to work in order to supplement their husbands' wages, and artisan and middle-class widows in reduced circumstances, often became trapped by the dependency of their young children, relying on their elder children as their primary support networks.[31] Maria Luddy suggests that 'children often worked, not to support themselves alone but often to support their families'.[32] The available evidence, primarily DPOS application files, confirms that elder siblings as well as widows benefited from the admission of younger dependents: after the admission of younger dependents, widows could seek out employment thereby reducing the burden of responsibility on their eldest children.

> T. P. employed by the Claremount Institution as a shoemaker earned a comfortable subsistence. His son (16) trained in father's business is now employed to the Committee of Claremont Institution as a shoemaker. His mother attends to the gate of the institution but does not seem to be able to earn sufficient to support so large a family and thus their entire support is thrown almost entirely on the young lad.[33]

Revd Gibson Black, DPOS secretary, referred to a similar case in 1852: 'she is in a state of complete destitution wholly unable to support either of these orphans. She has another son of about twelve who minds some cattle on the land where she is at present allowed to live, a miserable house scarcely habitable but the boy receives no wages, food or clothing or anything else'.[34] In other cases, girls worked for a pittance to supplement their widowed mothers' meagre wages and elder sisters were frequently called upon by their mothers to watch their younger siblings.

In 1892 Rosa Barrett drew attention to cases of child mistreatment in London where it was found that despite making significant contributions to the family economy, child workers were neglected and assaulted by their parents: 'a coroner in Whitechapel stated that out of 216 children under ten years of age who died in six months, 118 (more than half of the total number – nearly 55 per cent) brought money to those who let them die; in 84 other cases of children who died of neglect or suspected violence, 49 (over 58 per cent) brought in money'.[35] In 1896 Barrett raised the issue again referring this time to a case in Dublin, in which 'a boy of 11 was the chief support of the family'.[36] In the cycle of poverty endured by labouring families and single women – widows with dependents – the impact on elder siblings was significant. Often it was they who had experienced the greatest hardship because they had to forgo their own futures in order to provide for their families.[37]

PO Societies and the Industrial Schools Act, 1868

Despite the introduction of a comparable public measure such as the Industrial Schools Act, the charity's subscribers argued in favour of maintaining PO Societies as they had done after the Poor Law was extended to Ireland. The Cork POS was adamant that it should continue its work among Protestant orphans:

While we are sensible of the benefits conferred on certain classes of children by the operation of the Industrial Schools Act, at the same time we believe that the destitute children of our Protestant brethren, though coming within the provisions of this act, retain, nevertheless, their peculiar claim upon our Christian sympathy and charity and are still to be considered destitute orphans such as it is the object of the Protestant Orphan Society to provide for.[38]

The DPOS observed that while the industrial schools were doing 'a splendid job', they did not 'take the place of the orphan society', for through its 'peculiar' system, 'an opportunity was given for the children to be brought up as it would have been had the father lived and remained in prosperous circumstances'.[39] In the 1870s, Mrs O'Connell,[40] who advocated the reform of English pauper schools, proposed that boarding out should be combined with institutional training. William Neilson Hancock, secretary of the Statistical and Social Inquiry Society of Ireland, observed in 1879, 'Mrs. O'Connell's proposition has in favour of it the experience of half of a century of the largest Protestant Orphan Society'.[41]

POS training homes

DPOS orphans attended classes at Percy Place and remained there until they began their apprenticeships. Percy Place was managed by a matron and a warden, generally a married couple. Mrs Jepps, the DPOS secretary's wife, resigned from her position as matron of the home in October 1857:

> with extreme regret we accept the resignation of the matron of our House Percy Place – a regret increased by the fact that impaired health has induced Mrs Jepps to give up a post which for more than sixteen years she has filled to the entire satisfaction of the committee, during which time she has invariably enjoyed the most perfect confidence and esteem of every committee to which has been entrusted the management of the Protestant Orphan Society. The ability, the assiduous and maternal sympathy displayed by Mrs Jepps has been most beneficial to the children under her care – to many of whom she appears to have greatly endeared herself. We trust that, relieved from the arduous duties and anxieties of her position as matron, her health may be so far restored as to enable her to pursue her career of usefulness in her own family[42]

A year after Mrs Jepps's resignation, the Commissioners of Education in Ireland gave a less than satisfactory account of Percy Place. It stated that despite the 'eminent success' of the DPOS boarding-out system, there were problems at the training home. The accommodation was considered overcrowded; a gender imbalance in terms of instruction was also identified: 'the attention of the girls is not sufficiently directed to the attainment of knowledge and mental discipline'.[43] Girls were educated in housework and needlework 'with a view to making them as proficient as possible in the business of servants to which most of them will be apprenticed'.[44] (Children from orphanages, industrial schools and reformatories were also typically placed in service.[45]) The quality of instruction for the boys and the girls was deemed of 'inferior quality'.[46] The report recommended that the Society's funding would be better spent on the extension of its impressive boarding-out scheme rather than on the training home, which required updating.[47] In light of the report the committee catalogued the existing Percy Place library collection and recommended the addition of new volumes.[48]

PO Societies throughout Ireland followed Dublin's lead and founded associated training homes to offer the orphans further training in preparation for their apprenticeships. The Tipperary POS managed two training schools: the Abbey Training School for girls and the Clonbeg Training School for boys.[49] From the 1870s onwards, the Monaghan POS sent girls for training to Mrs J. G. Taylor, The Servant's Training Home, 76 Pakenham Place, Belfast.[50] The Westmeath POS sent the majority of its orphans to Wilson's Hospital School, a boarding school in Mullingar which was aimed at poor Protestant boys.[51] The admission age was between eight and eleven and children remained in the school for five years, after which they were apprenticed to trades.

Figure 6.1 DPOS apprentice c.1880s to 1890s.

Wilson's reported a fine record of educational achievement with a substantial number of its pupils passing the Intermediate Examination in the 1880s.[52] In 1888 sixty-six pupils received free education and board.

The Farra School provided boarding, clothing and apprenticeships for up to a hundred children. Competitive examinations were held annually and four to five children were awarded scholarships – free education and board – for four years. Boys between the ages of twelve and sixteen from Meath and Westmeath could sit the examinations. Boys who had completed the four years could extend their education at the training institution at Santry.[53] Intermediate Examination results for the Farra pupils were also 'very favourable'.[54] The Westmeath POS typically sent

Figure 6.2 DPOS apprentice c.1880s to 1890s.

girls to domestic service.[55] Girls from the Dublin POS and other local PO Societies were trained for domestic service in the Providence Home.

Health in the training homes

The maintenance of children's health and their access to medical care while in Percy Place appears to have been satisfactory.[56] It was imperative that the children remain in good health in order to secure apprenticeships. In March 1859, it came to the DPOS committee's attention that one of the children of the newly appointed matron of Percy Place had become ill with scarlatina. [57] The master of the house was implored by the committee to remove his child, 'lest the infection be communicated to the children'.[58] As the annual meeting was fast approaching, committee members feared that all the children due to arrive with their nurses would contract the illness. In order to prevent an outbreak, and at considerable inconvenience, they managed to secure St Mark's school rooms in Westland Row as an alternative location.[59] The apprentices who had been in contact with the matron's child were unable to attend the meeting.[60]

Typhoid fever broke out in Percy Place in the 1870s. The committee reported on 2 December 1878 that two orphans had been ill for days. Dr Harley had diagnosed them with typhoid fever, and ordered their transferral to Baggot Street Hospital. He also reported 'that – is now ill with the same disease and that she be removed to hospital without delay'.[61] The committee resolved that 'parents of the above named children be at once informed of their state'.[62] Children were occasionally taken on holidays primarily for health reasons. In 1878, the committee resolved that the orphans should be given a holiday on Whit Monday and directed the manager of the home to take them to the country.[63]

Dr Hobart, dispensary doctor and Cork POS medical officer, identified problems at the Cork POS training home in February 1869.[64] He reported the 'dilapidated, dark cheerless condition of the kitchen scullery in which a considerable portion of the working time is spent and also the cheerless state of the room in which the meals are served; the insufficiency of food; the dabbling in hot and cold, exposure to getting wet feet and carrying heavy weights'.[65] He concluded by stating it was 'at present a disgrace to the Society'.[66] He recommended that if the Society wished to continue with the home, it should be made 'really comfortable, with suitable furniture as the girls are brought there to make them servants not washerwomen; I would give up all washing except that of the home and oblige them to keep all parts of the house and furniture in order and scrupulously clean'.[67] He also recommended the formation of a 'ladies' committee' to assist the matron in the management of the home, which was duly formed, the appointment of a gentleman to inspect and, finally, improved diet – with meat served three to four times a week.[68]

The Working Boys' Home

The Dublin Working Boys' Home and Harding Technical School was founded in 1876 and originally located in Denzille Street and later Lord Edward Street. In the late 1880s, Miss Anna Middleton Harding left a bequest to fund the establishment of a technical school. The 1896 annual report for the Working Boys' Home stated:

The object of the Home is to provide a safe and comfortable residence for Orphans and other Boys, who are earning small wages as Apprentices or otherwise in Dublin, and who are, from any cause, without a suitable home in the city. The object of the School is to give a general elementary education to the Boys residing in the home, and others of the same class, and to afford instruction in Handicrafts, Experimental Science, Drawing, Shorthand, Book-keeping, and such other technical or commercial subjects as would help to advance the Boys in life. Religious instruction is provided for each boy in the home and in the school upon biblical and Protestant principles. Each boy, on admission to the Home or School, must produce a certificate of good character from a clergyman, from his employer, or from some other person worthy of credit. The age for admission is 12 to 16 years; but, under special circumstances, the limit of age may be extended to 18 years.[69]

By 1896 the home had sufficient accommodation for sixty-three boys and boasted a swimming club, gymnasium, cricket club and bell-ringing club among other 'healthy amusements'.[70] For a moderate fee, the boys had the option of attending evening classes after work. The report also recommended the foundation of a 'Supplement Home' for the admission of older boys.[71] The goal of these homes was to ensure that impressionable young boys progressed in their education, maintained good health, and did not succumb to the temptations of city life. The home's motto was 'prevention is better than cure'.[72] Thomas Spunner, former secretary of the Protestant Orphan Refuge Society, previously known as the Charitable Protestant Orphan Union, was superintendent of the Working Boys' Home from 1879 to 1896.

Industrial school ships

The Hibernian Marine Society was co-founded by the Lord Mayor, the Archbishop of Dublin in 1774. It was aimed at the orphans of seafarers in the Merchant and Royal Navy and was supported by voluntary subscription. With subsequent parliamentary grants the Society established a nursery and school which was situated at Rogerson's Quay.[73] In England children had been sent to sea as a form of punishment from the seventeenth century.[74] Disciplinary action was considered a necessary response to juvenile delinquency. Poor Law reformers in the nineteenth century such as Edwin Chadwick, James Kay, and Edward Tufnell endorsed military training for pauper children.[75] They promoted naval training in response to poor military performance during the Crimean War. Children's early training was viewed as essential to future military success.[76]

School ships began to be commissioned in the 1850s following the introduction of reformation and industrial schools legislation. The *Akbar*, the *Cornwall* and the *Clarence* were reformation school ships while, for example, the *Havannah*, the *Endeavour* and the *Cumberland* were industrial school ships.[77] The school ships were envisioned as a means of reducing 'juvenile delinquency' by providing better prospects for young boys who 'through poverty, parental neglect, or being orphans, are left destitute and homeless, and in danger of being contaminated by association with vice and crime'.[78] Generally, boys trained on industrial school ships were recruited into the merchant navy rather than the Royal service which required stronger, healthier boys. Industrial school ship trainees, many of whom had experienced hardship early in life, were considered at a distinct disadvantage in this respect.[79] Barnardo's had attempted to establish a training ship in the 1870s but did not secure funding to do so until 1901.

In 1875 the *Clio*, an industrial school ship, was certified under the provisions of the Industrial Schools Act, 1866, and moored off Bangor in the Menai Straits, north Wales. It was intended to serve Liverpool, Manchester and other Lancashire towns with a view to training the children as sailors for the mercantile navy. Voluntary subscriptions

Figure 6.3 *Clio* training ship.

Figure 6.4 Captain Moger, *Clio* training ship.

provided the funds to fit out the ship.[80] There were also voluntary training ships in England which catered for boys whose apprenticeships had
fallen through, 'the sons of poor widows unable to cope with large families', and workhouse children.[81]

Despite a strict admission age limit of twelve years, in the early 1880s
it was not uncommon for charities and workhouses, which were under
pressure to place homeless children, to seek the admission of eleven-year-
old boys; however, officials considered it unwise: 'I think this should be
declined both on the ground that a child under twelve is not well fitted
for an industrial school ship and on the ground that the whole question
of industrial schools is about to be considered by a Royal Commission

Figure 6.5 *Clio* boys, compass instruction.

Figure 6.6 *Clio* boys on deck.

and therefore it is inexpedient to make any considerable change, especially by way of extension'.[82] DPOS orphans were sent to the training
ship in Bangor for three main reasons: first, as a form of punishment
and a means of reform and discipline; second, for health purposes; and,
third, as a path to seamanship. The DPOS committee could not send
the children to the *Clio* without the consent of a surviving parent. The
DPOS committee asserted that boys who repeatedly ran away from their
nurses or apprenticeships would benefit from the disciplined regime on
board the *Clio*; however, only a relatively small number of children were
sent.[83] It was also used as a threat of punishment: 'Miss Routledge told
her brother was "wild" and needed rigid discipline before their trip to
New Zealand. Miss Routledge given advice on how to handle him and
Assistant Secretary warned the boy that if he was unruly he would be at
once taken from his sister and put on a training ship. He promised not
to act out'.[84]

There were nineteen orphans on board the *Clio* when DPOS inspectors visited the ship in 1889: 'They were greatly pleased with all they
saw, and consider that the discipline, cleanliness and general management of the ship reflect great credit upon Captain Moger'.[85] Inspectors
dismissed the fact that the boys did not wear shoes or hats: 'regarding
their clothing we have been informed that they are shoeless and bare-
headed. We consider this to be a great advantage to them instead of
injury; they seemed nothing the worse for it, but all the better, while
it should be remembered that in winter, they are supplied with boots
and caps'.[86] They concluded that they could see no need for additional
resources for the children, that the stores, hospital and bathroom were
sufficient for 'growing lads'. The ship was viewed as an excellent means
of 'turning out industrious and strong men'.[87] No mention was made of
the cramped living quarters or that the same covered deck was used as a
dining hall, dormitory and school room.[88]

While the health benefits were observed, 'the locality is most healthy,
the ship anchored as it is between Bangor and Beaumaris',[89] there had
been health problems on board in previous years. One boy had died
from pneumonia and another developed rheumatism because the ship
was positioned in an unsheltered spot exposed to battering winds and
rain.[90] Captain Moger had raised concerns for the children's well-
being and recommended the ship's relocation to a more sheltered area.
Widows in some cases objected to their children's placement on the ship.
For example, an orphan was sent to the *Clio* when he was thirteen and
remained there for over a year. He returned home in 1888 to lodge with
his mother and was apprenticed to a printer for six years. Significantly,
months later when the DPOS committee advised that it should send his

younger brother to the *Clio*, his mother refused to allow it, after which the Society 'gave him up to his mother'.[91]

By 1890 a great deal had changed on board the ship: the deck had been covered to protect the boys while at play; they were able to leave the ship to go on land more after a playing field was obtained for their use; they could visit the newly opened swimming baths in Bangor; the boys played in the *Clio* band which performed at local events; they attended a summer camp every summer a 'for a change of air'; parents could write to the boys and visit them once every two months.[92] Medical officers also visited the ship twice a week.[93] While it was officially recommended that 'as far as possible such boys were only to be sent to ships who were

Figure 6.7 *Clio* boys, DPOS orphans (brothers).

stout and robust in health',[94] the DPOS committee expressed confidence
that the sea air would improve the children's health. In 1890 the DPOS
sent a boy to the *Clio* for this very reason, 'this course being considered
necessary by the doctor'.[95]

Summary convictions, which were held at Anglesey County Record
Office, detail some of the offences for which the *Clio* boys were punished. A fifteen-year-old boy who coerced another to bring tobacco on
board and to steal biscuits was 'imprisoned at H.M.P. Carnarvon for
one month hard labour, thereafter detained at a Reformatory for four
years'.[96] Nevertheless, there was a relatively high success rate among the
discharged boys: over eighty out of 120 went to sea.[97] Twin brothers,
farmer's sons, who had been boarded out together in Carnew County
Wicklow by the DPOS were sent to the *Clio*. On 16 April 1888, having
completed his training, one of the brothers was 'shipped in a vessel called
the General Lee of Dublin Coasting Service';[98] the berth was found by
the *Clio* authorities. Two days later, on 18 April 1888, his twin brother
was 'provided with a berth in a ship "Paladia" trading to the Brazils';
the berth was also secured by the *Clio* managers.[99]

Isolation and exploitation

By the 1850s, the DPOS had become familiar with the legal status of
both the apprentice and the Society, knowledge which proved vital in
legal wrangles over indentures; however, while legally binding indentures were always used as a means of protection for the orphans,[100]
inspections were also absolutely crucial. It was highly likely, if not inevi-
table, that even with formal indentures, in some cases children would be
mistreated by their masters and mistresses.

As discussed in chapter 3, the DPOS introduced forward-thinking
measures to prevent children's mistreatment such as the careful selection of employers and maintaining close contact with the apprentices
through social events. Inspectors endeavoured to speak to the apprentices privately away from their masters in order to allow them to speak
freely. A young apprentice shoemaker complained of his master's
'severity'; the inspector interviewed the master who claimed the apprentice was 'idle and insolent' and 'hard to manage'.[101] In this case, the
inspector recommended that the boy 'talk to him directly'[102] with any
further problems. There is evidence that apprentices having difficulties
with their employers called upon elder siblings for assistance. In 1863
an elder sister wrote to the DPOS committee on her brother's behalf
and provided him with warm clothes after he deserted his master who
had mistreated him.[103]

Generally, PO Societies sent girls to domestic service where they were subservient to their master and mistress, and, therefore, most vulnerable to mistreatment.[104] Local clergymen were expected to visit the orphans regularly and report on their progress. In August 1860, the Senior Curate of Armagh expressed concern that a DPOS orphan girl who had been placed in service in his parish was being isolated by her master.[105] He reported that her master preferred his servants to attend church with him as he was a member of the cathedral choir.[106] Consequently, the girl no longer attended Sunday School and was 'very much withdrawn from the notice of the parochial clerk'.[107] Although her master 'complained a little of want of cleanliness and uneven temper on the part of the girl' and did not seem 'altogether satisfied with her', the curate concluded that in his opinion there 'may well be faults on both sides'.[108] Despite the overall effectiveness of inspections, there were reports that girls had been overworked, treated cruelly, denied adequate training and exploited as cheap labour. For example, a fourteen-year-old children's maid employed in Dublin was prevented from writing to the Society or to her mother, and was subjected to great cruelty at the hands of her mistress, which went undetected by the Society until she ran home to her mother who alerted the authorities.[109]

The following case concerns two boys apprenticed by the DPOS to the same master and mistress. The DPOS inspector reported that the first boy, who had only recently been placed there, stated he 'had little to complain of', but 'when master and mistress fought they felt the tension'.[110] In contrast, the second boy provided a detailed list of the mistreatment he had suffered at the hands of his mistress:[111]

1 His letters were intercepted.
2 His food has been withheld and his bread sometimes soaked in cold water.
3 His indenture destroyed.
4 His clothes have been torn and part of his outfit destroyed.
5 He received personal violence.
6 He has frequently and publicly been addressed as a rogue and bastard. (The mistress admitted that she had referred to her apprentice in these terms but later retracted the statement that he was dishonest.)[112]

The committee members took his allegations seriously and began an 'intensive investigation', in the course of which the mistress admitted the boy's indenture had been 'destroyed by fire'; however, although the committee believed that 'she was the doer',[113] she refused to accept responsibility. In light of the inspector's findings, both boys were removed.

In 1894 inspectors found that the apprentices were giving 'every satisfaction as reported by their respective masters' and that 'further to enquiries made to the apprentices themselves as to how they were taught their trades, the committee or the secretary learned that the apprentices were duly instructed in the particular trade to which they had been bound'.[114] In the same year the committee reported only two unsuitable apprentice placements and in both cases it decided against sending children to either master again. Thus, in much the same way as it had done with respect to 'good' nurses, over time the DPOS committees came to depend on 'good' masters and mistresses.

'Good' and 'bad' apprentices

The level of progress made during the period of apprenticeship depended on two factors: the Society's commitment to the children's welfare and the apprentices' determination to succeed, a point which is well illustrated in the following two case histories. In the first case an orphan was apprenticed as a general draper outfitter for five years in 1894. Shortly after he started his apprenticeship, the DPOS committee received a letter from his master regarding the boy's 'aversion to general drapery' and his desire to work instead as a baker.

The master stated, 'you may remember me speaking about –'s wishes to be a baker and how I could not keep him from the bake house; he is still inclined to stick to this trade and take it in preference to any other'.[115] He went on to say that he hoped – would receive the committee's consent to 'have him transferred to my brother's care and business in Main Street. I greatly fear now that he has developed a taste for this trade that if compelled it would be with the greatest reluctance he would work at any other business'.[116] The boy wrote to the committee to plead his case, 'I would rather be a baker than serve my time to do anything else'.[117] Four years later, the committee received a letter from the boy's new master who stated, 'I am glad to say – turned out a first class baker'.[118]

In the second case the associated problems of curbing juvenile delinquency are explored. A young apprentice found himself in trouble with the managers of the aforementioned Dublin Working Boys' Home and Harding Technical School in July 1898:

> endless lies, not paying for his board – we cannot inflict any punishment of the ordinary on such a character and there appears to be nothing in – to

appeal to him morally in order to arouse his sense of responsibility, he appears to have no idea of what it is to speak truthfully or act straightforwardly. Unless some arrangements can be made to act differently we would be much better without him in the home.[119]

In October 1898, the DPOS was informed by his employer that, 'I am very sorry to say I had to send back – as I could get no good of him, he went to the races nine miles away in the night without getting permission or leave from anyone in the house and when he returned he stopped out in the town and no good work either'.[120] Five days later the DPOS received another letter this time from the apprentice: 'will you be so kind as to ask Mr – to take me back I would like very much to learn my trade. I am very sorry for doing wrong and will in future obey my master's commands. And serve my full term that is on my indentures now'.[121] The master, Mr –, wrote a second letter stating 'cannot keep – from associating with corner boys … He is really unmanageable there is no use of me striving to get good of him'.[122] Eventually, despite his misgivings, Mr – agreed to take the boy back: 'will give him another chance even though he ran away as he has been good for a while'.[123] However in November, the employer informed the committee that if the boy returned he would have him arrested.[124]

The boy was spotted in Dublin weeks later: 'I thought it hard to see him wandering about the streets and got him something to eat and a bed for the night';[125] however, the Working Boys' Home refused to take him back. The DPOS committee stated on the 18 November 1898, 'Couldn't put him in industrial school. Decide to threaten him with reformatory school because he is an absconding apprentice which may keep him at his work. I judge he is rather a weak boy than positively bad'.[126] In December 1898 he was, by direction of the committee, 'brought before a magistrate and sentenced to five years in Malone Protestant Reformatory in Belfast'.[127] The case illustrates most clearly the boy's downward spiral into eventual destitution. Evidently a well-liked boy, there is little doubt that committee members went to extraordinary lengths in order to guide and protect him.

Emigration

Children were sent to Canada and Australia throughout the nineteenth century under the aegis of a number of emigration schemes, the most influential of which was the Barnardo Homes. PO Societies did not support the emigration of its orphans except when absolutely necessary as, in many cases, the children's mothers were still alive. Thomas

Spunner, secretary to the PORS, who had spent time with Mrs Rye in Canada, advocated orphan emigration. On 22 November 1882, the secretary to the county Monaghan POS publicly opposed Spunner's idea: 'The real question for benevolent people to consider in the matter is not the advisability of emigration in general, nor the possible advantages American domestic servants enjoy over Irish; but is it necessary to send out into the world, with, at best, but scant superintendence a number of young children'.[128] Revd Digby Cooke, who was a member of the Female Orphan House committee, also rejected his proposal. 'I cannot think it desirable to send out to a distant colony a number of children of tender age separating them from all ties of kindred possibly from a respectable mother'.[129] According to its 1884 annual report, only one orphan was assisted to emigrate by the Tipperary POS.[130]

In the majority of cases examined in the course of this study, young orphans emigrated with surviving parents and extended kin (often subsidised by the DPOS) rather than through emigration schemes. In numerous cases, elder siblings wrote to the DPOS committee requesting their permission to take their younger sisters and brothers with them when they emigrated.[131] A minor number of orphans aged under eighteen were sent to the Liverpool Sheltering Home, which was founded by Louisa Birt in 1872.[132] The LSH provided chaperones and a degree of protection for the youngsters on their voyage to Canada. While many children found stability and good homes, the lack of supervision provided for the children after they arrived led to cases of exploitation.[133] Other Protestant homes, such as Miss Carr's Homes, the Cottage Home for Little Children and the Ragged Schools, sent a small number of children from Ireland to Canada through the MacPherson and Birt schemes.[134]

Extended family and children's futures

Widows, siblings and extended kin assisted their young relatives who were beginning their working lives in a number of ways; first, if necessary, they objected to unsuitable apprenticeships arranged by the DPOS committee;[135] second, they drew the committee's attention to suitable placements or arranged apprenticeships themselves with the Society's permission; and, third, they monitored the children during their apprenticeships. Lydia Murdoch argues that, 'like histories of child philanthropy, studies of poor law institutions often ignore parents' roles in finding external aid for their children'.[136] The DPOS regularly apprenticed the orphans to their extended relatives in the first half of the nineteenth century, if the opportunity arose; the same was true to a greater extent in the second half of the nineteenth century.[137] For example, in some of these cases, widows in service found employment for their daughters in the same house.[138]

Generally speaking, the committee was most accommodating and agreed to any suggestion which would prove beneficial to the children. It also appears to have done its utmost to assist the widows and children in every way possible; for example, in 1883 the committee 'made the girl a present of a sewing machine as the mother intends having her instructed in dressmaking'.[139] In a second case, a widow, whose husband had been a government clerk, informed the committee in 1887 that she could secure a situation for her fourteen-year-old son. The committee agreed to return the child to his mother.[140] In another case, a widow proposed apprenticing her daughter to a dressmaker 'if the committee agree'.[141] The committee approached the recommended dressmaker. The lady stated, 'I would gladly take one of your girls as an apprentice to dressmaking but your fee is much under my fee'.[142] In fact it was five times that of the ordinary apprentice fee given for orphans; however, given the child's poor circumstances she charitably agreed to lower her normal rate. It was also common for elder siblings to arrange further training for their younger brothers and sisters.[143]

The DPOS raised its admission age limit to thirteen in 1898, after which applications increased: 'many children who were formerly sent to industrial schools would now come to that society'.[144] The flexibility with which the DPOS dealt with surviving parents and extended families when compared to the industrial schools, which did not permit any interference,[145] along with other changes to its general management were additional reasons for renewed public support.

By the late nineteenth century, the orphans were allowed greater freedom to make their own decisions and encouraged to be assertive, which is demonstrated in the following extract from a letter written to the DPOS committee by a young apprentice.

I beg of you to reconsider your decision as I have no taste for printing and as it is such an unhealthy trade I do not think I would get on at it. Besides I hear from a boy who was there that it was not a good place to be in. I am quite willing to work at anything but I should like to get into a nice place. I am answering all advertisements I can see. I hope you will reconsider this and that I shall soon get settled into a good place … Mr. Day is perfect right by saying that no boy ought to be put to anything against his will and this is a very unhealthy trade.[146]

For some orphans, the transition from apprentice to independent adult proved challenging; however, the DPOS maintained an interest in their well-being. 'One of the great objects that a parent has in view in general is to get children comfortably settled in life – to make provision for them. The society, in regard to those children whom it brings up to man's and woman's estate, really does stand in the place of a parent, and not only with regard to the girls but also with regard to the boys'.[147] There is evidence to support claims that the 'committee endeavour as far as possible, to keep in sight the orphans even after they have served their apprenticeships'.[148] The following cases attest to the Society's continued support of the orphans long after the removal of their names from the Society roll. One young man wrote to the Society on 7 January 1898:

> I, a boy reared by the Protestant Orphan Society, just come up lately to Dublin and having no one to get lodging for me shortly before Christmas I took sick and not till then did I learn what kind of house I was in. Of course being sick I got into debt, I therefore ask if the committee would lend me one pound. I would pay it back in instalments fit for any young man. It would take a good time with what I am charged for my lodging to get out of the house. I would gladly pay it back if the committee would consent to give it to me, as I would like to get respectable lodgings as soon as possible.[149]

The curate of St Thomas's described him as a very respectable young man, suggesting, 'I think as he is one of our children the committee would be right in helping him it would be in every best interest for him to enter into the boy's home Lord Edward Street but he has obligations at his present lodgings at 54 Lower Gloucester Street'.[150] The Working Boys' Home, Lord Edward Street, also founded the 'Rutland Club', which was based in Rutland Square for the benefit of elder boys, typically eighteen or nineteen years of age without accommodation. The Home's committee noted in 1896, 'we feel the gravity of such a responsibility, and how necessary it is for us to try to know them individually, so as to be able to help or advise them in case of difficulty or distress. Most of them are orphans and have no one else to look to for sympathy and guidance'.[151] Canon Francis B. Ormsby was Honorary Secretary of the Rutland Club and also a member of the DPOS committee.

Another former orphan, who approached the committee for assistance in 1898, informed the secretary that he had applied to the navy but had been rejected on account of his small build and 'stoppage in his speech'.[152] His apprenticeship to a farmer had left him with limited training and no savings:

It is a hard thing on a fellow to be brought up as a Protestant orphan and then thrown to the waves of the world without any one to look up to or down at. I might get work in a busy time and then I might starve afterwards. I would be thankful if they would send me to New Zealand or Australia where I could get something for my time. I conclude by thanking you for your kindness to me and trusting that you will help me.[153]

The feelings of loneliness expressed in the letter reflects the social reality of independence for the orphans, particularly those without any extended relatives. The letter also suggests that for many young people emigration was a sought-after survival strategy.

Annual reports from the 1890s reflect educational advances and a growing emphasis on the importance of quality training:

Your committee, fully aware of the influence of education, religious and secular on the future welfare of the young, devoted special attendance of this important branch of their work. The orphans are periodically examined in the different schools they attend and as a result, fees are granted to the teachers according to the progress made by the children during the year. They also aim at a higher class education for as many of their orphans as they can afford with a view of gratifying them for such positions as teachers, clerks, type writers; at present they have 16 girls in training at schools in the city, they have 2 boys at the Morgan school Castleknock and four boys at the Swords Borough School. From this latter school it might be mentioned one of the orphans at a competitive examination last year obtained an exhibition which entitled him free board and education for three years at the Farra Endowed school. From the same school another orphan won quite recently an exhibition of £20 with free board and education.[154]

The Morgan Endowed School, Castleknock, Dublin, a Protestant school endowed by Richard Morgan, was taken over by the King's Hospital in 1957. Revd J. C. Irwin was a governor of the school and also a member of the DPOS committee. Many of the boys who attended Morgan's passed the Intermediate Examination and pursued further training.

The main objective of PO Societies was to give children a good start in life. The Meath POS reported that it had apprenticed boys to the following trades: 'painter, tailor, saddler, gardener, shoemaker, carpenter, weaver, printer, baker, blacksmith, iron-moulder, grocer, watch and clock maker'.[155] Others joined the navy or army. As in Dublin, the mainstay for girls was domestic service and dressmaking. Girls were also apprenticed 'to grocers, chemists and confectioners' and became nurses, teachers and clerks.[156]

Table 6.1 Cavan POS orphans, 1850–63

How provided for	Girls	Average age	Boys	Average age
Baker			1	15
Blacksmith			3	15
Bootmaker			8	14
Carpenter			1	15
Confectioner	1	15		
Dressmaker	6	14		
Employment			1	16
Merchant			1	15
Miller			1	14
Painter			2	14
Printer			1	15
Returned to friends	35	13	27	13
Service	26	14	11	14
Shoemaker			13	14
Tailor			7	13
Taken by mothers	2	8		
To be apprenticed			3	15
To be sent to service	2	15	1	15
Other homes				
Female Orphan House	1	15		
Providence Home	2	14		
Wilson's Hospital			1	10
Emigration/migration				
America	3	12		
Australia	1	15		
Canada	2	11		
England	1	14		
Dublin	1	15		
Scotland	1	14		

Source: Cavan POS annual reports, 1850–63, NLI.

Conclusion

By 1895, PO Societies in Ireland had apprenticed or 'otherwise provided for' approximately 18,525 children ('otherwise provided for' referred to children who might have returned home to their mothers or extended kin, emigrated, or secured employment). From its foundation in 1828 to 1899, the DPOS provided apprenticeships for 1,769 of the 4,122 orphans admitted. The Society appears to have made every effort to

Table 6.2 Children apprenticed or otherwise provided for by PO Societies in Ireland[a]

PO Society	Annual average[b]	Total[c]	PO Society	Annual average	Total
DPOS	44	2,838	Tyrone	13	664
PORS	12	827	Carlow	3	175
Cork	24	1,598	Cavan	4	207
Limerick	25	1,635	Meath	6	314
Clare	5	335	Louth	4	193
Kildare (Naas)	4	276	Newry	2	74
Tipperary	14	845	Donegal	8	360
Kilkenny	4	289	Fermanagh	7	296
Ferns Diocesan	5	289	Galway	7	258
King's County	6	369	Mayo	6	199
Leitrim	6	353	Waterford	3	288
Sligo	16	905	Londonderry	9	273
Kerry	6	337	Antrim &		
Westmeath	7	413	Down	86	2,506
Roscommon	3	173	Armagh	15	430
Longford	7	394	Monaghan	3	81
Queen's County	6	331	**Total**	370	**18,525**

Notes:
[a] As a number of children were returned to their mothers/extended kin, not all children who were admitted to the Societies required its assistance with apprenticeships.
[b] Average number of children apprenticed or otherwise provided for annually, which included employment, small loans in lieu of apprenticeship fees, assisted emigration. Typically, children emigrated with siblings or other family members rather than through emigration schemes.
[c] Total number of children apprenticed or otherwise provided for by PO Societies from foundation to 1895.
Source: DPOS annual reports, 1830–95.

arrange suitable apprenticeships. It generally only accepted applications for apprentices from respectable employers; however, it claimed to stand in the place of a parent and had to make difficult decisions during periods of hardship just as parents did: when funds were low and apprenticeships scarce, orphans were sent to less than ideal situations. In certain cases masters did not train their apprentices adequately, treated them harshly and viewed them only in terms of cheap labour. Nevertheless, the apprentices were inspected and removed if necessary. They were also given practical guidance during and after apprenticeship which helped them to become independent and productive adults.

Notes

1 'Address to the British public on behalf of the Protestant Orphan Society for Ireland', p. 334.
2 Robins, *Lost Children*, p. 221.
3 Publicity material, 1866, NAI, POS papers, 1045/6/2.
4 Coolahan, *Irish Education*, p. 191.
5 Pim, 'On the importance of reformatory establishments', p. 5.
6 Sir J. Lentaigne, 'The treatment and punishment of young offenders', *JSSISI*, 8:63 (1884), pp. 31–40, p. 32.
7 Robins, *Lost Children*, p. 296.
8 21 & 22 Vic., c. 103 (2 Aug. 1858).
9 P. O'Mahony, *Criminal Justice in Ireland* (Dublin: Institute of Public Administration, 2002), p. 200.
10 Robins, *Lost Children*, p. 299.
11 Lentaigne, 'The treatment and punishment of young offenders', p. 33.
12 Revd B. Waugh, *The Gaol Cradle, Who Rocks It?* (London: Strahan and Co., 1873).
13 *First Report of the Inspector appointed to visit reformatory schools in Ireland*, p. 131 [2949], HC 1862, vol. xxvi.
14 Coolahan, *Irish Education*, p. 191.
15 *Inspector of Reformatory Schools of Ireland: fifteenth report*, p. 94 [C 1821], HC 1877, vol. xlii.
16 30 & 31 Vic., c. 25 (May 1868).
17 E. D. Daly, 'Neglected children and neglectful parents', *JSSISI*, 10:78 (1897/98), pp. 350–66, p. 352.
18 Robins, *Lost Children*, pp. 302–3; Barnes, *Irish Industrial Schools*, p. 32.
19 Barnes, *Irish Industrial Schools*, p. 154.
20 41 & 42 Vic., c. 66.
21 S. M. Parkes, 'Higher education, 1793–1908', in W. E. Vaughan (ed.), *A New History of Ireland, VI: Ireland Under the Union, II* (Oxford: Clarendon Press, 1996), pp. 539–70, p. 540.
22 D. Keenan, *Ireland within the Union: 1800–1921* (Philadelphia: Xlibris, 2008), p. 399.
23 O'Mahony, *Criminal Justice in Ireland*, p. 201.
24 NSPCC annual report, 1890, p. 21, NLI.
25 Daly, 'Neglected children and neglectful parents', p. 352.
26 Luddy, *Women and Philanthropy*, p. 71.
27 Robins, *Lost Children*, p. 240.
28 Jordan, *Victorian Childhood*, p. 128.
29 *Ibid.*
30 D. H. Akenson, *The Irish Education Experiment: The National System of Education in the Nineteenth Century* (London: Routledge and K. Paul, 1970).

31 J. Parr, *Labouring Children: British Immigrant Apprentices to Canada, 1869–1924* (London: Croom Helm, 1980), p. 15.
32 Luddy, *Women and Philanthropy*, p. 71.
33 Registered application files, Feb. 1855, NAI, POS papers, 1045/5/3.
34 *Ibid.*, 1852, (1152–72) (1153).
35 Barrett, 'Legislation on behalf of neglected children', p. 617.
36 R. M. Barrett, 'Foreign legislation on behalf of destitute and neglected children', *JSSISI*, 10:76 (1896), pp. 143–215, p. 145.
37 Parr, *Labouring Children*, p. 14; Frost, *Victorian Childhoods*, p. 73.
38 Minutes, 27 Nov. 1871, RCBL, CPOS papers, PRIV MS 519.1.
39 DPOS annual report, 1868, NAI, POS papers, 1045/1/1/66–93.
40 M. A. Bianconi, daughter of C. Bianconi of Longfield House, Cashel, was born 16 Sept. 1840 and died in 1908. She wrote her father's biography and married M. J. O'Connell, a lawyer.
41 W. N. Hancock, 'Statistics on points raised by Mrs. O'Connell's and Miss Smedley's papers', *JSSISI*, 8:40 (1879), pp. 38–41, p. 38.
42 Minutes, 2 Oct. 1857, NAI, POS papers, 1045/2/1/6, p. 123.
43 *Report of her Majesty's Commissioners Appointed to Inquire into the Endowments, Funds and Actual Condition of all Schools Endowed for the purpose of Education in Ireland*, p. 173 [2336–I], HC 1857–58, vol. xxii, pt. i.
44 *Ibid.*
45 M. Hearn, 'Life for domestic servants in Dublin, 1880–1920', in Luddy and Murphy (eds), *Women Surviving*, pp. 148–79, p. 149.
46 *Report of her Majesty's Commissioners Appointed to Inquire into the Endowments*, p. 173.
47 *Ibid.*, p. 282.
48 Minutes, 29 Oct. 1858, NAI, POS papers, 1045/2/1/6, p. 206.
49 *Ibid.*
50 Minutes, 4 Nov. 1886, RCBL, MPOS, PRIV MS 619.1.
51 *Irish Times* (9 October 1888).
52 *Ibid.*
53 *Irish Times* (18 June 1869).
54 *Irish Times* (9 October 1888).
55 Westmeath POS annual reports, RIA.
56 Minutes Percy Place Home inspection committee, 1877, NAI, POS papers, 1045/16/4.
57 Minutes, 25 Mar. 1859, NAI, POS papers, 1045/2/1/6, p. 241.
58 *Ibid.*
59 *Ibid.*
60 *Ibid.*, 4 Apr. 1859, p. 247.
61 Minutes Percy Place Home, 1877–78, NAI, POS papers, 1045/16/4.
62 *Ibid.*
63 *Ibid.*
64 Minutes, 22 Feb. 1869, RCBL, CPOS papers, PRIV MS 519.1.1.

65 *Ibid.*
66 *Ibid.*
67 *Ibid.*
68 *Ibid.*
69 Dublin Working Boys' Home, annual report, 1896, NAI, POS papers, 1045/1/1/63–93.
70 *Ibid.*
71 *Ibid.*
72 *Ibid.*
73 *The Tenth Report of the Commissioners enquiring into the State of all Schools on Public or Charitable Foundations in Ireland*, p. 249, HC 1810 (243), vol. x.
74 S. Millham, *Locking up Children: Secure Provision within the Child-Care System* (Farnborough: Saxon House, 1978), p. 16.
75 Murdoch, *Imagined Orphans*, p. 121.
76 *Ibid.*, p. 134.
77 T. Brassey, *The British Navy: Its Strengths, Resources, and Administration, Vol. 5* (London: Longmans, Green and Co., 1883), pp. 66–7.
78 *Ibid.*
79 *Ibid.*, p. 69.
80 *Freeman's Journal* (23 October 1876).
81 J. Duckworth, *Fagin's Children: Criminal Children in Victorian England* (London: Continuum International Publishing Group, 2002), p. 224.
82 *Clio* papers, Kew National Archives, HO45 9553 65394.
83 Register orphan histories, NAI, POS papers, 1045/5/1/6.
84 Minutes, March 1882, NAI, DPOS papers, 1045/2/1/10, pp. 369–70.
85 DPOS annual report, 1889, NAI, POS papers, 1045/1/1/55–60.
86 *Ibid.*
87 *Ibid.*
88 *Ibid.*
89 *Ibid.*
90 See E. W. Roberts, *The 'Clio', 1877–1920: A Study of the Functions of an Industrial Ship in North Wales* (Gwynedd: Llygad Gwalch, 2011), p. 69.
91 Register orphan histories, NAI, POS papers, 1045/5/1/6.
92 *Ibid.*
93 Roberts, *The 'Clio'*, p. 70.
94 *Clio* papers, Kew National Archives, HO45 9553 65394.
95 Minutes subcommittee nurses and education, 1890, NAI, POS papers, 1045/2/3.
96 6 Sept. 1886,. Kew National Archives, WQ/S/1886/M435.
97 *Clio* papers, Kew National Archives, HO45 9553 65394, C502987.
98 Register orphan histories, 1876, NAI, POS papers, 1045/5/1/6.
99 *Ibid.*
100 Parr, *Labouring Children*, p. 84.
101 Apprentice inspection reports, 1860, NAI, POS papers, 1045/6/7/9.

102 *Ibid.*
103 Letter in registered application files, 1863, NAI, POS papers, 1045/5/1.
104 Hearn, 'Life for domestic servants in Dublin', p. 149.
105 Apprentice inspection reports, NAI, POS papers, 1045/6/7/9.
106 *Ibid.*
107 *Ibid.*
108 *Ibid.*
109 Letter apprentice indenture files, 1892, NAI, POS papers, 1045/5/7/11.
110 Minutes, 11 Oct. 1878, NAI, POS papers, 1045/2/1/10, pp. 52–3.
111 *Ibid.*
112 *Ibid.*
113 *Ibid.*
114 Minutes subcommittee nurses and education, 1894, NAI, POS papers, 1045/2/3.
115 Apprentice inspection reports, 1894, NAI, POS papers, 1045/6/7/9.
116 Notes with apprentice indenture, 7 Feb. 1894, NAI, POS papers, 1045/5/7/11 (1268).
117 Apprentice indentures, 1894, NAI, POS papers, 1045/5/7/11 (579–1045).
118 Bound volume of incoming letters, 1898, NAI, POS papers, 1045/3/1/25.
119 *Ibid.*
120 *Ibid.*
121 *Ibid.*
122 *Ibid.*
123 *Ibid.*
124 *Ibid.*
125 *Ibid.*
126 *Ibid.*
127 Minutes, 16 Dec. 1898, NAI, POS papers, 1045/2/1/13, p. 26.
128 Book of press cuttings, NAI, POS papers, 1045/6/1.
129 Book of press cuttings, NAI, POS papers, 1045/6/3.
130 *Clonmel Chronicle* (17 May 1884) in scrapbooks, 1849–84, RCBL, CPOS papers, PRIV MS 519.16.1.
131 DPOS minutes and registers of orphan histories, 1850–90.
132 Parr, *Labouring Children*, p. 32.
133 *Ibid.*
134 Luddy, *Women and Philanthropy*, p. 87.
135 One widow refused to allow her son to be sent to the *Clio* because her husband had died at sea, register orphan histories, 1880s, NAI, POS papers, 1045/5/1/6.
136 Murdoch, *Imagined Orphans*, p. 68.
137 Register orphan histories, 1840–50, NAI, POS papers, 1045/5/1/3.
138 Register orphan histories, 1870 and 1880s, NAI, POS papers, 1045/5/1/6.
139 *Ibid*, 1883, p. 61.
140 *Ibid.*, 1887, p. 55.
141 Bound volume of incoming letters, 1898, NAI, POS papers, 1045/3/1/25.

142 *Ibid.*
143 *Ibid.*
144 *Irish Times* (8 April 1899).
145 Duckworth, *Fagin's Children*, p. 222.
146 Bound volume of incoming letters, 1898, NAI, POS papers, 1045/3/1/25.
147 DPOS annual report, 1880, NAI, POS papers, 1045/1/1/50–54, p. 12.
148 DPOS annual report, 1890, NAI, POS papers, 1045/1/1/61–65.
149 Bound volume of incoming letters, 1898, NAI, POS papers, 1045/3/1/25.
150 *Ibid.*
151 Dublin Working Boys' Home annual report, 1896, NAI, POS papers, 1045/1/1/50–54, p. 6.
152 Bound volume of incoming letters, 1898, NAI, POS papers, 1045/3/1/25.
153 *Ibid.*
154 DPOS annual report, 1895, NAI, POS papers, 1045/1/1/66–93.
155 Athey, 'A short history of the Meath Protestant Orphan Society', p. 7.
156 *Ibid.*

7

Tradition versus change, 1898–1940

As far as possible the children were left with their mothers. Children brought up in orphanages were like children brought up in workhouses – institutions which he regarded as hot beds of crime and pauperism.[1]

Poverty carries with it many evils, and the object of this and other Orphan Societies is to save the children, and that they shall go out into the world to live honest, Godly lives.[2]

Introduction

As the nineteenth century drew to a close social reforms were introduced to raise living standards and reduce dependency on the Poor Law, and children's health increasingly became a matter of national importance. The DPOS remained convinced that children could not thrive and become independent and productive adults if placed in institutions, particularly workhouses. Although it continued to support boarding-out in principle, the Society revised its rules in the late nineteenth century. The penultimate chapter discusses the marked shift in DPOS policies, its changing role, and the parallels between PO Societies and the NSPCC. Through case history analysis, it examines the ways in which bereaved families, including Irish playwright Sean O'Casey's sister, were assisted by the Society in the twentieth century and identifies the benefits of its policy changes for widows and children. It also analyses the children's transition from dependence to independent adulthood, evidence which serves as a barometer of the Society's success in the twentieth century.

'A new departure'

By the end of the nineteenth century, fifteen boards of guardians had appointed women's committees to oversee the boarding out of workhouse children.[3] The Pauper Children (Ireland) Act was passed in 1898 and the Boarding Out of Children in Unions Order, 1899, increased the age limit to fifteen[4] and from this point onwards, workhouse children were boarded out in greater numbers.[5] Inspectors were introduced to the state-run boarding-out scheme in 1902 and under the Children Act 1908 they were called upon to supervise the placement of children who were boarded out privately (for the most part illegitimate children) as well as children boarded out from workhouses.[6] (A professional, quali-fied social worker was appointed in 1948.[7]) Nevertheless, while 2,230 children were boarded out in 1908, 5,645 children remained in work-houses which was 72 per cent of the total number of children depend-ent on poor law relief.[8] Under the jurisdiction of the Irish Department of Local Government and Public Health in 1922 boarding out was not universally adopted despite the promotion of its benefits, particularly for illegitimate children.[9]

Though social reformers had held up its boarding-out system as an example in the 1860s and 1870s, and despite its continued support of the boarding-out system, by the 1890s it had become apparent that the DPOS, which had been serving the Protestant community for seventy years, was clinging to tradition and somewhat antiquated rules, par-ticularly with respect to the placement of orphans with nurses in the country as opposed to with their own kin. The Society had lost favour with the public because of the 'old rule', particularly as other local PO Societies had for a number of years formally adopted the new policy; moreover, by the 1890s public outdoor relief had become more widely available,[10] thereby broadening the scope of widows' relief options and simultaneously reducing the appeal of the DPOS. In order to retain its place among the growing network of prominent Dublin charities, and among local PO Societies, and keep pace with new child welfare trends, it became necessary to re-evaluate its policies. The DPOS stated in 1895:

> Hitherto, it has been the almost invariable custom on the election of orphans to remove them from their mothers and place them with the Society's nurses in the country. Within the past year, your committee have decided upon dealing with each case on its own merits and where they find, after careful enquiry, that the mother is a proper person, residing in a respectable locality, they will appoint her as nurse to her own children. On their election, the committee will allow a *weekly* sum for their main-tenance, provided that such an arrangement does not interfere with her earning her bread.[11]

In November 1898 the DPOS unanimously agreed to officially change its rules in order to permit widows to care for their own children with a paid allowance 'in cases which seem advisable'.[12] The Society continued to board out orphans in other cases.

One of the reasons for its reluctance to change its rules was the belief that urban children were disadvantaged on two fronts – health and morals. Throughout its history, the DPOS had always favoured the placement of children in the country for health purposes; however, its committee stated in 1899, 'when a mother is appointed nurse to her own children, she may with the committee's consent reside in a city parish'.[13] Even in 1912 there were still concerns that the city was not 'a safe, moral place to bring young people up in. It sharpened their wits but, at the same time, it blunted their moral sense'.[14] By 1915 there were 280 children cared for by their mothers with a paid allowance from the DPOS and 144 children boarded out.[15] (The relatively high number of children on the Society roll was a result of the amalgamation of the DPOS and the PORS in 1898 discussed in the next chapter.) There were times when various committee members expressed regret at the rule change: the placement of children with their mothers or extended relatives did not always prove to be in the children's best interests. In the broader context, the NSPCC detected multiple cases in which orphans were taken in by relatives and terribly mistreated.[16] Furthermore, public inspectors of children 'at nurse' also reported that relatives often only applied for children once they were of working age.[17]

Concerns over depopulation, infant mortality and the poor physical condition of Boer War recruits in the *fin de siècle* period informed later child rearing literature and stressed the importance of motherhood as a major factor in the maintenance of children's health.[18] Children were increasingly viewed as a national asset which required investment in order to produce healthy soldiers of the future.[19] In Ireland the Health Committee, the Society for the Prevention of Infant Mortality and the Women's National Health Association guided mothers in the care and feeding of infants. The WNHA also set up a milk depot for the distribution of pasteurised milk.[20] Shannon Millin read a paper before the Statistical and Social Inquiry Society entitled 'Child life: a national asset' in 1915 in which he stated that 'Speaking broadly, one baby out of every eleven born in Ireland in 1914 died within the year of its birth'.[21] He also argued that the nation should protect future generations who represented 'prospective wealth producers'.[22] The objective of the NSPCC, now the leading authority on child welfare issues, was to 'deal directly with the parents and to reform the home'.[23] It recommended that children were best placed with their 'parents and kinsfolk' and 'the very worst thing for a community' was 'to encourage the parental class to leave that care to private charity or to the state'.[24]

Applicants to the DPOS

Sanitary reform and public health were prevailing social issues in the early twentieth century. Deaths caused by typhus fever had significantly decreased while deaths caused by phthisis (consumption of the lungs) were reportedly double those of London. The WNHA, led by Lady Aberdeen, spearheaded a TB prevention campaign in 1908. The negative impact of tenement overcrowding in Dublin was repeatedly cited in public health enquiries. Unemployment was also a recurrent problem in the 1900s and by 1909 relief for the unemployed was given throughout the year rather than the usual winter months.[25] The religious composition of Dublin in 1911 was Catholic (83 per cent), Church of Ireland (13 per cent), Methodists (2 per cent) and Presbyterians (2 per cent), with a small percentage of 'other' religious beliefs including a small Jewish community. The widows of the Protestant lower middle class, whose numbers had declined considerably,[26] and professionals as well as tradesmen and labouring families continued to seek assistance from the DPOS.

The DPOS and local PO Societies regularly refused applications due to insufficient funds. In 1900 the Antrim and Down POS approved only thirty-nine of the eighty applications it had received that year.[27] In an appeal for funds in the early 1900s the DPOS committee referred to the numerous applications it had received and the many cases in which widows reported that they had 'no income'. In one such case eight children were left behind after their father's death, six of whom were provided for by the Society.[28] In 1910 a widow applied to the DPOS following the death of her husband, described as a young man, who had been on a high salary, and 'furnished a house suitable to his income'.[29] In the same year four children were elected following the death of an 'industrious and respectable tradesman'.[30] Also in 1910 a 'man of the labouring class', with seven children 'gave way to habits of intemperance and died'.[31] The family was left destitute and six of the seven children were elected. In 1915 applicants included widows of a shop assistant, brush maker, blacksmith, clerk, bootmaker, builder's labourer, plumber, shopkeeper and gunsmith.

Shortly after the 1916 rebellion, the DPOS was informed that a Protestant family from Dolphin's Barn had been 'put to considerable loss at the time of the rebellion'.[32] According to the report, 'their clothes and belongings were riddled with bullets. The soldiers were in the house for some days firing at the rebels and the –s had to take refuge in the kitchen and the back garden. The destruction of their clothes etc has made a considerable loss to them which they could ill afford'.[33] In addition, 'several applications came from widows, whose children had become orphans through the rebellion', and eleven children were elected to the Society roll.[34]

In some cases women were widowed abroad; for example, a young woman, aged twenty-seven, had married in November 1916 at St Peter's Rectory, in Manhattan, New York. Her husband died on 20 March 1918, leaving her a widow with an infant son. His death was likely to have been caused by the Spanish influenza virus, which hit Queens, New York, in 1918 and tended to cause mortality among young adults. He had worked as a head waiter at the Woodstock Hotel, New York. A chocolate moulder by trade, his widow had worked in Jacob's biscuit factory in Dublin before she left for America. It took all her husband's small savings to pay for her passage home.[35]

The Society expected a rise in the number of applications as 'the clouds of war are being swept away'.[36] As well as casualties of war, accidental deaths were also reported. In 1919 the DPOS assisted two families from Arklow, County Wicklow: 'At a meeting of the committee during the year under review no less than ten orphans, members of two brothers' families were elected from the parish of Arklow. Both fathers perished in a disastrous collision at sea in December, 1919, leaving 14 orphans to the tender mercies of humanity. Another son perished with his father and uncle'.[37]

The influenza pandemic also had a devastating effect in Ireland which caused substantial loss of life; there were a staggering 10,651 deaths registered in 1918.[38] Other applicants to the Society in 1919 included the widows of a blacksmith, insurance collector, bootmaker, builder's labourer, gunsmith, shopkeeper, plumber, clerk, painter and inspector of police (whose widow was a nurse and subsequently moved to England with her children). There was an increase in applications from the widows of ex-soldiers in 1919 and 1920. In 1923 the orphans of an engineer, labourer (and sexton), chauffeur, steward, caretaker, bookbinder, clerk, park ranger, boiler maker, mechanical engineer and postman were admitted to the Society.

Sean O'Casey, his sister Isabella and the Dublin POS

Sean O'Casey, originally John Casey, was born to Michael and Susan Casey née Archer on 30 March 1880 at 85 Upper Dorset Street in St Mary's parish. O'Casey had suffered from poor eyesight since childhood and was one of thirteen children, eight of whom died in infancy.[39] O'Casey's sister, Isabella Charlotte Casey, married Nicholas Beaver, a drummer in the Liverpool Regiment, in 1889. Her husband later worked as a 'checker on the railway'[40] and died on 10 November 1907 aged thirty-four.[41] Alderman Healy inspected the case on behalf of the DPOS: 'I visited Mrs Beaver at – today ... The children go to St Barnabas Day and Sunday Schools. I recommend the children to be taken on by the committee and left with their mother'.[42] The DPOS approved the case and the names of Isabella's three children then aged eleven, eight and three were added to the Society roll in December 1907.[43] The committee provided a small grant for each child and permitted them to remain with their mother. Once they had reached the age limit of fifteen, the boys' names were removed from the Society roll – the eldest in 1911, the middle child in 1914, and the youngest in 1918.[44] The family received assistance from the DPOS for a total of twelve years. Isabella passed away in January 1918 followed by O'Casey's mother, Susan, in November of the same year.[45]

In his autobiographies, O'Casey recalls a meeting he had with Mr Robert John Henchy, the secretary of the DPOS, to discuss his nephew's poor attendance at Sunday School.[46] O'Casey, who was working as a labourer at the time, told Mr Henchy that he would not force his nephew to attend Sunday School. Henchy replied that if he did not adhere to the rules the DPOS would have no option but to discontinue the grant; however, O'Casey remained adamant. Henchy warned, 'but, my friend, if the Society take away the grant, the child will suffer'.[47] O'Casey claimed that the DPOS grant was insufficient to bring up a child. (The grants were intended more as a supplementary payment than full maintenance grants.) Overall, while pointing out the class difference, and their opposing views on Jim Larkin, O'Casey portrayed Mr Henchy in a positive light, describing him as 'essentially a kind man'.[48] He noted the smile on his 'handsome face' and that he shook his hand before he departed. As he left, Henchy remarked that O'Casey's nephew 'didn't look too well';[49] he also reminded O'Casey that he was bound by the Society's rules to request that children attend Sunday School.[50] In many respects the O'Casey story epitomises the sad reality of bereavement and child mortality in late nineteenth and early twentieth-century Dublin. Moreover, the meeting between O'Casey and Mr Henchy highlights the Society's attempts to unify Church of Ireland parishioners from distinct backgrounds through its charitable work.

Cottage homes

Cottage homes were intended to replicate family life as much as possible and were in stark contrast to most orphanages which, according to Rosa M. Barrett, founder of the Cottage Home for Little Children, Kingstown

(1879), were often too large, 'for individual care, and the love these poor children so supremely need',[51] the much smaller cottage homes were intended to replicate family life as much as possible. From the late nineteenth century, the DPOS placed children in cottage homes, typically only in the event that both parents had died, if a surviving parent was in poor health, at the surviving parent's request, or, alternatively, if no foster families were available. In 1895, Miss Charlotte Burroughs established Sunnyside Home for girls in Kilternan, County Dublin. The home was situated 1½ miles from the Carrickmines railway station. The DPOS committee sent inspectors to visit the home to judge its suitability for the placement of girls on the Society roll:

> It is beautiful and most healthfully situated in the parish of Kilternan. It is under the immediate supervision of Miss Burroughs who lives quite close to the home. The matron who lives on the premises seemed a superior woman and very capable of looking after the children under her care. The sanitary arrangements are outside the house and consist of an earth closet which is emptied every morning. The house – sitting room, bedrooms beds, etc were all scrupulously clean. There seemed to be ample accommodation for about eighteen or twenty children. There are about eight children in the Home who all looked well cared for and in good health. There is a good school within a short distance.[52]

Following Miss Burroughs' retirement in 1916, it came under the management of a matron and local committee: the rector, his wife and three other ladies. Dr Ellerker was the medical superintendent at Sunnyside. The wider community contributed regularly to the home; for example, they purchased a pony for the girls on 27 October 1916 and later a gramophone. The home received fixed rates from the DPOS to pay for the children's upkeep. Sunnyside also held its own collections and other fundraising events. Reports from Sunnyside suggest that the local committee pro-actively made the home as family oriented as possible. The girls usually joined the Kilternan Girl Guides and a select number spent summer holidays, generally for one week, in a camp at Greystones, County Wicklow.[53] The children were also 'well supplied with toys from the Harvest Gift Service'.[54] In order to increase the transparency of its work among the orphans, the local committee also arranged 'Home Days' which gave Sunnyside supporters the opportunity to visit the home, observe its healthy surroundings and witness the children's progress. (The home closed in 1953.)

Colonel Kemmis, County Wicklow, offered a cottage for DPOS orphans on his grounds in 1898; nevertheless, at this juncture, the committee expressed reluctance and declined the offer, not wishing to 'depart from their established custom of boarding the children out in the houses of farmers'.[55] That same year, Revd J. S. Lindsay, Rector of Malahide, also offered premises for the benefit of Protestant orphans.[56] The house was situated on a high and open space within two or three minutes' walk of the church and the schools. The accommodation was generous:

> On the right hand side of the hall door as you enter there is a large day room for the children, running the entire length of the house from front to rear. On the left side is the matron's sitting room. Behind the main building there is a commodious kitchen, with excellent range, with hot water cylinder. There are also several pantries, lockups, clothes-room etc. Off the first landing there is sleeping accommodation for the matron a servant and one child with Bathroom and W.C. adjoining. The second story consists of two large dormitories with ample sleeping accommodation for twelve persons in each – 25 altogether. Over one of these there is a comfortable attic with fire place.[57]

The home was approved by the DPOS committee and officially titled 'The Church of Ireland Orphan Home in connection with the Protestant Orphan Society', though it was more commonly known as the Malahide Home.

It came under the management of Revd Lindsay who was assisted by a local ladies' committee, 'which shall have – subject to the control of the committee of the Society – the supervision of all domestic matters including food, clothing and education, medical supervision, and [be] subject to periodical inspection by the officers and committee of the Society, who shall report at least quarterly to the committee'.[58] In addition, some of the beds were set aside for use by the Society for 'delicate children under its care ordered a change of air'.[59] Children's names were removed from the Society roll at the age of fifteen; however, the Society envisaged that the ladies' committee would contribute to 'the future disposal of the children when the limit of age has been attained'.[60] On an inspection in June 1900, the children 'seemed well cared [sic] and happy. In education they have been making fair progress. The dormitories and sleeping arrangements were scrupulously clean'.[61] The following year it reported that, 'up to the present twenty girls have been placed there, and the arrangement so far has given hope that it will work out satisfactorily. The orphans are regularly inspected and the reports of the inspectors have been placed before the committee and everything is done to make the children happy and comfortable'.[62] However, in later years, a lady inspector criticised the manner in which the children were disciplined. The Malahide Home continued to receive children from the DPOS until its closure in 1915 due to lack of funds.

The less well known Clondalkin Cottage Home, which was the select vestry's concern,[63] was proposed by Revd Dr Ferguson in 1899. After some discussion it was decided that the Clondalkin Cottage Home, which catered for ten girls, aged between eight and twelve, should be managed by Dr Ferguson and a local ladies' committee. Both Ferguson and the local committee were subject to the authority of the DPOS committee, which had agreed to contribute annual payments for the girls' maintenance.[64]

In 1901 Miss Neville proposed a cottage home for Swords after which a DPOS subcommittee was formed to visit the property which had the capacity to accommodate twenty-five boys. The committee reported that, 'there is a fine garden in which the boys can either engage in gardening operations or Athletic Sports. Miss Neville who met the subcommittee was extremely considerate in her proposals'.[65] The garden often produced a surplus of vegetables which were then sold. The home built up an admirable reputation for health which is discussed later in the chapter.

In a minor number of cases, the DPOS also sent children to other highly reputable children's homes located in Dublin such as the Cottage Home for Little Children, Kingstown, Miss Carr's Homes and the Female Orphan House. Local PO Societies, such as the Monaghan and the Cork PO Societies, also placed children in cottage homes.

The aforementioned Cottage Home for Little Children, Kingstown admitted Protestant children only. Revds W. E. Burroughs, Dowse and Day assisted both the Cottage Home, Kingstown and the DPOS. The DPOS occasionally called upon Rosa Barrett to receive children under its guardianship. In March 1899, three siblings, two boys and a girl were sent to Kingstown. The DPOS committee resolved 'That the following three children which were elected on 3rd be sent to the Cottage Home Trivoli Road Kingstown and that a sum of £– per annum be paid to the committee of management for their maintenance. This committee undertaking not to remove any of the children without giving one month's previous notice'.[66] There is also evidence that Miss Rosa Barrett requested that the DPOS receive children from the Cottage Home.

The DPOS was often the first port of call for parish clergymen who wished to place children in one of the Protestant cottage homes in Dublin. For example, a widow whose Protestant husband, a compositor, had died of acute pneumonia applied to the DPOS in 1906. 'There are two children left with the widow whose husband died after one day's illness ... The mother proposes getting her into Miss Carr's Home. The younger child is an invalid having some affection which the mother hopes to get attended to in the Children's Hospital, Harcourt Street'.[67] The DPOS was approached first, with a view to assisting the child's admission into Miss Carr's.

In 1910 the DPOS ventured to assist in the case of an infant aged just one year nine months old. The committee received an application for his admission from a Dr Piggot who wrote on behalf of the child's widowed mother. Her husband, a plasterer, had died after a long illness; he had been disabled through heart disease and paralysis. Having ascertained that all the relevant supporting evidence such as marriage and baptismal certificates could be procured, Dr Piggot stated, 'I am most anxious if elected he should get to Miss Barrett's Home as he wants care. He suffered illness in his infancy. I hope the poor little child will be elected'.[68] An inspector visited the widow's home: 'I saw the child who is a nice little fellow and was in charge of a woman who lives in the same house while the mother is at work. The room is clean and respectable though small, but the child would be decidedly better in such a place as Miss Barrett's Home'.[69] The mother decided 'not to part with her little child' until he was older.[70]

In 1916 the committee entered into a working scheme with the Female Orphan House, North Circular Road, by which they were enabled to send a certain number of orphans to the home to be trained and educated.[71] Generally, children were placed in the orphanage only in the event that their mothers had died. The DPOS committee acted as child welfare coordinators in all of these cases.

Children in the family home

In 1898, out of the 2,067 cases dealt with by the NSPCC, 1,987 children were mistreated by their own parents, 21 children were illegitimate, 22 were step-children, 29 were nurse children and in 8 cases they were 'otherwise related'.[72] Neglect was the leading complaint (631), followed by assault and ill treatment (57), abandonment (52), and exposure and begging (27).[73] In the late nineteenth century, the NSPCC reported drunkenness and unsuitable surroundings as the leading factors in neglect cases: 'in nearly every case drink is the dominating cause of cruelty and neglect to children'.[74] The NSPCC recommended that 'the improvement of tenement houses and the strict enforcement of sanitary laws, temperance legislation, and especially the prevention of the sale of drink to children, are all needed, and have alike our cordial support'.[75,76] The NSPCC sought out neglect in family homes and its duty was to 'enforce parental responsibility'. The DPOS and county PO Societies had always given priority to the selection of 'suitable nurses', and condemned immoral surroundings and drunkenness. The NSPCC's 'carefully trained inspectors' used 'warnings' and inspections to prevent neglect.[77] It referred to several cases in which the threat of prosecution improved parental behaviour towards their children;[78] moreover, in other cases the NSPCC, like PO Societies, attempted to 'reform the parents by persuasion'.[79] PO Societies had operated a warning and inspection system to raise nursing standards from the 1830s. It, like the NSPCC, and as discussed in chapter 5, rewarded nurses' good work with gratuities for the care of sick children and threatened to remove children if standards of care were not met. It also did all in its power to vet step-parents prior to children's return to their mothers. In the majority of cases the NSPCC was informed of cases of neglect by the public and liaised with the police. In like manner, members of the community informed the DPOS committee or local superintendents of cases of neglect and members of auxiliaries were also relied upon to watch over the children. The NSPCC offices and shelter were located at 20 Molesworth Street and the DPOS office at 28 and later 33 Molesworth Street.

From the late nineteenth century onwards, women became more involved in orphan inspections on an official basis. In June 1899 the DPOS appointed the committee of inspection and clothing for that year, 'that each member of the committee be requested to inspect a certain number of the orphans each half year in addition to the inspections of the Clerical Secretary and that where possible the co-operation of ladies be invited'.[80] Clergymen were 'empowered to invite the assistance of the following ladies'.[81] The ladies were the committee members' wives. In 1904, a visiting committee was organised to include six women.[82] The general committee remarked in 1905 that the work of the 'Visiting Committee' was of great benefit to the children's welfare and happiness.[83]

The DPOS monitored the children's progress while in their mothers' care identified problems, offered widows advice, which was not always welcome, and in some cases recommended the children's transferral from their mothers' care.

> I regret to be compelled to write to you to say that the orphans named – living in our parish under the care of their mother are being greatly neglected. The mother is not a thrifty woman and is being very careless about their attendance at church, Sunday school and day school. But she says she will not part with her children so I must wash my hands of them all together as they are now not of our parish. And I am persuaded that my advice is best for her and them and yet she refuses to help herself in any way.[84]

The inspector's concerns seem justified yet the Society had always met with widows' resistance when it came to the possible removal of their children from the family home.

Inspectors also visited widows' homes to establish whether they could realistically afford to care for their children in the long term. The identification of inferior housing was a recurrent theme in both DPOS and NSPCC annual reports. A DPOS inspector observed in May 1901, 'This room is rather small – top front in a tenement house – I don't particularly care for the surroundings. I am of the opinion however with Revd J. Haythornwaite's supervision that she may be allowed to reside where she is at present'.[85] Certain applications were approved on the strict condition that widows would find superior accommodation: 'election of child confirmed. To be left with mother on condition that she finds suitable quarters containing *two* rooms at least'.[86]

An inspector, a clergyman, visited a Protestant family in Townsend Street in April 1914 and found that, apart from her two grown-up daughters who contributed a small weekly sum, the widow, a 'general worker', had no relatives to assist her. He indicated that the widow and her late husband, a coal porter, had been 'from humble means' and that the widow was 'very poor'.[87] While he admitted he had 'no experience of tenements',[88] he expressed disapproval of the widow's home: 'I must confess I do not like her room and I doubt if anything could improve it'.[89] Nevertheless, he suggested that the widow's children remain with her as he considered her a 'strong woman' and 'very capable'.[90]

Conversely, in June of the same year, a DPOS inspector reported on a separate case in which he felt that the children's removal from the home was necessary:

> I visited this case today and saw Mrs – and the children who appear to be well cared for from their condition, but I fear the food she is able to supply them with is very meagre for the means are very small. She said she had saved a few pounds which is now nearly come to an end. And she got nothing from her husband's trade society head quarters at Liberty Hall … The rector says we ought to leave the children under the mother's care; I do not think it is possible for her to keep them, feed them, clothe them, and pay rent, as she is earning nothing so I told her and she promised to consider by Friday [whether] she would give them up to the Protestant Orphan Society for the homes.[91]

As the case suggests, the Society thoroughly investigated widows' circumstances in order to make arrangements which best suited their individual needs.

DPOS inspectors closely monitored children's attendance at day school and Sunday school and regularly reported their findings to the committee. The visiting committee and a lady inspector were expected to visit the widows to resolve cases of truancy and unexplained absences from school.[92] If a compromise could not be reached with the widow regarding school attendance, the Society sent, or threatened to send, the children to Protestant Industrial Schools, or stopped the widow's allowance altogether.[93] Susanne Rouvier Day, Poor Law Guardian, Cork, recommended that parents who neglected their children's education should no longer be entitled to outdoor relief and should instead be provided with indoor relief.[94] Under the terms of the School Attendance Act, 1926, parents were obligated to ensure their children's attendance at elementary school.

Support for widows

Church of Ireland widows worked in Dublin as charwomen, dressmakers, house-keepers, domestic servants, cooks, teachers and nurses.[95] A number of widows also took in lodgers.[96] As discussed in previous chapters, many did not seek out or accept charity or public relief of any kind unless they had young dependents, their health had deteriorated and they could no longer work. The DPOS provided widows with vital targeted assistance on a case-by-case basis which ranged from facilitating access to their children, providing children with temporary care, and assistance with finding better accommodation, to easing the burden of single motherhood during periods of crises.

Many widows whose children were boarded out or placed in DPOS children's homes, wished to maintain close contact with them and there are numerous references to cases in which the Society facilitated access; for example, in 1900, when a widow asked to have her children 'home for the holidays' the secretary agreed without question.[97] In another case a widow requested that the Society place her children with a nurse who lived close by. Unwilling to unsettle the children who were doing well in another location, yet eager to compromise, the committee instead 'granted tickets for two excursions per year'.[98] The Society also regularly provided widows with grants to partially fund children's vacations with them.

Widows who had remarried occasionally postponed their children's return for various reasons. For the most part, the DPOS agreed to keep the children under its guardianship and arrange suitable placements until it became possible for their mothers to receive them. In one such case, which was reported in 1899, the committee informed the 'intending stepfather' that he would be required to pay towards his step-son's maintenance as a boarder in the Swords School.[99] The following year, a widow, who had recently remarried, requested that the Society 'retain her children for the present'.[100] In response, the committee enquired, 'what is she prepared to pay towards maintenance of the children (3)?'.[101]

A widow, assistant matron of the Newcastle Sanatorium, County Wicklow, originally placed her child in the Cottage Home for Little Children. The boy was subsequently admitted to the DPOS for a short time while the widow was 'training in the Rotunda Hospital'. The widow was appointed matron of the Sherborne Preparatory School, Dorset, after which she requested the return of her son and both left for England.[102] Typically, in cases of this kind, the children were accommodated in the Society's associated children's homes and schools as short-term boarders. The DPOS represented a source of child care for widows which gave them the opportunity to establish themselves and prepare financially for their children's return.

In 1902 the committee reported that a child under her mother's care had been assaulted, advising that 'the child be sent to Dr – to be examined and that the mother be directed to seek the assistance of the Police with a view to bringing to justice the man whom she charges with assault on her child'.[103] The assistant secretary stated that 'he waited with orphan – on Doctor – on Saturday Morning 3rd September who directed him to bring the child to the Dispensary on the following Monday morning. He brought the child accompanied by her mother as instructed, the Doctor in charge refused to have anything to say to the case and the mother expressed a desire to let the matter drop'.[104] The DPOS secretary provided the widow with crucial support and encouraged her to seek justice for her child, which were highly significant responses to a difficult case.

Although most widows preferred to keep their children with them and while many excelled in their role as mothers when healthy, there were others in poor or deteriorating health for whom the social reality of single motherhood was too great to bear. The ladies of the visiting committee made every effort to assist these widows particularly during bouts of illness. They reported such cases to the managing committee and requested additional grants for the families in the greatest distress. In 1907 a young boy and his mother were brought to the office to explain his non-attendance at school, which would in normal circumstances have led to a harsh warning and the threat of discontinuance of allowance. However, when it came to light that his mother was in poor health, the committee 'recommended that they get another chance'.[105] In a second case, a lady visitor informed the committee that one of the widows was 'at present incapacitated from looking after her children'.[106] The secretary wrote to the widow stating that the Society was responsible for the children and 'that she should go into hospital and hand the children pro term to the Society'.[107] There is also evidence that the DPOS kept children on the Society roll after the normal age if widows were ill. As discussed in chapter 5 widows were admitted to asylums and/or became physically ill under the burden of single motherhood. Records of provincial mental asylums suggest that widows continued to be admitted, albeit in smaller numbers, into the twentieth century.[108]

The Society also assisted widows to find better accommodation if necessary. As discussed earlier, DPOS inspectors identified poor housing as one of the leading problems for widows. A lady visitor reported that the room in which a widow and her children resided was 'overcrowded' and therefore 'unsatisfactory' and that unless there was some change she would call for the children's removal. In this case the same lady visitor approached the visiting committee to 'help Mrs – to get better quarters than her present home'.[109] The secretary agreed to assist and promised to 'make further enquiries and make the best arrangements possible'.[110] In this case, the Society increased the widow's allowance in line with the higher rent.[111]

During the war, the DPOS distributed bonuses to supplement DPOS widows' allowances and made Christmas appeals: 'owing to the present high price of living our nurses and mothers find it very hard to support the orphans under their care on the amounts they receive from the Society'.[112] Moreover, just after the Great War had ended, the secretary, R. J. Henchy, appealed for support for an upcoming jumble sale being held in aid of the Society: 'Old clothing and boots are a very great help to the widows and orphans, as the price of these commodities is so high at present'.[113]

Home Assistance was introduced in 1924 and was essentially another name for the system of outdoor relief. The issue of stigmatisation of widows in receipt of home assistance was raised in the 1927 report of the Poor Law Commission.[114] The solution was the Widows' and Orphans' Act, 1935.[115] Widows had to be aged between sixty and seventy or have a dependent child under fourteen; widows who remarried or lived with a man were no longer eligible.[116] At an annual meeting of the Kilkenny POS, a committee member stated: 'The government has made it known that they were about to introduce a scheme of insurance for widows and orphans. That was a very wise and good move'.[117] The DPOS investigated the terms and found that as many of the widows whose children were already under its care had not been insured under the National Health Insurance Act, the dependents were consequently precluded from state pensions.[118] In relevant cases, adjustments had to be made to widows' grants in light of the legislation.[119] If widows were ineligible for either contributory or non-contributory pensions they could benefit from 'home assistance'.[120] The age limit and other criteria for non-contributory pensions were eventually removed and the 1937 amendment abolished the insurance test,[121] which made pensions more widely available.

The DPOS continued to assist widows after the Widows' and Orphans' Act and appealed to the public for funds on their behalf again in the 1940s due to rising living costs. The numerous written expressions of gratitude sent by widows to the DPOS committee attest to the effectiveness of its system.[122]

Health and medical care

As the DPOS, and local PO Societies, increasingly left children with their mothers rather than place them with nurses in the country, widows became directly responsible for their children's health and medical care. It was perhaps no coincidence that a number of widows in receipt of DPOS allowances were trained nurses. It is highly likely that these widows were permitted to care for their own children, firstly, due to the respectability associated with nursing,[123] and, secondly, their ability to care for sick children particularly at a time when the NSPCC continued to report the prevalence of medical neglect.

While the ladies who managed the DPOS cottage homes in various locations were responsible for the children's general and medical care, they also relied upon and corresponded with the DPOS committee regarding medical matters.[124] Dr S. J. Gordon became a DPOS committee member in the early twentieth century. Both Dr Gordon and other members of the committee agreed that the Swords Home's location had contributed greatly to low levels of illness: 'in the open country with large garden and playground, good sanitation, and water supply ensures health and we have an almost unbroken record of freedom from serious illness'.[125] Swords reported in 1933 that 'there has been complete absence again of serious illness during the year and the more recent arrivals among the boys show a marked improvement in health and physique – good evidence of their healthy surroundings'.[126] The home's medical officer was thanked regularly 'for the care and attention to the boys' welfare at all times'.[127] Sunnyside had also established an excellent reputation for good health.[128] The available evidence suggests that the DPOS committee and local committees responsible for the cottage homes prioritised children's health and ensured their access to medical care.

The DPOS continued to pay widows an allowance beyond the ordinary

Table 7.1 Children's medical care, 1899–1940

Year	Gender	Age	Location	Illness	Treatment
1899	boy	n/r	Swords	Influenza	Cod liver oil & malt extract
1900	boy	n/r	Working Boys' Home	Scarlatina	Cork St Hospital
1900	girls (9)	9–12	Malahide	Whooping cough	Recovered
1904	boy	n/r	with mother	Consumption	Consumptive Hospital, Newcastle[a]
1906	boy	n/r	Swords	Fits	n/r Removed from the school temporarily
1910	boy	n/r	n/r	Weak back, feet	Medical boots
1910	girl	n/r	Stewart Inst.	Pulmonary TB	Died
1913	boy	n/r	Swords	Tonsillitis	Adelaide, removal tonsils (5 wks hospital)[b]
1914	girl	n/r	with mother	Wasting away	Adelaide Hospital, mother removed her[c]
1914	girl	n/r	Sunnyside	TB	Crooksling Sanatorium[d]
1914	boy	n/r	Swords	TB	Peamount Institution[e]
1915	girl	10	Sunnyside	Spine	To mother fitted with a medical corset
1915	girl	n/r	with mother	Affection of eye	Treatment arranged
1918	boy	n/r	Swords	TB	To local doctor then Peamount Institution
1919	girl	n/r	n/r	Scarlatina	In hospital progressing well
1922	boy	4	with mother	Pneumonia	Adelaide Hospital[f]
1923	girl	8	with mother	Eye weakness	Given spectacles on prescription
1924	girl	9	with mother	Scarlatina	Cod liver oil after recovery, to Sunnyside
1925	girl	6	with mother	Very delicate	Robeleine, Virol, cod liver oil, to Sunnyside
1925	girl	9	with mother	Rickets	Malt & cod liver oil, Adelaide, Sunshine Home
1926	boy	n/r	n/r	Pneumonia after measles	Died
1926	n/r	12	with mother	Meningitis	Died

Table 7.1 (Continued)

Year	Gender	Age	Location	Illness	Treatment
1926	girl	6	with mother	Eye weakness	Given spectacles on prescription
1927	boy	13	with mother	Flat feet, weak back	Surgery orthopaedic hospital, steel supports
1928	girl	9	with mother	Operation on arm	Hand removed, Stevens' Hosp. (1 yr) Sunnyside
1928	girl	10	Sunnyside	Eye weakness	Given spectacles on prescription
1930	boy	n/r	n/r	Adenoids, tonsils	Drumcondra
1931	girls	n/r	Sunnyside	Measles, mumps	Prolonged holidays, no bad cases
1933	girl	n/r	Sunnyside	Influenza	Newcastle Sanatorium
1937	boy	n/r	Swords	Weak ankles	Orthopaedic Hospital
1939	girls	n/r	Sunnyside	Spring – mumps	In quarantine for a very long time, all recovered
1939	girls	n/r	Sunnyside	chicken pox	In quarantine, all recovered
1939	girl	n/r	Sunnyside	Appendicitis	Operation, recovered
1939	boy	n/r	Swords	Knee injury	Children's Hospital, Harcourt Street

Notes:
[a] Newcastle Sanatorium, the National Hospital for Consumption, was founded in 1896. It was modelled on the sanatoria which had flourished in England and Scotland. Its design was based specifically on the National Hospital of Ventor on the Isle of Wight. Lord Fitzwilliam provided nineteen acres between Newcastle and Newtown Mount Kennedy, County Wicklow. It was the first open air hospital of its kind in Ireland.
[b] To mother, then to Stillorgan Convalescent Home.
[c] DPOS intervened to ensure she received necessary medical care and admitted her to Steven's Hospital, Dublin.
[d] The Crooksling Sanatorium was established by the Dublin Joint Hospitals Board, at Brittas, County Dublin in 1911 and aimed at the poor to prevent consumption (TB). The expansive building was situated on a hill known as Crooksling; over 300 acres surrounding the site were also purchased.
[e] The Women's National Health Association founded the Peamount Institution in 1912 as a TB sanatorium.
[f] Four months later mother given grant to bring children on holidays to Glendalough, County Wicklow.
Source: DPOS register of orphan histories; minutes of visiting committee; annual reports, 1899–1940.

term if their children were ill; moreover, it arranged children's holidays to the country for health purposes.[129] The Country Air Association also funded similar excursions for children while the WNHA formed the Children's Fresh Air Fund in 1919 which arranged for children to spend two week holidays in the country, known as the Fresh Air Fortnight.[130]

Further training and work

In the early twentieth century, when DPOS girls turned fourteen they were 'in the opinion of the committee to be fitted for domestic service', and transferred to the Providence Home or other similar homes for technical training in domestic service.[131] At this time, the DPOS committee warned widows if they disapproved of their daughters' placement in domestic service they would no longer receive its assistance. The Dublin Domestic Training Institute, 37 Charlemont Street, Dublin was founded in 1906 under the Board of Education of the General Synod of the Church of Ireland, and, in connection with the Department of Agriculture and Technical Instruction for Ireland scheme as a residential school for training girls in domestic economy.[132] Seven girls from various PO Societies received scholarships, along with 'six from the Girls' Friendly Society, and twenty-seven were supported by assisted scholarships and private payment'.[133] These scholarships in domestic training were provided by the County Councils. However, due to poor uptake, in 1911, the Institute foresaw its imminent closure unless matters improved. The managers, such as Canon Charles Dowse, lamented the possible loss of advantages for 'young women of Ireland' should it close.[134] Despite a rise in domestic service wages, girls received comparatively less pay, based on the assumption that girls were not workers in their own right but rather worked for a short period prior to marriage.

While most girls entered domestic service, a minor number availed themselves of other training opportunities. Miss – was sent for trial in the postal and telegraph business 'in accordance with the instructions of the committee in February 1900'.[135] In the same year another girl was 'to be taught shorthand and typewriting and qualified in both these branches of education'.[136] Shorthand and typewriting remained in demand; a number of mothers requested that the DPOS assist their daughters to train in office work which was typically of six months' duration in a technical school.[137]

The visiting committee reported in 1908 that one of the girls aged fourteen 'desires to be trained as a teacher and is going in for the Intermediate'.[138] In October 1919, a widow requested assistance from the committee to purchase a uniform for her daughter who was 'going as probationer to the Rest for the Dying', which was duly provided.[139] In 1933 a girl obtained a scholarship to Alexandra College and trained as a school teacher at the Kildare Street Training College.[140] The committee informed the widows when suitable positions arose for their daughters and also encouraged them to seek out placements for their children.

Training for boys included the agricultural schools, technical schools, and Hibernian Marine School. Apprentices who lived outside Dublin continued to lodge at the Working Boys' Home with the Society's assistance.[141] The Morgan Endowed School, Castleknock, was among the other training options. The Love and Gardiner's Charity provided educational grants to members of the Church of Ireland whose 'parents have lived within the old city limits; the children must also have attended a primary school in the city or County of Dublin; the proposed employer must be Protestant'.[142] The managers stated that they would 'give a favourable consideration to orphans under the care of this Society whose case falls within their scheme'.[143] While the charity was aimed primarily at boys, it also contributed to DPOS girls' training fees.[144] In a number of cases, the DPOS retained children beyond the ordinary term for periods of between four and six months, or longer if necessary, in order that they could complete their training. The Commission on Technical Instruction identified the inadequate number of valuable apprenticeship schemes.[145] The Apprentice Act was passed in 1931.

Independence

The main objective of PO Societies was to guide children through adolescence into independent adulthood. The Tipperary POS reported in 1905 that since its foundation in 1835 it had assisted 1,027 orphans and apprenticed 400 and that it currently had 58 children under its care.[146] The Cork POS updated subscribers on the orphans' progress in 1914: one entered the Royal Navy Hospital School Greenwich; one joined the Royal Engineers as a mechanic; one joined the Royal Navy; one was elected to the Masonic Orphan Boys' School Dublin; one accompanied his mother to the USA; two went with their mother to England; one went with her mother to Dublin.[147]

Eighteen men who had once been on the DPOS roll, most of whom were educated at Miss Neville's home Swords, 'gave up their brave lives for the sake of their King and country ... The Society has erected in their boardroom a roll of honour which bears the names of the eighteen heroes. Simple as it is the committee felt it was the least they could do to keep in perpetual memory the names of which they are so proud'.[148] A committee member's son also died in action.

The challenges associated with securing young people of the church employment were discussed at the 1929 Youth Conference convened by the Church of Ireland.[149] In the 1930s, children who had grown up in the cottage homes found work, for example, as assistants on farms or in grocers' shops, while others secured jobs locally. Occasionally, girls were employed by Sunnyside and the Cottage Home, Kingstown. For example, a girl who had been raised in Sunnyside, but who 'was not very strong', was employed as a maid in the home.[150] The Meath POS referred to the clergymen, officers in the army, and successful men of business who had 'once belonged to the Protestant Orphan Society'.[151] Tables 7.2–7.4 provide an overview of the paths taken by some of the orphans raised by the Dublin POS and Galway POS.

The following excerpts are from letters written by former orphans to the DPOS which were included with their applications for marriage portions. The first is from a letter dated 1898:

Table 7.2 Galway POS orphans, 1890–1909

	Boys		Girls
Church sexton	1	Post office assistants	2
Clerk	2	Post mistress	1
Engine driver	1	Hospital nurse	1
Artillery	2	Domestic service	3
Royal Navy	1	Emigrated to America	7
Australian Police	1	Killed in Boer War	1

Source: Galway POS annual report, *Irish Times* (11 November 1909).

Table 7.3 Dublin POS orphans, 1903

	Girls		Boys
Domestic service	5	Other homes/orphanages	3
Training for domestic service	13	Emigrated to America	5
Other homes and orphanages	10	South Africa with mother	1
Dressmaking	2	England with mother	1
Shop assistant	1	Apprenticed shop assistants	2
Post office	1	Placed in offices in the city	6
Typist	1	Given up to mothers	11
Returned to mothers	13	Adopted by nurse	1

Source: Dublin POS annual report, 1903, pp. 14–15.

Table 7.4 Dublin POS orphans, 1910–40

Employment/apprenticeship		Further information
Housemaid	Girl	Married[a]
Children's nurse (worked in munitions factory during WWI)	Girl	Married[b]
Imperial Tobacco Factory	Boy	Died of consumption
Railway Bus Service	Boy	Married
Heley's, Dame Street	Boy	Married
Woolworths, Belfast	Girl	Married
Motor driver, Belfast	Boy	n/r
Joined British Army, bugler	Boy	n/r
Bugler in artillery, Woolwich	Boy	Married
Hibernian Marine School	Boy	n/r
Irish Signs Limited	Boy	Married
Jacob's Factory	Boy	n/r
NKM Irish Cream Toffee	Girl	n/r
Shoemaker	Boy	America
Messenger on motor van	Boy	America
Motor mechanic	Boy	Married
School teacher (scholarship Alexandra College and training Kildare St Training College)	Girl	Baltinglass
Gravesend School, steward	Boy	Australia
Benson's Jewellers	Boy	Married
Ferrier & Pollocks	Boy	n/r
Killed in Active Service Field Ambulance	Boy	n/r 1940
Infantry	Boy	Wounded in action
Hopkins Tailors Outfitters, Dublin	Boy	n/r
Irish Salt Company, 40 Lr Mayor Street	Boy	n/r
Joined Navy	Boy	n/r
Peugeot Motor Co., Dawson Street	Boy	n/r
Messenger SN Railway	Boy	n/r
Typist	Girl	n/r
Joined SS *King City* Cardiff	Boy	Died[c]
Posting dept Arnott & Co.	Boy	n/r
Harland & Wolfe, Belfast	Boy	n/r

Notes:
[a] Her husband had carried out two years' active service as a Lance Corporal with the 13th Lancers and suffered serious wounds on three separate occasions.
[b] Married a soldier who 'was awarded the Divisional Parchment Certificate for Gallantry in action on 1 July 1916 and was awarded the Belgian War Cross for conspicuous bravery in the last battle of Flanders'.
[c] Casualty of SS *King City* lost by enemy action Aug. 1940.
Source: Dublin POS register of orphan histories.

Gentleman, Mr Hewitt informed me that you were annoyed with me at my getting married and changing my address without telling you. I am very sorry if I have caused you any trouble by doing so. Thanking you for all past kindnesses and anticipating a continuance of the same. P.S. Gentleman I wish to let you know that my husband – was one of your orphan boys.[152]

A former orphan wrote to the committee in 1917 to apply for a Kinsey marriage portion. He was living in England at the time, where he worked as a tramcar driver for sevenpence an hour 'when there was work'.[153] He had married in 1908 and had four children aged eight, six and (twins) three. 'You will find that I have never been an apprentice also I have got no trade of any kind. Owing to my own fault for not taking same when required to do so'.[154]

In another letter of application to the Kinsey Marriage Portion Fund received in 1924, a former DPOS orphan stated he had served his time as a saddler in Newtown, Barry, Wexford, continued to work for the same employer after his apprenticeship and subsequently joined the army. He informed the committee that he was no longer in the army and that he could not find work. 'Times are bad with me, owing to the motor business there is very little doing in the saddlery line and I tried several times to see if I could get a job and could not. So I would be very grateful if you could send me a little help as I have a wife and child to keep also hope you will forgive me for troubling you'.[155] In a second letter received months later, the applicant's wife wrote, 'cannot get a job, so we have made up our minds, if we can get our fare, to go to Canada as my husband has a sister there and perhaps he would find work there'.[156]

Orphans who had settled all the over the world from England to New Zealand also contacted the Society in Dublin to request their 'birth lines'. The Society appears to have consistently released the requested information.[157] The DPOS stood out from contemporary child welfare agencies in this respect primarily because children typically emigrated with relations or joined family members in the destination country.[158] Thus, DPOS and most local PO Society orphans did not generally experience the often long-term emotional distress and stigmatisation described in studies of child emigration schemes to Canada and Australia and did not share the same sense of 'lost identity' as the children in Margaret Humphreys' study *Empty Cradles* who were denied access to their family histories in adulthood.[159]

The personal testimony of a family whose forebears were assisted by the DPOS in the early 1900s presents further convincing evidence of the Society's commitment to the welfare of bereaved families. In this case

Figure 7.1 Adult DPOS orphan c.1880s to 1890s.

a mother with three young dependents was placed under considerable financial strain after her husband's death. The Society stepped in to assist and the widow was able to remain in the family home, which may not have otherwise been possible. The boys were sent to boarding school where they thrived and received a good education. The widow lived into her eighties in the same home and the boys grew up to be well-rounded individuals, found success in their chosen careers, married and became supporters of Church of Ireland associated charities.[160]

Conclusion

The DPOS underwent considerable change in the late nineteenth century: widows cared for their own children often in urban locations; DPOS

Figure 7.2 Adult DPOS orphan with his wife c.1880s to 1890s.

committee members increasingly assumed the role of child care coordinators while the visiting committee and secretary carried out many of the duties of modern social workers. The DPOS and local PO Societies provided widows with targeted assistance and acted as reliable support networks in the absence of, or as an addition to, their families. In many respects, the NSPCC's vision of cruelty prevention mirrored the earlier work of PO Societies particularly with respect to its inspection system. The DPOS and the ladies' committees in charge of its associated cottage homes invested much time, effort and money in the children's health and medical care. The children's aftercare was no less important and there is ample evidence to support the view that the charity did its utmost to secure valuable training and stable employment for the orphans. The final chapter examines the broader religious and social context in which the DPOS operated in the second half of the twentieth century.

Notes

1 Revd J. W. Mervyn, 'Protestant Orphan Society annual meeting', *Irish Independent* (6 April 1907).
2 Monkstown POS annual report, 1908.
3 Luddy, *Women and Philanthropy*, p. 91.
4 M. Carroll and A. Lee, 'Community work: a specialism of social work?' in Kearney and Skehill (eds), *Social Work in Ireland*, pp. 146–64.
5 See Robins, *Lost Children*, p. 282.
6 Skehill, 'Child protection and welfare social work', p. 136.
7 *Ibid.*
8 S. S. Millin, 'The duty of the state towards the pauper children of Ireland', *JSSISI*, 12:89 (1908/1909), pp. 249–62.
9 Maguire, *Precarious Childhood*, pp. 56–7.
10 Crossman, 'Welfare and nationality', p. 84.
11 Loose document found in minute book, NAI, POS papers, 1045/15/2. See also *Irish Times* (15 December 1896) in book of press cuttings, NAI, POS papers, 1045/6/1.
12 Minutes, 1898, NAI, POS papers, 1045/2/1/13–14, p. 20.
13 Minutes, 17 Mar. 1899, NAI, POS papers, 1045/2/1/14, p. 61.
14 Extracts from DPOS annual report, 1912, book of press cuttings, 1045/6/3.
15 See DPOS annual report, 1905, NAI, POS papers, 1045/1/1/66–93.
16 NSPCC annual report, 1901, p. 29, NLI.
17 Skehill, 'Child protection and welfare social work', p. 136.
18 C. Urwin and E. Sharland, 'From bodies to minds in childcare literature: child care advice literature and infant mortality', in R. Cooter (ed.), *In the Name of the Child* (London: Routledge, 2002), pp. 174–99, p. 177.
19 H. Hendrick, *Child Welfare in England, 1872–1989* (London: Routledge, 1994), p. 14.
20 J. V. O'Brien, *Dear, Dirty Dublin: A City in Distress, 1886–1916* (Berkeley, London: University of California Press, 1982), p. 109.
21 S. S. Millin, 'Child life as a national asset', *JSSISI*, 13:96 (1915), pp. 301–16, p. 307.
22 *Ibid.*
23 H. Hendrick, *Child Welfare: Historical Dimensions, Contemporary Debates* (Bristol: Policy Press, 2003), p. 25.
24 Daly, 'Neglected children and neglectful parents', p. 354.
25 M. Daly, *Dublin the Deposed Capital: A Social and Economic History, 1860–1914* (Cork: Cork University Press, 1984), p. 112.

26 M. Maguire, 'A socio-economic analysis of the Dublin Protestant working class, 1870–1926', *Irish Economic and Social History*, 20 (1993), pp. 35–61, p. 38.

27 'Antrim & Down POS', *Belfast News-letter* (6 April 1900).

28 Appeal for funds, 1902, NAI, POS papers, 1045/1/1/116–44.

29 DPOS annual report, 1910, NAI, POS papers, 1045/1/1/66–93, p. 14.

30 *Ibid.*

31 *Ibid.*

32 Kinsey Marriage Portion Fund applications, 12 May 1916, NAI, POS papers, 1045/5/9.

33 *Ibid.*

34 DPOS annual report, 1916, NAI, POS papers, 1045/1/1/66–93, p. 10

35 Orphan case files, 7 Feb. 1919, NAI, POS papers, 1045/5/5/A1.

36 DPOS annual report, 1919, NAI, POS papers, 1045//1/1/66–93, p. 13.

37 Kinsey Marriage Portion Fund applications, NAI, POS papers, 1045/5/9.

38 Sir W. J. Thompson, 'Mortality from influenza in Ireland', *JSSISI*, 14:1 (1920), pp. 1–14.

39 P. G. Hill, *Our Dramatic Heritage: Classical Drama and the Early Renaissance* (New Jersey: Farleigh University Press, 1992), p. 253.

40 *Ibid.*

41 Registered appliction files, NAI, POS papers, 1045/5/3/3 (803–4101).

42 Register orphan histories, June 1903 – 5 July 1912, NAI, POS papers, 1045/5/1/8, pp. 167–8.

43 *Ibid.*

44 *Ibid.*

45 R. Ayling, *Sean O'Casey's Theatres of* War (Vernon: Kalamalka Press, 2004), p. 23.

46 S. O'Casey, *Mirror in my House: The Autobiographies of Sean O'Casey, Vol. I* (London: Macmillan, 1956), pp. 319–40.

47 *Ibid.*, p. 320.

48 *Ibid.*

49 *Ibid.*

50 *Ibid.*

51 Raftery and O'Sullivan, *Suffer the Little Children'*, p. 58.

52 *Ibid.*, May 1900.

53 DPOS annual report, 1924, NAI, POS papers, 1045/1/1/95–114.

54 *Ibid.*, p. 40.

55 Minutes, 7 Oct. 1898, NAI, POS papers, 1045/2/1/14, p. 71.

56 *Ibid.*, 16 Dec. 1898, p. 32.

57 *Ibid.*

58 *Ibid.*, 30 Dec. 1898, p. 35.

59 *Ibid.*, p. 36.

60 *Ibid.*

61 *Ibid.*, 17 June 1900, p. 148.

62 *Ibid.*, 26 Apr. 1901, p. 191.

63 *Ibid.*, 14 Apr. 1899, p. 70.
64 *Ibid.*, p. 71.
65 *Ibid.*, 26 Apr. 1901, p. 191.
66 Unregistered applications (refused and postponed), NAI, POS papers, 1045/5/4.
67 *Ibid.*
68 *Ibid.*
69 *Ibid.*
70 *Ibid.*
71 DPOS annual report, 1916, NAI, POS papers, 1045/1/1/66–93.
72 NSPCC annual report, 1898–99, p. 2, NLI.
73 *Ibid.*
74 NSPCC annual report, 1899–1900, p. 10, NLI.
75 *Ibid.*
76 *Ibid.*
77 NSPCC, annual report, 1903–1904, p. 15, NLI.
78 NSPCC, annual report, 1898–99, p. 12, NLI.
79 *Ibid.*, p. 13.
80 Minutes, 2 June 1899, NAI, POS papers, 1045/2/1/14, p. 85.
81 *Ibid.*
82 DPOS annual report, 1905, NAI, POS papers, 1045/1/1/66–93.
83 *Ibid.*
84 Bound volume of incoming letters, 1898, NAI, POS papers, 1045/3/1/25.
85 Registered application files, NAI, POS papers, 1045/5/3.
86 Minutes, 7 August 1903, NAI, POS papers, 1045/2/1/14, p. 271.
87 Unregistered applications (refused and postponed), NAI, POS papers, 1045/5/4.
88 *Ibid.*
89 *Ibid.*
90 *Ibid.*
91 *Ibid.*
92 Minutes visiting subcommittee, 17 Oct. 1919, NAI, POS papers, 1045/2/8/1, p. 198.
93 *Ibid.*, 18 June 1915, p. 137.
94 Crossman, 'Middle-class attitudes', p. 142.
95 Census 1911.
96 Maguire, 'A socio-economic analysis of the Dublin Protestant working class'.
97 Minutes, 6 July 1900, NAI POS papers, 1045/2/1/14.
98 *Ibid.*, Oct. 1906, p. 394.
99 *Ibid.*, 17 Feb. 1899, p. 52.
100 *Ibid.*, 15 June 1900, p. 149.
101 *Ibid.*
102 Minutes executive subcommittee, 1929, NAI, POS papers, 1045/2/7/1.
103 Minutes, 1902, NAI, POS papers, 1045/2/1/14, p. 8.

104 *Ibid.*
105 *Ibid.*, 15 Feb. 1907, p. 36.
106 *Ibid.*, 1910, p. 76.
107 *Ibid.*
108 See A. McCarthy, 'Hearts, bodies and minds: gender ideology and women's committal to Enniscorthy Lunatic Asylum, 1916–25', in A. Hayes and D. Urquhart (eds), *Irish Women's History* (Dublin: Irish Academic Press, 2004), pp. 115–35.
109 Minutes visiting subcommittee, 19 May 1911, NAI, POS papers, 1045/2/8/1, p. 89.
110 *Ibid.*
111 *Ibid.*
112 *Irish Independent* (21 December 1917).
113 *Irish Times* (18 January 1919).
114 See Cullen, 'Widows in Ireland, 1830–1970', p. 610.
115 *Ibid.*
116 *Ibid.*
117 *Irish Times* (18 June 1935).
118 DPOS annual report, 1935, NAI, POS papers, 1045/1/1/95–114.
119 *Ibid.*
120 Cullen, 'Widows in Ireland'.
121 *Ibid.*
122 Letters registered application files, NAI, POS papers, 1045/5/1–9.
123 See Cronin, '"You'd be disgraced"', p. 115.
124 Minutes, 1903, NAI, POS papers, 1045/2/1/14, p. 275.
125 DPOS annual report, 1933, NAI, POS papers, 1045/1/1/95–114, p. 44.
126 *Ibid.*, p. 43.
127 *Ibid.*, 1939, p. 39.
128 *Ibid.*, 1939, p. 37.
129 Register orphan histories.
130 'Children's Fresh Air Fund', *Irish Times* (8 April 1939).
131 Minutes, May 1903, NAI, POS papers, 1045/2/1/14, p. 313.
132 *Irish Times* (11 March 1911).
133 *Ibid.*
134 *Ibid.*
135 Minutes, 16 Feb. 1900, NAI, POS paper, 1045/2/1/14, p. 123.
136 *Ibid.*, Nov. 1900.
137 Minutes visiting subcommittee, 19 Jan. 1919, NAI, POS papers, 1045/2/8/1, p. 33.
138 *Ibid.*, 16 Apr. 1908, p. 53.
139 *Ibid.*, 17 Oct. 1919, p. 181.
140 Register orphan histories, NAI, POS papers, 1045/5/9, p. 236.
141 Minutes, May 1904, NAI, POS papers, 1045/2/1/14.
142 *Ibid.*, 27 Jan. 1899, p. 26.
143 *Ibid.*

144 Minutes executive subcommittee, 16 Feb. 1917, NAI, POS papers, 1045/2/7/1, p. 158.
145 Coolahan, *Irish Education*, p. 101.
146 'Tipperary POS annual meeting', *Nenagh Guardian* (8 November 1905).
147 Minutes, 1914, RCBL, CPOS papers, PRIV MS 519.1.
148 DPOS annual report, 1919, NAI, POS papers, 1045/1/1/66–93, p. 10.
149 M. Maguire, '"Our People": the Church of Ireland and the culture of community in Dublin since disestablishment', in Gillespie and Neely (eds), *The Laity and the Church of Ireland*, pp. 277–303, p. 294.
150 DPOS annual report, 1930, NAI, POS papers, 1045/1/1/95–114.
151 'Meath POS', *Irish Times* (30 September 1893).
152 Bound volume of incoming letters, 24 Aug. 1898, NAI, POS papers, 1045/3/1/25.
153 Kinsey Marriage Portion Fund applications, 29 June 1917, NAI, POS papers, 1045/5/9.
154 *Ibid.*
155 Letter found *ibid.*
156 *Ibid.*
157 Register orphan histories.
158 See M. Humphreys, *Empty Cradles* (New York, London: Corgi, 1996); R. Parker, *Uprooted: the Shipment of Poor Children to Canada, 1867–1917* (Bristol: Policy Press, 2010); Parr, *Labouring Children*.
159 Humphreys, *Empty Cradles*.
160 Personal and private testimony of a family whose forebears were assisted by the DPOS in the early 1900s.

8

Decline and resilience, 1898–1940

The Protestant Orphan Society supplied a great want in their benevolent and charitable institutions and he felt they could not get on without them.[1]

Introduction

Given the relatively significant decline in the Protestant population, the creation of the Free State, the growing authority of the Roman Catholic church as evidenced by its extensive network of convents, orphanages and schools, and the 1937 constitution, it stood to reason that PO Societies in the south would lose some, if not all, of the social influence built up in the nineteenth century. Yet, despite these changes as well as the removal of restrictions on outdoor relief or 'Home Assistance' and the introduction of the Widows' Pension in 1925 in Northern Ireland and in 1935 in the Free State, PO Societies endured. The final chapter examines the social service carried out by Dublin POS committee members and Church of Ireland women and identifies the distinguished figures from Douglas Hyde to Dr Ella Webb who lent the Society their support. It argues that in a rapidly changing Ireland PO Societies represented a link to the past that bound together heterogeneous elements in the Church of Ireland in the north and south of the country into the twentieth century.

Social reform

Women were at the forefront of social service provision and the driving force behind social reform in Ireland. Founded in 1897, the Philanthropic Reform Association, with leading members such as Rosa Barrett, sought workhouse reforms and initiated the Police Aided Children's Clothing Society.[2] The Alexandra Guild followed Octavia Hill's lead in terms of social work and formed the Tenement Company in 1897. Alexandra College offered courses in social work and its trainees obtained work placements in the Jacob's factory. Owned by Quakers, the working conditions were unrivalled: a welfare department catered for all the employees' medical needs and promoted their good health.[3]

In addition to its foundation of mother and baby clubs and its successful TB prevention campaign discussed in chapter 7, the Women's National Health Association (WNHA) promoted women's and children's health in a number of other ways, for example, free school meals, children's dental clinics, maintenance of district nurses, playgrounds and school gardens. The WNHA contributed significantly to the professionalisation of social work in Ireland.[4] Susanne Rouvier Day was appointed a Poor Law Guardian in Cork in 1911 and later became convinced of the flaws in the Poor Law system particularly with respect to women and children.

Maud Gonne and Hanna Sheehy Skeffington, along with Stephen Gwynn, advocated a state funded free meals initiative (a scheme previously opposed by the Roman Catholic church), which led to the Education (Provision of Meals) (Ireland) Act, 1914.[5] Lady Aberdeen, WNHA, also played a leading role in the Irish Home Industries Association, founded 1886, and the Civics Institute formed in 1914,[6] which promoted public health and housing reform. The Congested District Board and other departments offered classes in cookery and hygiene from the 1890s[7] and the Dublin Corporation worked with the Civics Institute on specific projects related to tenement housing.[8]

The Joint Committee of Women's Societies and Women Social Workers was founded in 1935 and represented the Irish Country Women's Association (originally the United Irishwomen), Irish Housewives Association, the Irish Women Citizens' Association, Saor an Leanbh, the Irish Women's Workers Union and the Mothers' Union.[9] In Belfast, the Council of Social Welfare was formed, voluntary hospitals built and charitable initiatives for the disabled founded.[10]

Nuns assumed a pivotal role in Catholic voluntary activism through their tireless work in orphanages, hospitals and schools and attempts were made to organise the Catholic laity to counteract the influence of socialism.[11] St Vincent De Paul's membership increased steadily during the early twentieth century and laymen such as Professor O'Rahilly set up the Catholic Social League in 1917 in Cork.[12] Later in the century, Catholic lay women were involved in the Catholic Social Service Conference and the Legion of Mary.[13]

Women and PO Societies

Church of Ireland women contributed consistently, generously and unobtrusively to PO Societies in their vital roles as nurses and matrons, collectors and fundraisers. In 1919 the level of parish work undertaken by Church of Ireland women was emphasised in a petition submitted to the General Synod by Archbishop Gregg to support the restoration of women's rights to hold vestry office.[14]

Women continued to collect and fundraise on behalf of PO Societies in the twentieth century. Though perhaps not as well attended as in former years, bazaars were often utilised to clear outstanding debts.[15] The Sunnyside local ladies' committees arranged 'Pound Days' at which attendees were invited to donate 1 lb of household provisions. It also organised Gift Days at Sunnyside and Gift Services at local churches, 'to keep the children well supplied with toys'.[16] There were also 'Protestant Orphan Days' when sermons were preached on behalf of the charity in every Church of Ireland parish.[17]

Women also continued to hold concerts to raise funds for the Societies, which, for example, contributed to children's excursions to the seaside during the summer. Women were also adept at raising the Society's profile among prominent businesses in order to encourage donations: Moët and Crosse & Blackwell were two of the more well known businesses. The Monkstown POS committee stated in 1914 that 'the lady collectors had proved the Society's main reliance'.[18]

Apart from their more traditional roles as nurses and fundraisers, women gradually became involved in other important duties. In the nineteenth century the DPOS employed men as clerks and secretaries; however, the position of assistant secretary was filled by a woman in 1909.[19] It was a key role which involved direct correspondence with bereaved families and required a high level of organisational skills. (By 1914, approximately 8,000 women were employed as office clerks in Ireland.[20]) While clergymen's wives and daughters had assisted in overseeing boarded-out children in the nineteenth century, their later more official role proved an immense asset to the Society: members of the visiting committee could identify more easily with the widows' trials and could therefore provide those who had the charge of their own children with the assistance they needed.

Women gained valuable experience from their time spent with the Society, which stood them in good stead to find other related voluntary work; for example, a member of the ladies' visiting committee was offered a position as assistant to the Church of Ireland Temperance Society in 1915, which she duly accepted.[21] In 1919 the DPOS employed a lady inspector to carry out inspections of every orphan on the Society roll. Initially envisaged as a temporary role, the woman's work was so impressive it was made a permanent position.[22]

Miss Charlotte Burroughs and Miss Neville, who founded cottage homes in association with the DPOS in the late nineteenth century, contributed enormously to the overall management of the DPOS. On 14 April 1917 their endeavours were commended publicly: 'to both these ladies the Protestant Orphan Society owed a debt which could never be discharged'.[23] These lay women consistently contributed to social service in connection with their church. Charlotte Burroughs, who died in China in January 1929 and who left Sunnyside to the Society, and bequeathed a large sum towards its future management, was the sister of Revd W. E. Burroughs. Revd Burroughs had been a friend of both the PORS in the 1880s and later the Cottage Home, Kingstown. He praised his sister's efforts on behalf of Protestant orphans in September 1916 in an entry in the home's visitors' book.

> Visited Sunnyside after some time and found that while some had come, and some had gone in the interval, there was no change in the spirit and tone of the home or its management. It is still a home rather than a house … I cannot but add my conviction that the departure of my sister – founder and ceaseless friend of Sunnyside will be an almost irreparable loss only to be met by the continued services of Mrs Harris, who so thoroughly knows and values the rules and principles laid down from its commencement and never departed from. May Sunnyside for years to come send with its bright supply of happy, pure and god fearing young lives to serve god and their generation by his will.[24]

Both Miss Neville and Miss Charlotte Burroughs were single women who had dedicated most of their lives to the care and support of Protestant orphans.

Apart from the direct care of the children, the names of lady doctors featured on the annual reports of the DPOS as medical officers for the first time in the 1930s. Dr Dorothy McEntire Bennett became a medical adviser for the DPOS in 1936 and remained so until 1944.[25] It is likely that Bennett was sympathetic to the needs of the Society as she herself had been widowed less than a year before. Dorothy McEntire was the daughter of Alexander Knox McEntire and widow of Captain Frank Bennett, the son of the late William Massy Bennett of Glenesy, County Tipperary.[26]

Women and local PO Societies

Although women had become members of visiting committees, for example, in the cases of Limerick and Cork PO Societies from the 1840s and late 1850s, respectively, in other cases, women were not invited to become members of POS managing committees until the late nineteenth and early twentieth century. The Armagh POS, for example, formally recognised women as members of the committee in 1898. A motion was passed which read that, 'the Rules be altered to admit of ladies being elected on the Committee of the Armagh Protestant Orphan Society', and subsequently, on 21 June 1898, at the meeting held in the Diocesan Rooms, Armagh, there was 'an expression of heartfelt self congratulation on the part of the Committee at the presence of Ladies for the first time at their meeting'.[27]

In February 1917 the honorary secretary of the Meath POS, the Revd R. J. Merrin, died: 'The wife of the Reverend Lancelot Coulter of Ardbraccan was appointed in his stead. At the annual meeting, the same year, ladies were for the first time elected members of the committee'.[28] Women tended to pave the way for other women to join the committees. In Monaghan, women were not recorded as members of the managing committee in the late nineteenth century; however, by the early twentieth century four women had been appointed.[29] The Ferns POS welcomed women in 1920, one year after vestry rights were restored: 'his Lordship expressed pleasure at the introduction of ladies to the Committee of the society';[30] four women were appointed committee members, one of whom was Revd Wilkinson's daughter, and another was the Countess of Courtown.

Dublin POS (DPOS) committee members and social service

In the post-disestablishment era, Church of Ireland clergymen could participate in social service in a way not previously possible;[31] for example, they founded the highly successful Dublin Hospital Sunday Fund in 1874 to raise funds for Dublin hospitals.[32] The fund enabled investigations into hospital management which identified the problem of inadequate nurse training.

In the late nineteenth century, Church of Ireland clergymen in Dublin took part in several other social service initiatives. Revd Paterson Smyth, who was mentioned in the DPOS minutes of committee meetings as an attendee, and a committee member of the Monkstown POS, founded the Church of Ireland Social Service Union in 1898.[33] Smyth viewed poverty as a social problem rather than a personal one based on morals alone.[34]

(A year later 1899 Revd R. M. Gwynn founded the Dublin University Social Service Society.[35])

The overcrowding of the Dublin slums and the immorality associated with multiple families living in one house or of people of all ages and both sexes living in the same room were identified as particularly pressing problems in proposals for the Church of Ireland Social Service Union.[36] Miss Rosa Barrett, and other speakers including Dr Paterson Smyth, delivered lectures on the theme of 'Work in the Slums' at a meeting of the union in 1898 and a year later the Union highlighted the fact that children of 'tender years' were being 'employed as messengers for intoxicating liquor'.[37] Professor Brougham Leech, TCD, Mr Ernest Swifte, Divisional Police Magistrate, and Revd J. C. Irwin, also a DPOS committee member, became members of the Dublin Central Committee of the Church of Ireland Social Service Union in December of that year.[38] Alderman Healy, an inspector for the DPOS, was also a member of the Clontarf branch of the Social Service Union.[39]

Revd Maurice Day became a DPOS committee member in the 1890s, supported the Clergy Widows' and Orphans' Society,[40] and became chairman of the St Matthias branch of the Social Service Union. In 1899 he reiterated the Union's aims, 'to rouse the Christian conscience of the country; to assert Christ's claim; and to teach Christ's will in dealing with social problems'.[41] Day stressed that the Church of Ireland was but one branch of the Social Service Union, which he claimed should 'appeal to Christian men and women of every denomination. There are Roman Catholics, Nonconformists, and Irish Churchmen whose hearts are sore at the social evils which lie around them and which could be largely remedied if a sufficiently strong public opinion were brought to bear upon them'.[42] Revd Day's son, the Most Revd Canon John Godfrey Day, later primate of Ireland, also supported the DPOS in subsequent years. Moreover, his uncle Maurice Fitzgerald Day had been a prominent evangelical clergymen and incumbent of St Matthias parish in the 1860s, and served as vice-patron of the DPOS in 1867.

By the late nineteenth century, a number of Church of Ireland clergymen had given generously of their time in the wider field of social service as well as to the care of Protestant orphans. In 1901 the Archbishop of Dublin, Joseph Peacocke, then aged sixty-five, proudly reflected on the extensive social service carried out by the Dublin POS.

> He was very glad to find that at the opening of the twentieth century this social service was being taken up and pushed forward. And yet it ought to be borne in mind that social service work had been done by the Protestant Orphan Society for the last seventy years. The work of the society had

been to make provision for the orphans of their poor Protestant people, to throw some protection around them, and to prevent them from falling down to paths of degradation, and possibly crime. The society felt that prevention was better than cure.[43]

There were two types of charity identified in the early twentieth century – preventative and those that dealt specifically with urgent need.[44]

Clergymen's daughters, PO Societies and social service

Miss Catherine Drew, daughter of Revd Dr Drew, supporter of the Belfast auxiliary to the DPOS in the 1840s, endorsed a similar system for the bereaved families in her own field. An authoress and journalist, Miss Drew was a generous contributor to the Institute of the Journalists' Orphan Fund, from its foundation in Dublin in 1891.[45] The idea for an orphan fund was in fact proposed by Drew in that year.[46] She was also a co-founder of the Ladies' Press Association.

Kathleen Lynn, daughter of Revd Robert Young Lynn, a Church of Ireland clergymen, was born in Mayo in 1874. Revd Lynn was secretary to the Mayo POS in the late 1870s. Among numerous other achievements, Kathleen Lynn was one of the founders of the Irish Citizens' Army,[47] and established St Ultan's Hospital for Infants in 1919. Archbishop Edward Byrne opposed a proposal to merge St Ultan's, a multi-denominational hospital, with the Children's Hospital, Harcourt Street, a Catholic hospital, in 1935. Byrne opposed the scheme unwaveringly on the basis that he believed Catholic children would be at risk of Protestant proselytising.[48]

Like Dr Kathleen Lynn, and Catherine Drew, Dr Ella Webb was also the daughter of a Church of Ireland clergyman, Revd Charles Thomas Ovenden, Dean of St Patrick's.

In July 1908, Webb visited Sunnyside Home, the DPOS affiliated cottage home in Kilternan, and that day left a message in the visitors' book:

I have been greatly pleased by the appearance of the children. Their healthy looks and pretty manners leave nothing to be desired. I consider the house excellently situated the number of children not too great for the air space, and the sanitary arrangements perfect. The general management and diet of the children seems to be admirable.[49]

Webb was likely to have been influenced by much of the work carried out by ladies such as Miss Charlotte Burroughs, Sunnyside, and Rosa Barrett, Cottage Home for Little Children. Webb opened a dispensary for children in the Adelaide Hospital in 1918[50] and in 1925 founded the Children's Sunshine Home for Convalescents, Stillorgan, County

Dublin[51] (a Catholic home also called the Sunshine Home was established ten years later); she became a close associate of Kathleen Lynn at St Ultan's. In 1935 Webb praised the work of the DPOS, noting 'that it did one good to see the pleasure which mothers experienced when they were told the children would be provided for after the death of the bread-winner. The Society was carrying on a great work in that direction, and deserved every support'.[52] Her words echoed her father's earlier sentiments. Based in Fermanagh for a time, Revd Ovenden, when rector of Enniskillen, spoke in favour of the County Fermanagh POS, stating in 1893 at an annual meeting 'that the society deserves the warmest and heartiest support of every member of the Church of Ireland in this country'.[53]

Miss Emily Hyde, daughter of Revd A. Hyde, contributed extensively to the Leitrim POS in the nineteenth century and her nephew Douglas Hyde, the first President of Ireland, carried on the tradition. Hyde's vision of de-anglicising Ireland and the importance he placed on the Irish language won him wide acclaim. The Leitrim POS reported in June 1939, 'His Excellency the President of Éire, if in the district, has signified his intention of being present, for his grandfather, the Revd A. Hyde, was one of the Society's early secretaries, and Miss Emily Hyde acted for some time as lady secretary'.[54]

Dr Dorothy Stopford Price, daughter of Jemmett and Constance Stopford (whose father was Evory Kennedy, master of the Rotunda Lying In Hospital), also supported the DPOS. At a DPOS meeting in 1935, a 'resolution expressing the thankfulness of the Society to the contributors and collectors was proposed by Dr Dorothy Stopford Price'.[55] Price brought the vaccination for TB to St Ultan's, which was the first hospital to introduce the BCG vaccine in Ireland or Great Britain.[56] Price was extremely well connected and her extended family were also keen supporters of PO Societies. For example, Price's grand-uncle, Archdeacon Edward Alderly Stopford of Meath, who liaised with Gladstone to formulate the Church Act, was also a member of the Meath POS committee. Archdeacon Stopford's daughter was Alice Stopford, historian and nationalist.

This sense of tradition and support, which stretched over time and across generations, was mirrored by the bereaved families assisted by PO Societies and general subscribers. The same families subscribed to the DPOS in the twentieth century as had done in the nineteenth. Orphans who had passed through the POS system frequently donated to its funds as adults. Moreover, in a number of cases, orphans who had been helped by the Society reached adulthood and married, and tragically became dependent on the Society themselves. For example, the DPOS admitted a nine-year-old boy and paid his aunt an allowance to cover his upkeep. When he was twelve he applied to the British Army (boys' service); he failed the medical examination. Three years later the Society provided him with apprentice fees which paid for his entry to Gravesend Sea School, one of the premier training facilities under the management of the Shipping Federation, which was established in 1918 to train boys for the Merchant Navy. He subsequently joined the British Navy and married at the age of twenty-two. Eight years later he died while on active service and within a year his son had been elected to the Society roll.[57]

Religious rivalry

Despite Parnell's and Isaac Butt's prominence in the Home Rule Movement in the nineteenth century, home rule was opposed by most members of the Church of Ireland.[58] Amid intense religious rivalry and against the backdrop of the Home Rule Movement, proselytism remained an inflammable issue. During Queen Victoria's visit to Ireland, a 'Children's Day' was held in the Phoenix Park on 9 April 1900. The DPOS was also closed 'on the occasion of Her Majesty's visit to Dublin',[59] and a member of the committee noted 'with satisfaction the large assemblage of children recently in the Phoenix Park'.[60] Nationalists regarded Children's Day as a 'scheme to use the Queen's visit for making loyal little Britons of the sons and daughters of Irish Nationalists' and an 'act of political souperism and possibly religious souperism'.[61] The ladies' committee refuted the claims, assuring the objectors that its only aim was to ensure that all poor children would be properly fed on that day.

Maud Gonne, founder of the Inghinidhe na hÉireann (1900), and a leading voice in the anti-conscription campaign, organised the 'Patriotic Children's Treat' in Clonturk Park, Drumcondra on 1 July 1900 as a nationalist display of defiance against the earlier 'Children's Day' event. Gonne regarded it as 'most encouraging' that so many children 'had the firmness and courage to refuse to attend the Queen's treat', pointing out that 'only 5,000 allowed themselves to be used for a Unionist demonstration, and these 5,000 were chiefly from the Masonic, industrial and workhouse schools'.[62] A DPOS committee member noted that Protestant orphans were among the children who attended.[63]

On the occasion of the 1902 coronation other events arranged by a ladies' committee, which aimed to 'entertain the poor children of Dublin',[64] also aroused suspicion.

> From the vivid language of certain resolutions passed by some branches of a well-known association that need not be named, it might be thought

that this notion of giving the children of Dublin a happy day at the seaside or in the country was a deep plot to turn little Roman Catholics into little Protestants. A glance at the list of the ladies forming the committee will be sufficient to dispel any such ridiculous idea, for they include a considerable proportion of Roman Catholics.[65]

During the hardship caused by the trade union strikes in Dublin, Mrs Dora Montefiore proposed the evacuation of children from Dublin to stay with trade unionist families in England.[66] Larkin, who had founded the Irish Transport and General Workers' Union in 1908, supported the proposal; however, despite Montefiore's assurances that the scheme had been successful elsewhere and that the children would be sent to Catholic families, Archbishop of Dublin, William Walsh (1885–1921) opposed it on the basis that the children would be in danger of proselytism.[67] The main aim of the Catholic Protection and Rescue Society of Ireland was the prevention of proselytism.[68] It regularly questioned the motives of the numerous Protestant children's homes in Dublin given the relatively small Protestant population. Canon A. E. Hughes stated with respect to the DPOS that 'the society was in no sense a proselytising organisation'.[69]

Ne Temere

The *Ne Temere* decree, which was issued in 1907 and came into force on Easter Sunday 1908, threw the spotlight on the issue of intermarriage.[70] The decree stated that both parties had to sign an agreement to baptise their children in the Roman Catholic church and the Roman Catholic partner was pressured into converting the other party.[71] While Canon Gregg, Blackrock, Cork, admitted in 1911 that, 'if a certain mixed marriage had not taken place in County Clare three generations ago, I should not be here to-night', he disagreed with these unions in principle:

> Our general synod did very rightly in protesting against its publication, at its meeting in 1908, the earliest opportunity that presented itself. I myself raised my voice on the subject on December 31st, 1908, in the cathedral; and I am glad to know that the warning I gave has not been altogether without effect. I flatly contradict a statement made by a public man in Cork a few weeks ago to the effect that nothing was heard about the Decree among us till the Belfast case of Mrs McCann came on. Our people had been duly put on their guard, but, when the inevitable fruits of the Decree began to manifest themselves, a more vigorous type of action was called for. A case of actual wrong and outrage inflicted upon a Protestant through

the ruthless working of the law called for a strong protest, which we would have been less than human if we had not made, but which was not called for by the mere threatening of danger.[72]

The McCann case in Belfast had provoked widespread condemnation of the decree, rioting in Belfast, and vehement opposition from the Presbyterian church on 8 June 1911. In the same year St John G. Ervine's 'Mixed Marriage' was performed at the Abbey Theatre Dublin.

In both the 1901 and the 1911 census, more than fourteen per cent of Protestant men in Dublin were returned as married to Catholic women.[73] Contemporary press reports also indicate that in a number of intermarriage cases Protestant women, who had changed their religion and baptised their children Catholic, returned to their own church when the marriages ended through death or desertion. For example, a Protestant woman was received into the Roman Catholic church before her marriage in 1931. In later years, her husband, while a patient in St Vincent's Hospital, claimed that his wife had attempted to 'interfere' with their children's religion, wishing to raise them Protestants. The husband's sister stated that she could care for the children after his death until arrangements could be made to send them to Catholic institutions. The judge concluded that the children be committed to their aunt's care, and they 'were then transferred to the custody of Miss – amid tearful scenes, the younger children having to be separated from their mother, to whom they clung, while the elder boys tried to protect them'.[74] The often difficult outcomes in cases of this kind, particularly for the children, served to reinforce already vehement opposition to intermarriages.

Divisions within Protestantism also emerged in the context of *Ne Temere*.

> The whole question was rendered more serious in Ireland in light of the persistent demand that was being made by the Nationalist party for legislative separation. If some sort of Home Rule were granted, what guarantee could be given that some such edict as the *Ne Temere* would not become the law of the land? Not one word of disapproval regarding it had fallen from the lips of any Nationalist member of Parliament. On the other hand, many of them had tried to justify its existence and the so-called Protestant members, on the whole had been discreetly silent.[75]

Numerous autobiographies and biographies also contain references to the *Ne Temere* decree and refer to Catholic opposition to intermarriage.[76] Ultan Macken documents the case of Tom Kenny, a member of the Church of Ireland, who wished to marry a wealthy Catholic farmer's daughter; however, in order to do so, he had to convert to Catholicism and sign the decree.[77] Others such as Phyllis Harrison Browne refer to the paucity of eligible bachelors for Protestant girls in the 1930s[78] which further elucidates the marginalising effects of the decree: men and women, regardless of class, were left with few choices – to marry outside their church, to migrate, emigrate or to passively accept a life of bachelor and spinsterhood.

PO Societies and the orphans of mixed marriage

The committee members of various PO Societies regarded themselves as the children's guide, a father to the fatherless, and it was their responsibility to ensure the children did not stray from the Church of Ireland. The DPOS had finally agreed to its amalgamation with the Protestant Orphan Refuge Society, formerly the Charitable Protestant Orphan Union, with effect from 1 November 1898. The amalgamated charity operated under the name the Protestant Orphan Society, and, consequently, it admitted 'destitute orphans, one, or both of whose parents was or were, a Protestant, or Protestants'.[79] While other PO Societies had admitted the Protestant orphans of mixed marriages since their foundation, the DPOS had only accepted children of strictly Protestant parentage. In 1901 Captain Wade Thompson, member of both the DPOS and the Adelaide Hospital committees, remarked that

> Protestants, who were in the minority in Ireland, should be most particular in seeing that children of their faith who were left without father or mother, or without either, were properly looked after and preserved in the religion of their parents. On the present occasion they were dealing with the Amalgamated Society, composed of the Protestant Orphan Society and the Protestant Orphan Refuge Society. The committee could now deal with the offspring of mixed marriages, and that was a branch of the work to which he attached great importance.[80]

Supporters had always maintained that PO Societies linked Protestants together: 'their Protestant Orphan Societies had been an immense blessing to the country. They had kept the Protestant people together to a large extent, and their existence had been a great source of comfort and consolation to their people when they were dying, because they had the knowledge that their children would be properly cared for'.[81] The DPOS dealt with a certain number of mixed marriages applications. One application was made for the admission of a young girl by her aunt, a Protestant. The child's mother was Catholic, her deceased husband a Protestant, who, in his will, asked that his children be raised Protestant. The DPOS responded to the recommender of the case:

The committee notice that on the form of application it is stated that the two eldest children are in institutions and they wish to know what institutions they are in. They have an idea that they may be in Roman Catholic institutions. They also note that the form is not signed by the mother as the person who applies for the children, but by an aunt (it should be signed by the mother). They wish to know why this is. They say that it will be necessary for the mother to attend here on the election day, to give her consent to the children being taken on by us.[82]

The chairman concluded that, 'if it were the wish of the mother, he would do what he could to set the child into some home or institution of her own religious persuasion'.[83] The case demonstrates the thorough manner in which the Society dealt with applications, particularly with regard to parental consent.

At a meeting of the DPOS in 1924, Archbishop Gregg stated that 'they were trying to avert what was a very serious loss to their church: that was mixed marriages. Their marriage portion fund was doing something in that direction'.[84] He also wished to make it clear that the Church of Ireland objected to these unions. In 1926 he again referred to the 'evils' of mixed marriages, which he described as a menace to the church; the future of the Church of Ireland, he asserted, was 'bound up, in the most serious way, with the next generation'.[85] The Catholic church in England, he claimed, had complained bitterly of serious 'leakages' from its flock due to such marriages.[86]

Dwindling Protestants and amalgamation

The dwindling Protestant population had many knock-on effects for a charity such as the DPOS, one of which was the decline in funding. There was a common belief that the 'Protestant Orphan Society was supposed to be a rich Society, and did not need funds'.[87] A clergyman assured the DPOS in January 1898 that he would try to obtain some further subscriptions for the Society, but informed the committee, 'that it has been represented in this neighbourhood that your Society is too well off and there is a schism in favour of Miss Carr's'.[88] The committee reported in 1900 that this was not the case and appealed for funds. It was the beginning of a steady decline; 'it is unhappily true that the Protestant Orphan Society has not of late occupied the prominent place among the Diocesan charities which its importance deserves'.[89] The foundation of new charities such as Miss Carr's Homes naturally resulted in a fall off in DPOS funding as donations were evenly dispersed among the new as well as the old good causes.

The Church of Ireland population in the Irish Free State was 249,535 in 1911 and 164,215 in 1928.[90] Losses from World War I, emigration and intermarriages contributed to the decline. The figures also included the departure of the crown forces in significant numbers post 1921.[91] The *Irish Independent* covered the subject of Protestant emigration in 1910. The article entitled 'Dwindling Protestants' outlined the grounds for Protestant emigration and suggested that artisans 'were finding themselves gradually elbowed out and unable to make a living in many localities'.[92] In its 1910 annual report, the DPOS reflected on emigration in a commentary which was strikingly similar to its reports from the early 1830s.

> Their Protestant population in Ireland was diminishing, like the whole of the population of the country, and there was a fear that in the not very distant future it might diminish still more. The Protestant Orphan Society in a small way tended to keep their people together, and prevent them from emigrating to other lands, where, possibly, they would do better than they were doing here. At all events, they were bound to do their best to keep their Protestant orphans here as a source of strength to their Church and their religion.[93]

Protestant migration north during the period from 1920 to 1925 reduced the Protestant population in the south by twenty four thousand; for example, over two thousand Protestants – ex-policemen, ex-Royal Irish Constabulary, shopkeepers, teachers, farmers, blacksmiths, servants, labourers – left Wicklow, Cavan, Monaghan, Dublin, Leitrim, Galway, Longford for Fermanagh.[94] In 1909 the Antrim and Down POS reported that it had 999 orphans on its roll and that 'they were bound to see that every child was given the chance of leading a good and honest life'.[95] It reported in 1924 that, unlike other local PO Societies in southern Ireland, which had in some cases been forced to reduce nurses' wages, it was in a position to maintain the fixed rate.[96]

As table 8.1 clearly illustrates, the number of children being cared for by PO Societies was relatively few in counties such as Waterford and Clare when compared with Antrim and Down POS, a reflection of the reduced Protestant presence in the future southern Ireland. The Armagh POS noted in 1914 that there were thirty four PO Societies caring for 2,500 children, 'in spite of their diminishing population'.[97] The majority of these children were assisted by the Antrim and Down POS. In total, 19,000 orphans (which included children with a surviving parent and children whose fathers were alive but incapacitated bodily or mentally) had been assisted through the combined efforts of all the PO Societies in Ireland from 1828 to 1914.[98]

Table 8.1 POS orphans in Ireland, 1914–18

PO Society	Year	Orphans
Antrim & Down	1917	1,025
Armagh	1917	20
Clare	1918	10
Cork	1917	76
Derry	1918	114
Donegal	1918	60
Ferns	1917	50
Galway	1914	20
Kerry	1917	24
Kings Co.	1918	16
Leitrim	1917	16
Limerick	1917	57
Lisburn	1917	21
Longford	1918	16
Louth	1918	23
Mayo	1918	16
Meath	1918	27
Monaghan	1918	50
Monkstown	1917	26
Newry	1918	18
Queen's co.	1914	18
Roscommon	1917	11
Sligo	1914	44
Tipperary	1918	28
Tyrone	1918	133
Waterford	1914	7

Source: Report relative to the amalgamation of PO Societies, 1919.

Given the general decline in population, the possible amalgamation of PO Societies was discussed in 1917 and again in 1919. PO Societies were organised, in most cases, as one separate Society for each county. The 1917 report suggested that this separateness which had 'endured for the greater part of a century' was justification enough to reject the proposal for amalgamation: 'The county is the unit for local government and administration ... and the people of each county have usually more knowledge of, and interest in, each other than in those of other counties. The county, would, therefore, seem to be prima facie a suitable unit for the organisation of the Protestant Orphan Societies'.[99] After careful consideration, those who compiled the reports concluded that despite the relatively low number of children cared for in certain parishes, amalgamation would reduce local support for the Society.[100] In 1928, on the occasion of the DPOS centenary, the issue of amalgamation was raised again: 'It was of tremendous importance that they should endeavour to link up all Protestant Orphan Societies, in order that the money collected and administered might be put to the best advantage of those who were beneficiaries of the Protestant Orphan Society'.[101] In 1929 a Youth Conference was organised by the Church of Ireland to attract the attention of the younger generation.[102]

In addition to the decline in Protestant numbers, the gradual changes to the structure of public poor relief also diminished the need for private charity. The Widows and Orphans Pensions act was passed in Northern Ireland in 1925 and the Poor Law retained until 1939. (Outdoor relief was provided though not extensively.[103]) Poor Law Guardians did not generally board out children and consequently many were under the care of charities. The Belfast Charitable Organisation Society was founded in 1906 and the Northern Ireland Council for Social Service in 1938.[104]

A link to the past and to the future

The closure of local PO Societies would have proven a considerable blow to Protestant voluntary service networks in the south,[105] and to some extent weakended the sense of Protestant community, purpose and cultural identity. There were a number of important social events associated with PO Societies such as annual meetings, fundraising events – bazaars, 'pound days', 'home days' – and local committee meetings for the cottage homes. While there was perhaps a less 'lively interest' in the charity, many subscribers still retained fond memories of bygone years. In 1901 Archbishop Peacocke recalled his childhood memories of the Queen's County POS, noting that few meetings were held in the country apart from those of the Society which were 'looked upon as the one great event of the year'.[106] He described the 'crowded rooms' and the 'immense display of enthusiasm'.[107] The same sentiment was expressed again in 1912 at a DPOS annual meeting when it was remarked that the 'meetings were not like they used to be in days gone by, when they were held in the Round Room of the Rotunda, which was filled end to end'.[108] Other voluntary associations such as the YMCA and the Mothers' Union were equally important social outlets for the Protestant community, particularly in smaller rural areas.[109]

Archbishop Gregg commented on the decline of the Protestant population in 1930: 'he could not but feel a certain amount of sadness, in the continued decline in the number of orphans coming on to the roll

Figure 8.1 DPOS committee members, 1937.

of the Society. From one point of view they ought to be glad, because there were fewer orphans, but he took it that the cause of it was that the constituency from which the orphans came was gradually getting smaller'.[110] The 'shrinkage' of voluntary contributions was considered a matter of grave concern.[111] He also expressed disappointment that former orphans no longer seemed to 'acknowledge in some ways their connection with it and the benefits that they received from it'.[112] A constant promoter of the charity, the archbishop stated the following year that despite waning support, it was 'one of the finest pieces of constructive work in the Church of Ireland'.[113] The first half of the twentieth century witnessed the deaths of many of the Society's most faithful supporters. Eugene O'Meara, who had been clerical secretary to the DPOS for thirty-five years, died in 1913. Charles H. Gick, secretary of the Irish Medical Association, the DPOS and the Institute for the Deaf and Dumb, died in 1932.[114]

In 1937 Gregg rebuked the 'rising generation' for their 'failure to shoulder the burden' of 'the community to which they belonged'.[115] Archbishop Gregg stressed again in 1946 that 'a church "which cannot count on a younger generation is doomed to early extinction"'.[116] Annabel Goff's autobiography, *Walled Garden: Scenes from an Anglo-Irish Childhood*, documents the gradual decay of her class.[117] Metaphors used by PO Societies, often naval in origin, included that the charity represented a 'lifeboat for poor Protestants'. Another commonly used metaphor for 'the Anglo Irish', was that of an 'orphan' who had been forsaken by its parent, England.[118] The Protestant Orphan Society of Ireland was a symbol of Protestant vitality and resilience that bound together 'all sorts and conditions' with one common goal – preservation.

Conclusion

Social service in the first half of the twentieth century took many forms and Church of Ireland clergymen in Dublin were involved in a number of these good causes in addition to their work among Protestant orphans, which in many respects gave them greater insights into the lives of the bereaved families they aimed to assist. Women had shaped the character of PO Societies in the nineteenth century, and they continued to exert their influence on the charity's policies in the twentieth. Local PO Societies, once a defining feature of church life, had a distinctive character which was a reflection of the individuality of the county and of the committee members. Prominent Protestant families throughout Ireland had been associated with the charity over generations. The gradual decline of the Protestant population in southern Ireland is plain to see through the lens of PO Societies – the corresponding diminution in financial support, consequent public appeals, and less well attended annual meetings. Yet, in spite of these losses, and the somewhat haunting predictions of further decline, PO Societies remained committed to the preservation of Protestant orphans, of Protestant posterity, and the Church of Ireland.

Notes

1 Archbishop of Dublin speaking at the DPOS annual meeting held in the Gregg Memorial Hall, Dawson Street; press cutting, *Irish Times* (15 April 1898) found in minute book, NAI, POS papers, 1045/2/1/14.

2 Luddy, *Women and Philanthropy*, p. 95.

3 G. Kirwan, 'Welfare and wedding cakes: an example of early occupational social work', in Kearney and Skehill (eds), *Social Work in Ireland*, pp. 196–210, p. 198.

4 E. Walsh, 'International social work over time: vignette', in Kearney and Skehill (eds), *Social Work in Ireland*, pp. 211–23, p. 212.

5 D. A. J. MacPherson, *Women and the Irish Nation: Gender, Culture and Irish Identity, 1890–1914* (Basingstoke: Palgrave Macmillan, 2012).

6 N. Kearney, 'Social work education: its origins and growth', in Kearney and Skehill (eds), *Social Work in Ireland*, pp. 13–32, p. 21.

7 C. Clear, 'Women of the house in Ireland, 1800–1950', in Bourke (ed.), *Field Day Anthology of Irish Writing*, p. 589–608, p. 590.

8 C. Delap and T. Kelleher, 'Local authority social work in Ireland: origins, issues and developments', in Kearney and Skehill (eds), *Social Work in Ireland*, pp. 51–76, p. 53.

9 See C. Skehill, *The Nature of Social Work in Ireland: A Historical Perspective* (Lewiston: Edwin Mellen Press, 1999), p. 83.

10 Acheson, Harvey, Kearney and Williamson, *Two Paths, One Purpose*, p. 25.

11 M. Curtis, *A Challenge to Democracy: Militant Catholicism in Modern Ireland* (Dublin: History Press, 2010), p. 35.

12 *Ibid.*, p. 40.

13 L. Earner-Byrne, '"Aphrodite rising from the waves"? Women's voluntary activism and the women's movement in twentieth century Ireland', in P. Thane and E. Breitenbach (eds), *Women and Citizenship in Britain and Ireland in the Twentieth Century: What Difference did the Vote Make?* (London: Continuum International Publishing Group. 2010), pp. 95–112, p. 100.

14 Acheson, *History of the Church of Ireland*, p. 219.

15 See DPOS annual reports, for example 1903, NAI, POS papers, 1045/1/1/66–93.

16 DPOS annual report, 1928, NAI, POS papers, 1045/1/1/95–114, p. 46.

17 *Irish Times* (14 November 1915).

18 'Monkstown Protestant Orphan Society', *Irish Times* (4 June 1914).

19 Minutes executive subcommittee, 1901–30, NAI, POS papers, 1045/2/7/1.

20 M. Hill, *Women in Ireland: A Century of Change* (Belfast: Blackstaff, 2003), p. 47.

21 Minutes executive subcommittee, 24 Sept. 1915, NAI, POS papers, 1045/2/7/1, p. 351.

22 DPOS annual report, 1920, NAI, POS papers, 1045/1/1/66–93.

23 *Irish Times* (17 April 1917).

24 Sunnyside visitors' book, NAI, POS papers, 1045/13/3.

25 DPOS annual report, 1936, NAI, POS papers, 1045/1/1/95–114.

26 'Obituary of Captain Frank Bennett', *Irish Times* (5 August 1935).

27 R. J. N. Portes, *In the Name of Jesus: A History of the County Armagh Protestant Orphan Society* (The author, 1986), p. 15.

28 Athey, 'A short history of Meath Protestant Orphan Society', p. 11.

29 Annual reports, 1871–1930, RCBL, MPOS papers, PRIV MS 692.6.

30 'Ferns POS', *Irish Times* (24 June 1920).

31 See M. C. Considere-Charon, 'The Church of Ireland: continuity and change', *Irish Quarterly Review*, 87:346 (Summer 1998), pp. 107–16.

32 See G. M. Fealy, *A History of Apprenticeship Nurse Training in Ireland: Bright Faces and Neat Dresses* (Oxford: Routledge, 2006), pp. 21–2.

33 Minutes, 10 Mar. 1899, NAI, POS papers, 1045/2/1/14, p. 60.

34 M. Maguire, 'The Church of Ireland and the problem of the Protestant working-class, 1870s – 1930s', in Ford, McGuire and Milne (eds), *As by Law Established*, pp. 195–203, p. 201.

35 Delap and Kelleher, 'Local authority social work in Ireland', p. 52.

36 *Irish Times* (24 October 1898).

37 *Ibid.*

38 *Irish Times* (13 December 1899).

39 Maguire, '"Our People"', p. 291.

40 *Irish Times* (2 November 1899).

41 *Irish Times* (10 November 1899).

42 *Ibid.*

43 DPOS annual report, 1901, NAI, POS papers, 1045/1/1/66–93.

44 Skehill, *The Nature of Social Work in Ireland*, p. 68.

45 *Irish Times* (29 August 1910).

46 F. Clarke and L. Lunney, 'Catherine Drew', *Dictionary of Irish Biography*.

47 See P. Comerford, 'A decade in which anarchy was loosed upon the world, a terrible beauty was born', *Church Review, Dublin & Glendalough Diocesan Magazine* (January 2012), pp. 4–5.

48 T. J. Morrisey, *Edward J. Byrne, 1872–1941: The Forgotten Archbishop of Dublin* (Blackrock: Columba Press, 2010), pp. 214–15.

49 Sunnyside visitors' book, NAI, POS papers, 1045/13/3.

50 M. Horne and E. O'Connor, 'An overview of the development of health-related social work in Ireland', in Kearney and Skehill (eds), *Social Work in Ireland*, pp. 165–83, p. 166.

51 See L. Kelly, 'Rickets and Irish children: Dr Ella Webb and the early work of the Children's Sunshine Home', in MacLellan and Mauger (eds), *Growing Pains*, pp. 141–59.

52 *Irish Times* (9 May 1935).

53 *Belfast News-letter* (5 October 1893).

54 *Belfast News-letter* (8 June 1939).

55 *Belfast News-letter* (10 May 1934).

56 M. Ó'hÓgartaigh, 'Dorothy Stopford Price', *Dictionary of Irish Biography*.

57 Register orphan histories, 1918, NAI, POS papers, 1045/5/1/9.

58 Neely, 'The laity in a changing society', p. 224.

59 Minutes, 30 Mar. 1900, NAI, POS papers, 1045/2/1/14, p. 134.

60 *Irish Times* (21 April 1900).

61 B. Payne, 'The Queen's Breakfast: a forgotten Dublin controversy', *Irish Times* (28 February 1961).

62 Pamphlet advertising and seeking donations for the Patriotic Children's Treat circulated by members of the ladies' committee: Maud Gonne, Alice

Furlong, May O'Leary Curtis, Judith Rooney, Nora Egan, Sarah White. 'Patriotic Children's Treat', 1900, NLI.

63 DPOS annual report, 1901, NAI, POS papers, 1045/1/1/66–93.

64 *Irish Times* (17 June 1902).

65 *Ibid.*

66 B. Winslow, *Sylvia Pankhurst: Sexual Politics and Political Activism* (London: Routledge, 2013), p. 63.

67 T. J. Morrissey, *William J. Walsh: Archbishop of Dublin, 1841–1921* (Dublin: Four Courts Press, 2000), p. 249–54.

68 Skehill, 'Child protection and welfare social work', p. 137.

69 *Irish Times* (4 May 1933).

70 F. S. L. Lyons, 'The watershed, 1903–7', in Vaughan (ed.), *A New History of Ireland, VI*, pp. 111–22, p. 119. See, J. White, *Minority Report: The Protestant Community in the Irish Republic* (Dublin: Gill and Macmillan, 1975), p. 129.

71 J. F. Lydon, *The Making of Ireland: From Ancient Times to the Present* (London: Routledge, 1998), p. 330.

72 Revd J. A. F. Gregg, BD, Incumbent of Blackrock, Cork, 'The "Ne Temere" Decree: a lecture delivered before the members of the Church of Ireland Cork Young Men's Association' (1911), p. 6.

73 Maguire, 'A socio economic analysis of the Dublin Protestant working classes', p. 49.

74 *Ibid.*, 4 Apr. 1931.

75 Revd John Crawford Irwin, *Irish Times* (13 March 1911).

76 S. Christie, *My Granny Made me an Anarchist: The Cultural and Political Formation of a West of Scotland 'baby boomer'* (2nd edn, Hastings, E. Sussex: Christie books: 2002), p. 44.

77 U. Macken, *W. Macken: Dreams on Paper* (Cork: Mercier Press, 2009), p. 75.

78 D. O'Byrne, 'Last of their line: the disappearing Anglo-Irish in twentieth-century fictions and autobiographies', in M. Busteed, F. Neal and J. Tonge (eds), *Irish Protestant Identities* (Manchester: Manchester University Press, 2008), pp. 40–53, p. 48.

79 General information attached to application form, NAI, POS papers, 1045/5/3.

80 'Protestant Orphan Society annual meeting', *Irish Times* (13 April 1901), book of press cuttings, NAI, POS papers, 1045/6/1.

81 DPOS annual report, 1898, NAI, POS papers, 1045/1/1/66–93.

82 Unregistered applications, 27 June 1914, NAI, POS papers, 1045/5/4.

83 *Ibid.*

84 *Irish Times* (24 April 1924).

85 *Irish Times* (10 November 1926).

86 *Irish Times* (13 November 1926).

87 DPOS annual report, 1900, NAI, POS papers, 1045/1/1/66–93, p. 11.

88 Bound volume of incoming letters, 1898, NAI, POS papers, 1045/3/1/25.

89 DPOS annual report, 1900, NAI, POS papers, 1045/1/1/66–93, p. 11.

90 Acheson, *History of the Church of Ireland*, p. 229.

91 *Ibid.*

92 *Irish Independent* (9 April 1910).

93 *Irish Times* (2 April 1910).

94 See T. A. M. Dooley, 'Protestant migration from the Free State to Northern Ireland, 1920–25: a private census for Co. Fermanagh', *Clogher Record*, 15:3 (1996), pp. 87–132.

95 *Irish Independent* (13 May 1909).

96 *Irish Times* (25 April 1924).

97 'Armagh POS: address by the primate', *Irish Times* (22 May 1914).

98 *Ibid.*

99 Note on proposed amalgamation of PO Societies, 1917, NAI, POS papers, 1045/6/2/6.

100 Report relative to the amalgamation of PO Societies throughout Ireland with the DPOS, 1919, NAI, POS papers, 1045/6/2/5.

101 *Irish Times* (29 November 1928).

102 Maguire, '"Our People"', p. 294.

103 Acheson, Harvey, Kearney and Williamson, *Two Paths, One Purpose*, p. 30.

104 *Ibid.*, p. 31.

105 See Maguire, '"Our People"', p. 292; see also P. Deignan, 'The importance of fraternities and social clubs for the Protestant community in Sligo from 1914 to 1949', in J. Kelly and R. V. Comerford (eds), *Associational Culture in Ireland and Abroad* (Dublin: Irish Academic Press, 2010), pp. 191–212.

106 'Protestant Orphan Society annual meeting', *Irish Times* (13 April 1901), book of press cuttings, NAI, POS papers, 1045/6/1.

107 *Ibid.*

108 Press cutting, 1912, *ibid.*

109 See Maguire, '"Our People"', and Deignan, 'The importance of fraternities and social clubs'.

110 'Protestant Society's work: Archbishop's tribute', *Irish Times* (24 April 1930) book of press cuttings, NAI, POS papers, 1045/6/1.

111 DPOS annual report, 1937, NAI, POS papers, 1045/1/1/95–114, p. 11.

112 *Ibid.*

113 'Help for Irish orphans'; loose pamphlet in book of press cuttings, NAI, POS papers, 1045/6/1.

114 *Irish Independent* (2 April 1932).

115 *Irish Times* (11 May 1937).

116 S. Mooney, 'Ghost writer: Beckett's Irish Gothic', in S. Kennedy (ed.), *Beckett and Ireland* (Cambridge: Cambridge University Press, 2010), p. 131–53, p. 135.

117 O'Byrne, 'Last of their line: the disappearing Anglo-Irish'.

118 *Ibid.*

Conclusion

In 1928 at the centenary meeting of the Protestant Orphan Society in Dublin, Revd Canon Thompson remarked that it would be the job of the 'future historian', 'to estimate the social influence of the work done by the Protestant Orphan Society'.[1] What legacy did the charity, founded in 1828 and developed on a country-wide basis, leave behind? The answer lies primarily, as Revd Thompson suggests, and as the author has emphasised throughout this study, in its social influence.

From its foundation the DPOS was a highly significant vehicle for moral reform. As the parent body it was more important than the later local PO Societies; it was responsible for the development of the boarding-out system and the implementation of imperative safeguards, which were adopted and modified to suit local needs. While PO Societies sent children to 'decent', 'respectable' families, this did not necessarily mean that their standards of care matched those set by committee members. There was often a class conflict between the committee members and nurses mostly related to the committee's perception of appropriate child care and the nurses' inability to meet such high standards, which were often impractical particularly with respect to hygiene, given the labour intensiveness of cleaning.

The nursing ideals and values promoted by PO Societies, essentially a form of nurse training, took hold gradually – over generations – and were likely to have influenced nurses' treatment of their own children as well as boarded-out children. Those who managed PO Societies – doctors, clergymen and their wives, laymen and women – raised awareness and imparted knowledge on issues such as public health, hygiene, containment and prevention of disease, prompt medical care, diet and nutrition, the health benefits of 'good milk', a change of air, sea air, fresh air, and the importance of education, recreation, and moderate punishment. The Societies expected nurses to treat every child in their care as one of the family for however long their placement lasted: children spent from months to years on the Society roll depending on individual circumstances. The institutional model did not afford the same opportunity as the boarding-out system to reach into the wider community. Women also shaped these standards: many were appointed as nurses because the local superintendents had observed the excellent care they had taken of their own children. Various POS committees held up their work as an example for others to emulate. At a time when respectability meant everything, women no doubt competed for the coveted title of 'good nurse', and thus 'good mother', which elevated their status in their church and parish.

Despite the religious rivalry and bitter divide that overshadowed their respective work, both Protestant and Catholic charities shared the same aim of improving the moral and physical condition of the poor.[2] Moreover, Margaret Aylward, the founder of St Brigid's Outdoor Orphanage, and PO Societies agreed on the merits of the 'family system'. The DPOS had decades of experience and unmatched insights into the workings of an extensive boarding-out scheme. Mr Greig's implementation of a boarding-out scheme in Scotland in the 1840s, which was based on the POS plan, established the Society's reputation as an authority on boarding out. Its system, which boasted consistently low mortality rates, represented an incredibly significant blueprint for Irish workhouse reforms in the early 1860s. St Brigid's, which reported impressively low mortality rates, and St Joseph's boarding-out scheme were noteworthy examples of the system in practice. Subsequently, in the 1870s, Scottish boarding out served as a paradigm for English workhouse reforms.

The DPOS system became the template for the Presbyterian Orphan Society which was founded in 1866 and the Methodist Orphan Society formed in 1870. Boarding out also became the answer to other social ills such as the accommodation of the insane. In Ireland, Dr Connolly Norman, whose name features in the list of donors to the DPOS, advocated boarding out for lunatic asylum inmates in the 1890s.

Middle and lower middle-class widows in reduced circumstances often became destitute in an instant. These women could avoid the stamp of 'pauper' by staying out of workhouses, referred to by most as the 'poor house' and by instead admitting their children to PO Societies. Many widows were obliged to send their children to unregulated nurses in the country or to leave their children with neighbours while they worked – the POS system was regulated. Moreover, PO Societies provided widows and elder siblings with the freedom to find work, at home or abroad, and re-establish themselves, for example, through remarriage or until such time as their elder children contributed enough to enable the younger children's re-entry to the household, or until the younger children were themselves economically productive. There is ample evidence to support the view that PO Societies preserved family ties in the long term through short-term separation. Typically, family reunions were facilitated in every way possible; full or partial payment of fares abroad was regularly made.

Were the Societies child and family oriented? The 'family system' was a more humane method of care than the institutional model for a number of reasons: the children were not subjected to a mechanical and artificial environment; they grew up with their siblings and as a member of a family; they were raised to become independent rather than dependent and 'fit for the battle of life'; children were supervised by local superintendents and subject to regular inspections. Moreover, boarded-out children often retained kin ties which to some extent at least eased the pain of bereavement. Widows, extended kin and elder siblings also watched over the children from a distance.

Throughout the nineteenth century local PO Societies appointed a combination of nurses as well as widows and extended kin to care for their own children with paid allowances. While with hindsight, various PO Societies considered the separation of children from widows harmful, widows had often requested the admission of their youngest dependents in order that they could work or emigrate with a view to reuniting the families when re-established. The introduction of a paid allowance for widows, which was adopted at different times by Monkstown, Cork, Limerick, Galway, Monaghan and most other PO Societies, was a forward-thinking approach which predated state policy by decades. From its foundation, the DPOS allowed children to remain with their mothers at different times – during bouts of illness and in infancy – until it took a more official line in the late nineteenth century. However, even after its rule change, it continued to express concerns that children were not always better off with their own kin. These concerns were reinforced by NSPCC reports of parental cruelty and exploitation of children.

In the twentieth century the DPOS and PO Societies provided widows with targeted assistance. Mothers, elder siblings and extended kin found work and apprenticeships for their children and the DPOS generally supported their endeavours as long as they were confident that it would serve the children's best interests. The DPOS provided mothers with respite if ill and additional support if they required superior housing. It was responsible for the placement of children in foster care, cottage homes, or with their mothers, inspection of orphans at all locations, primary education, secondary education, apprenticeship management, further training, marriage portion distribution, and, most importantly, medical care. The DPOS, which was in many respects a micro-social welfare system, aimed to provide children with an excellent start in life.

Consecutive committees responded to every case of neglect with a corresponding reform measure; for example, stricter inspections regulations were introduced and nurses' instructions amended. The founders of the DPOS had enshrined such reformative thinking in the original rules devised in 1828. While the majority of children appear to have been treated well, there were cases of mistreatment and exploitation of boarded-out children and apprentices which was a bleak reflection of children's precarious position in wider society. If placements were not vetted thoroughly or monitored vigilantly, children suffered.

Many of the clergymen who managed the DPOS and local PO Societies were also actively involved in other related social service initiatives such as the Social Service Union, the Country Air Association and other Protestant cottage homes. PO Societies represented a social service which was shaped by the laity it served. Religious polarisation was a major feature of life in nineteenth-century Ireland. The *Ne Temere* decree led to further Protestant insularism. PO Societies became more relevant following the decree when increased efforts were made to discourage mixed marriages. With support from prominent figures such as Dr Ella Webb and Douglas Hyde whose relatives had supported the Fermanagh POS and Leitrim POS respectively, it is not surprising that the DPOS retained its good reputation for so long and remained resilient in the midst of decline and social and political upheaval.

Preservation has been a key theme of this book: the founders of the DPOS viewed the Society, which aimed to preserve children's religion, health, physical and moral, widows' respectability, and the family, as a solution to the economic distress experienced by fellow artisans in Dublin. In addition to its significance as a benevolent cause and moral reform agency, in the broader context the charity also became regarded as a means of preserving Protestant posterity and the Church of Ireland, the future of which was dependent on the welfare of its rising generation. The Church of Ireland was perceived to be under threat from the time of emancipation and it was in this context that the children of the church – Protestant orphans – became worthy of investment to a nation within a nation.

Notes

1 Revd W. B. Thompson, 'A Dublin centenary', *Irish Times* (27 November 1928).
2 Prunty, *Dublin Slums*, p. 10.

Select bibliography

Primary sources

Archives

<small>NATIONAL ARCHIVES OF IRELAND</small>
Protestant Orphan Society, Dublin

<u>Minutes</u>
Apprentice subcommittee, 1836–78.
Executive subcommittee, 1901–30.
General committee, 1834–1908.
Nurses and education subcommittee, 1833–96.
Percy Place Home inspection committee, 1858–79.
Visiting subcommittee, 1904–22.

<u>Registers</u>
Applications, 1831–1914.
Clothing issued to girls and boys, 1861–87.
Health and education of newly elected orphans in order of election, March 1855.
Incoming letters, 1832–70; bound volume of incoming letters, 1898.
Marriage portions, 1875–97.
Orphan histories, 1829–1926.
Orphan movements, 1877–95.

<u>Miscellaneous records and reports</u>
'Constitution and rules of a proposed Protestant Orphan Society submitted by
   committee to general meeting; with amendments as passed in 1828'.
Fingal Home for Boys, Swords, 1919–29.
Orphans' upbringing and education, 1829–72.
Parish inspection forms, 1872–73.
Percy Place Home, visitors' book, 1858–70.
Publicity material (books of press cuttings), 1830–1928.
*Report relative to the amalgamation of PO Societies throughout Ireland with
   the DPOS*, 1919.

Sunnyside Children's Home, Kilternan, 1898–1940.
Unregistered application forms, 1840–1914.

NATIONAL LIBRARY OF IRELAND
National Society for the Prevention of Cruelty to Children. Dublin Aid Committee
Annual reports.
Tipperary Protestant Orphan Society papers
Annual reports.
Minutes.
Tyrone Protestant Orphan Society
Annual reports.

REPRESENTATIVE CHURCH BODY LIBRARY
Cork City and County Protestant Orphan Society (private collection)
Books of press cuttings re. the Society's activities, 1832–1900.
Apprentice indentures, 1838–78.
Inspectors reports, 1890–96.
Minute books of the committee, 1847–1914.
County Monaghan Protestant Orphan Society (private collection)
Annual reports, 1871–1930.
Minute books of the committee, 1870–90.
Registers of orphans, 1864–1932.

NATIONAL ARCHIVES, KEW
Clio Industrial School Ship papers.

ROYAL IRISH ACADEMY
Association for the Relief of Distressed Protestants annual report, 1842.
Cork Protestant Orphan Society annual report, 1832.
Westmeath Protestant Orphan Society annual report, 1842.

Contemporary works
'Address to the British public on behalf of the Protestant Orphan Society for Ireland', *Church of England magazine, Church Pastoral-Aid Society*, 29 (1850), p. 334.
Arnott, Sir J., Mayor of Cork, *The Investigation into the Condition of the Children in the Cork Workhouse with an Analysis of the Evidence* (Cork: Guy Brothers, 1859).
Athey, Revd R., 'A short history of the Meath Protestant Orphan Society compiled on the occasion of its centenary' (Privately printed, 1944).
Davenport Hill, F., *Children of the State: The Training of Juvenile Paupers* (1st edn, London: MacMillan and Co. 1868).
Davenport Hill, F., F. Fowke (ed.), *Children of the State* (London: Macmillan and Co., 1889).

Gregg, Revd J., *Misery and Mercy: A Sermon Preached in Trinity Church on Sunday, January 13, 1850 in aid of the Protestant Orphan Society* (Dublin: William Curry, 1850).

MacDonnell, R. L., 'Observations on the nature and treatment of various diseases', *Dublin Medical Press*, 16:311 (1846), pp. 306–8.

Maguire, E., *Roman Catholic Proselytisers Met and Answered: Recollections of a Visit to Lyons in 1858* (Dublin: Curry, 1858).

Massy, D., *Footprints of a Faithful Shepherd: a Memoir of the Rev. Godfrey Massy, B.A., vicar of Bruff, and hon. sec. of the Limerick Protestant Orphan Society; with a sketch of his times* (London, Dublin: Selley, Jackson & Haliday, 1855).

M'Crea, J. B., Minister Independent Church, *The Cause of Irish Protestant Orphans: The Cause of Godliness and Loyalty* (Dublin: Richard Moore Tims, 1833).

Missions in Ireland: Especially with Reference to the Proselytising Movement (Dublin: J. Duffy, 1855).

The Orphans of Glenbirkie: A Story Founded on Facts (Dublin: Protestant Orphan Society, 1841).

Pagani, G. B. (ed.), *Life of the Rev. Aloysius Gentili L.L.D. Father of Charity, and Missionary Apostolic in England* (London, Dublin: Richardson and Son, 1851).

Ryland, R. H., *The History, Topography and Antiquities of the County and City of Waterford* (London: J. Murray, 1824).

Shore, Revd T. R., *Case of Rev. Thomas R. Shore, and the Protestant Orphan Society with a statement of the circumstances under which he was removed from the Society* (Dublin: William Leckie, 1851).

Stanley, W., *Facts on Ireland* (Dublin: R. Milliken and Son, 1832).

Tod, I., 'Boarding out of pauper children', *Journal of the British Association for Advancement of Science*, 54 (1878), pp. 293–8.

JOURNAL OF THE STATISTICAL AND SOCIAL INQUIRY SOCIETY OF IRELAND

Barrett, R. M., 'Legislation on behalf of neglected children in America and elsewhere', 9:72 (1892), pp. 616–31.

Bastible, C. F., 'Emigration and immigration', 9:67 (1887), pp. 300–15.

Brooke, W. G., 'Report on the differences in the law of England and Ireland as regards the protection of women', 6:43 (1872), pp. 202–29.

Carre, N. W., 'The law of marriage in its bearing on morality', 8:59 (1881), pp. 289–96.

Daly, E. D., 'Neglected children and neglectful parents', 10:78 (1897/98), pp. 350–66.

Dawson, C., 'The Children Act and the Oldham League', 12:90 (1909), pp. 388–95.

Dickie, A., 'State insurance and mothers' pensions', 13:97 (1917), pp. 675–9.

Eason, C., 'The tenement homes of Dublin: their condition and regulation', 10:79 (1898), pp. 383–98.

Falkiner, F. R., 'Report on homes of the poor', 8:59 (1881), pp. 261–71.

Gibson, E., 'Employment of women in Ireland', 3:20 (1862), pp. 138–43.

Hancock, W. N., 'On the importance of substituting the family system of rearing orphan children for the system now pursued in our workhouses', 2:13 (1859), pp. 317–33.

Hancock W. N., 'The difference between the English and Irish Poor Law as to the treatment of women and unemployed workmen', 3:18 (1861), pp. 217–34.

Harty, S., 'Some considerations on the working of the artisans' dwellings acts, as illustrated in the case of the Coombe area, Dublin', 8:62 (1883), pp. 508–22.

Houston, A., 'The extension of the field for the employment of women', 4:32 (1866), pp. 345–53.

Lentaigne, J., 'The treatment and punishment of young offenders', 8:63 (1884), pp. 31– 40.

Mapther, E. D., 'The sanitary state of Dublin', 6:27 (1864), pp. 62–76.

McCabe, E. W., 'The need for a law of adoption', 28:2 (1948), pp. 178–91.

Millin, S. S., 'Child life as a national asset', 13:96 (1915), pp. 301–16.

Pim, H., 'On the importance of reformatory establishments for juvenile delinquents', 3:7 (1853/54), pp. 1–20.

Secondary sources

Books

Acheson, A., *History of the Church of Ireland, 1691–1996* (Dublin: Columba Press, APCK, 1997).

Acheson, N., B. Harvey, J. Kearney and A. Williamson, *Two Paths, One Purpose: Voluntary Action in Ireland, North and South: A Report to the Royal Irish Academy's Third Sector Research Programme* (Dublin: Institute of Public Administration, 2004).

Akenson, D. H., *The Irish Education Experiment: The National System of Education in the Nineteenth century* (London: Routledge and K. Paul, 1970).

Barnes, J., *Irish Industrial Schools, 1868–1908: Origins and Development* (Dublin: Irish Academic Press, 1989).

Bebbington, D. W., *Evangelicalism in Modern Britain: A History from the 1730s to the 1980s* (London: Routledge, 1989).

Begley, J., *The Diocese of Limerick from 1691 to the Present Time, Vol. 3* (Dublin: Browne and Noble, 1938).

Bowen, D., *The Protestant Crusade in Ireland, 1800–70: A Study of Protestant-Catholic Relations between the Act of Union and Disestablishment* (Dublin: Gill and Macmillan, 1978).

Cassell, R. D., *Medical Charities, Medical Politics: The Irish Dispensary System and the Poor Law, 1836–1872* (Woodbridge: Boydell Press, 1997).

Clarke, B. P., *Piety and Nationalism: Lay Voluntary Associations and the*

Creation of an Irish-Catholic Community in Toronto, 1850–1895 (Quebec: McGill-Queen's Press, 1993).

Connolly, S. J., *Religion and Society in Nineteenth-century Ireland* (Dundalk: Dundalgan Press, 1985).

Coolahan, J., *Irish Education: its History and Structure* (Dublin: Institute of Public Administration, 1981).

Cosgrove, A. and W. E. Vaughan (eds), *A New History of Ireland: A Chronology of Irish History to 1976* (Oxford: Clarendon Press, 2005).

Crawford, J., *The Church of Ireland in Victorian Dublin* (Dublin: Four Courts Press, 2005).

Dalton, K., *That Could Never Be: A Memoir* (Dublin: Columbia Press, 2003).

Daly, M., *Dublin the Deposed Capital: A Social and Economic History, 1860–1914* (Cork: Cork University Press, 1984).

Davin, A., *Growing up Poor: Home, School and Street in London 1870–1914* (London: Rivers Oram Press, 1986).

Digby, A. and P. Searby, *Children, School and Society in Nineteenth-century England* (London: Macmillan, 1981).

Duckworth, J., *Fagin's Children: Criminal Children in Victorian England* (London: Continuum International Publishing Group, 2002).

Fealy, G. M., *A History of Apprenticeship Nurse Training in Ireland: Bright Faces and Neat Dresses* (Oxford: Routledge, 2006).

Frost, G. S., *Victorian Childhoods* (Westport, CT: Praeger Publishing, 2009).

Frost, N., *Child Placement and Children Away from Home* (Oxford: Routledge, 2005).

Gallman, J. M., *Receiving Erin's Children: Philadelphia, Liverpool and the Irish Famine Migration, 1845–55* (Chapel Hill, NC: University of North Carolina Press, 2000).

Geary, L. M., *Medicine and Charity in Ireland, 1718–1851* (Dublin: UCD Press, 2004).

George, V., *Foster Care: Theory and Practice* (London: Routledge and K. Paul, 1970).

Gordon, L., *Heroes of their Own Lives* (New York: Viking, 1988).

Gray, P., *The Making of the Irish Poor Law, 1815–43* (Manchester: Manchester University Press, 2009).

Greven, P., *The Protestant Temperament: Patterns of Child-rearing, Religious Experience and the Self in Early America* (New York: Routledge, 1977).

Harrison, P. (ed.), *The Home Children: Their Personal Stories* (Winnipeg: Watson and Dwyer, 1979).

Hearn, M., *Below Stairs: Domestic Service Remembered in Dublin and Beyond, 1880–1922* (Dublin: Lilliput Press, 1993).

Hendrick, H., *Children, Childhood and English Society 1880–1990* (Cambridge: Cambridge University Press, 1997).

Hill, J. R., *From Patriots to Unionists: Dublin Civic Politics and Irish Protestant Patriotism, 1660–1840* (Oxford: Clarendon Press, 1997).

Hill, M., *Women in Ireland: A Century of Change* (Belfast: Blackstaff, 2003).

Jalland, P., *Death in the Victorian Family* (Oxford: Oxford University Press, 1996).

Jenkins, B., *Era of Emancipation: British Government of Ireland, 1812–1830* (Quebec: McGill-Queen's Press, 1988).

Jordan, T. E., *Victorian Childhood: Themes and Variations* (New York: SUNY Press, 1987).

Jordan, T. E., *Ireland's Children: Quality of Life, Stress and Child Development in the Famine Era* (Westport, CT: Greenwood Publishing Group, 1998).

Keenan, D. J., *The Catholic Church in Nineteenth Century Ireland: A Sociological Study* (Dublin: Gill and Macmillan, 1983).

Kinealy, C. and G. MacAtasney, *The Hidden Famine: Hunger, Poverty and Sectarianism in Belfast, 1840–50* (London: Pluto Press, 2000).

Larkin, E. J., *The Historical Dimensions of Irish Catholicism* (New York: Arno Press, 1984).

Lindsay, D., *Dublin's Oldest Charity: The Sick and Indigent Room Keeper's Society 1790–1990* (Dublin: Anniversary, 1990).

Luddy, M., *Women and Philanthropy in Nineteenth Century Ireland* (Cambridge: Cambridge University Press, 1995).

MacLellan, A. and A. Mauger (eds), *Growing Pains: Childhood Illness in Ireland, 1750–1950* (Dublin: Irish Academic Press, 2013).

Magee, S., *Weavers and Related Trades, Dublin, 1826* (Dublin: Dun Laoghaire Genealogical Society, 1995).

Matthews, A., *Renegades: Irish Republican Women, 1900–1922* (Cork: Mercier Press, 2004).

McCarthy, K. D., *Women, Philanthropy, and Civil Society* (Indiana: Indiana University Press, 2001).

McDowell, R. B., *The Church of Ireland: 1869–1969* (London: Routledge, 1975).

Miller, K. A., *Emigrants and Exiles: Ireland and the Irish Exodus to North America* (Oxford: Oxford University Press, 1985).

Milne, K., *Protestant Aid, 1836–1936: A History of the Association for the Relief of Distressed Protestants* (Dublin: APCK, 1986).

Milne, K., *The Irish Charter Schools, 1730–1830* (Dublin: Four Courts Press, 1997).

Moffitt, M., *The Society for the Irish Church Missions to the Roman Catholics, 1849–1950* (Manchester: Manchester University Press, 2010).

Morrissey, T. J., *William J. Walsh: Archbishop of Dublin, 1841–1921* (Dublin: Four Courts Press, 2000).

Murdoch, L., *Imagined Orphans: Poor Families, Child Welfare, and Contested Censorship in London* (Brunswick, NJ: Rutgers University Press, 2006).

O'Connor, S., *Orphan Trains: The Story of Charles Loring Brace and the Children he Saved and Failed* (Chicago: University of Chicago Press, 2004).

O'Mahony, P., *Criminal Justice in Ireland* (Dublin: Institute of Public Administration, 2002).

Owens, C. R., *A Social History of Women in Ireland, 1780–1939* (Dublin: Gill and Macmillan, 2005).

Parkes, S. M., *Kildare Place: The History of the Church of Ireland Training College and College of Education 1811–2010* (Dublin: CICE, 1984).

Parr, J., *Labouring Children: British Immigrant Apprentices to Canada, 1869–1924* (London: Croom Helm, 1980).

Pollock, L., *Forgotten Children: Parent-Child Relations from 1500–1900* (Cambridge: Cambridge University Press, 1983).

Preston, M. H., *Charitable Words: Women, Philanthropy, and the Language of Charity in Nineteenth Century Ireland* (Westport, CT: Greenwood Publishing Group, 2005).

Prunty, J., *Dublin Slums, 1800–1925: A Study in Urban Geography* (Dublin: Irish Academic Press, 1998).

Prunty, J., *Margaret Aylward 1810–1889: Lady of Charity, Sister of Faith* (Dublin: Four Courts Press, 1999).

Rafferty, O., *The Catholic Church and the Protestant State* (Dublin, Portland: Four Courts Press, 2008).

Raftery, M. and E. O'Sullivan, *Suffer the Little Children: The Inside Story of Ireland's Industrial Schools* (Dublin: New Island Books, 1999).

Robins, J., *The Lost Children: A Study of Charity Children in Ireland, 1700–1900* (Dublin: Institute of Public Administration, 1980).

Robins, J., *The Miasma: Epidemic and Panic in Nineteenth Century Ireland* (Dublin: Institute of Public Administration, 1995).

Smyrl, S. C., *Dictionary of Dublin Dissent: Dublin Dissenting Meeting Houses, 1660–1920* (Dublin: Farmar & Farmar, 2009).

Tobin, R., *The Minority Voice: Hubert Butler and Southern Irish Protestantism, 1900–1991* (Oxford: Oxford University Press, 2012).

Walsh, O., *Anglican Women in Dublin: Philanthropy, Politics and Education in the Early Twentieth Century* (Dublin: UCD Press, 2005).

Whelan, I., *The Bible War in Ireland: The 'Second Reformation' and the Polarization of Protestant-Catholic Relations, 1800–1840* (Dublin: Lilliput Press, 2005).

White, J., *Minority Report: The Protestant Community in the Irish Republic* (Dublin: Gill and Macmillan, 1975).

Williams, G., *Barnardo: The Extraordinary Doctor* (London: Macmillan Press, 1966).

Yates, N., *The Religious Condition of Ireland, 1750–1850* (Oxford: Oxford University Press, 2006).

Essays in edited volumes

Brunton, D., 'The problems of implementation: the failure and success of public vaccination against smallpox in Ireland, 1840–1873', in G. Jones and E. Malcolm (eds), *Medicine, Disease and the State in Ireland, 1650–1940* (Cork: Cork University Press, 1999), pp. 138–57.

Clear, C., 'The limits of female autonomy: nuns in the nineteenth century', in M. Luddy and C. Murphy (eds), *Women Surviving: Studies in Irish Women's History in the 19th and 20th Centuries* (Dublin: Poolbeg Press, 1990), pp. 15–50.

Clear, C., 'Women of the house in Ireland, 1800–1950', in A. Bourke (ed.), *The Field Day Anthology of Irish Writing: Irish Women's Writing and Traditions* (New York: New York University Press, 2002), pp. 589–608.

Comerford, P., 'An innovative people: the Church of Ireland laity, 1780–1830', in R. Gillespie and W. G. Neely (eds), *The Laity and the Church of Ireland: All Sorts and Conditions 1000–2000* (Dublin: Four Courts Press, 2000), pp. 170–95.

Cronin, M., 'The female industrial movement, 1845–52', in B. Whelan (ed.), *Women and Paid Work in Ireland* (Dublin: Four Courts Press, 2000), pp. 69–85.

Cronin, M., '"You'd be disgraced!": middle-class women and respectability in post famine Ireland', in F. Lane (ed.), *Politics, Society and the Middle Class in Modern Ireland* (Basingstoke, New York: Palgrave Macmillan, 2010), pp. 107–29.

Crossman, V., 'Welfare and nationality: the poor laws in nineteenth-century Ireland', in S. King and J. Stewart (eds), *Welfare Peripheries: The Development of Welfare States in Nineteenth and Twentieth Century Europe* (Bern: Peter Lang, 2007), pp. 67–96.

Crossman, V., 'Middle-class attitudes to poverty and welfare in post-famine Ireland', in F. Lane (ed.), *Politics, Society and the Middle Class in Modern Ireland* (Basingstoke, New York: Palgrave Macmillan, 2010), pp. 130–47.

Cullen, M., 'Widows in Ireland, 1830–1970', in Bourke (ed.), *Field Day Anthology of Irish Writing: Irish Women's Writing and Traditions* (New York: New York University Press, 2002), pp. 609–18.

Deignan, P., 'The importance of fraternities and social clubs for the Protestant community in Sligo from 1914 to 1949', in J. Kelly and R. V. Comerford (eds), *Associational Culture in Ireland and Abroad* (Dublin: Irish Academic Press, 2010), pp. 191–212.

Hill, J. R., 'Protestant ascendancy challenged: the Church of Ireland laity and the public sphere', in R. Gillespie and W. G. Neely (eds), *The Laity and the Church of Ireland: All Sorts and Conditions 1000–2000* (Dublin: Four Courts Press, 2000), pp. 150–69.

Maguire, M., '"Our People": the Church of Ireland and the culture of community in Dublin since disestablishment', in R. Gillespie and W. G. Neely (eds), *The Laity and the Church of Ireland: All Sorts and Conditions 1000–2000* (Dublin: Four Courts Press, 2000), pp. 277–303.

Malcolm, E., 'Hospitals in Ireland', in A. Bourke (ed.), *Field Day Anthology of Irish Writing: Irish Women's Writing and Traditions* (New York: New York University Press, 2002), pp. 705–21.

McCarthy, A., 'Hearts, bodies and minds: gender ideology and women's committal to Enniscorthy Lunatic Asylum, 1916–25', in A. Hayes and D.

Urquhart (eds), *Irish Women's History* (Dublin: Irish Academic Press, 2004), pp. 115–35.

Neely, W. G., 'The laity in a changing society', in R. Gillespie and W. G. Neely (eds), *The Laity and the Church of Ireland: All Sorts and Conditions 1000–2000* (Dublin: Four Courts Press, 2000), pp. 196–225.

Neely, W. G., 'The Clergy, 1780–1850', in T. Bernard and W. G. Neely (eds), *The Clergy of the Church of Ireland 1000–2000: Messengers, Watchmen and Stewards* (Dublin: Four Courts Press, 2006), pp. 142–56.

Prunty, J., 'Mobility among women in nineteenth century Dublin', in D. J. Siddle (ed.), *Migration, Mobility, and Modernization* (Liverpool: Liverpool University Press, 2000), pp. 131–63.

Prunty, J., 'Battle plans and battlegrounds: Protestant mission activity in the Dublin slums, 1840–1880', in C. Gribben and A. Holmes (eds), *Protestant Millennialism, Evangelicalism and Irish Society, 1790–2005* (London: Palgrave Macmillan, 2006), pp. 119–43.

Skehill, C., 'Child protection and welfare social work in the Republic of Ireland: continuities and discontinuities between the past and present', in N. Kearney and C. Skehill (eds), *Social Work in Ireland: Historical Perspectives* (Dublin: Institute of Public Administration, 2005), pp. 127–45.

Walsh, E., 'International social work over time: vignette', in N. Kearney and C. Skehill (eds), *Social Work in Ireland: Historical Perspectives* (Dublin: Institute of Public Administration, 2005), pp. 211– 23.

Articles in journals

Chonaire, R. U., 'The Luther legacy: homeopathy in Ireland in the nineteenth century', *Journal of the Irish Society of Homeopaths* (2010), pp. 17–24.

Comerford, P., 'A decade in which anarchy was loosed upon the world, a terrible beauty was born', *Church Review, Dublin & Glendalough Diocesan Magazine* (January 2012), pp. 4–5.

Considere-Charon, M. C., 'The Church of Ireland: continuity and change', *Irish Quarterly Review*, 87:346 (Summer 1998), pp. 107–16.

Davidoff, L., 'Kinship as a categorical concept: a case study of nineteenth century English siblings', *Journal of Social History*, 39:2 (Winter 2005), pp. 411–28.

Dooley, T. A. M., 'Protestant migration from the Free State to Northern Ireland, 1920–25: a private census for Co. Fermanagh', *Clogher Record*, 15:3 (1996), pp. 87–132.

Drurie, A., 'Medicine, health and economic development: promoting spa and seaside resorts in Scotland c. 1750–1830', *Medical History* (2003), pp. 195–216.

Maguire, M., 'A socio-economic analysis of the Dublin Protestant working class, 1870–1926', *Irish Economic and Social History*, 20 (1993), pp. 35–61.

Neff, C., 'The Children's Friend Society in Upper Canada, 1833–37', *Journal of Family History*, 32:3 (Summer 2007), pp. 235–59.

Purdue, O., 'Poverty and power: the Irish Poor Law in a north Antrim town, 1861–1921', *Irish Historical Studies*, 37:148 (2011), pp. 567–83.

Wall, M., 'The rise of a Catholic middle class in eighteenth-century Ireland', *Irish Historical Studies*, 11:42 (1958), pp. 91–115.

Thesis

Enright, C., '"Take this child": a study of Limerick Protestant Orphan Society, 1833–1900' (MA dissertation, University of Limerick, 2003).

Index